Animal Symbolism in Hofmannsthal's Works

American University Studies

Series I
Germanic Languages and Literature

Vol. 56

PETER LANG
New York · Berne · Frankfurt am Main · Paris

Helen Frink

Animal Symbolism in Hofmannsthal's Works

PETER LANG
New York · Berne · Frankfurt am Main · Paris

Library of Congress Cataloging-in-Publication Data

Frink, Helen
  Animal symbolism in Hofmannsthal's works.

  (American university studies. Series I, Germanic languages and literatures; vol. 56)
    Bibliography: p.
    Includes index.
    I. Hofmannsthal, Hugo von, 1874-1929--Symbolism.
  2. Animals in literature. I. Title. II. Series.
  PT2617.047Z73624 1988 831'.912 87-3831
  ISBN 0-8204-0400-4
  ISSN 0721-1392

CIP-Kurztitelaufnahme der Deutschen Bibliothek

Frink, Helen:
Animal symbolism in Hofmannsthal's works / Helen Frink. - New York; Berne; Frankfurt am Main; Paris: Lang, 1987.
  (American university studies: Ser. 1,
  Germanic languages and literature; Vol. 56)
ISBN 0-8204-0400-4

NE: American university studies / 01

©Peter Lang Publishing, Inc., New York 1987
All rights reserved.
Reprint or reproduction, even partially, in all forms such as microfilm, xerography, microfiche, microcard, offset strictly prohibited.
Printed by Weihert-Druck GmbH, Darmstadt (West Germany)

TABLE OF CONTENTS

Introduction 7

Chapter I: Military Service: "Die Tücke des Pferdes und des eigenen Körpers" 19

Chapter II: "Ein Traum von großer Magie" 29

Chapter III: "Das Märchen der 672. Nacht" 41

Chapter IV: "Reitergeschichte" 65

Chapter V: *Die Frau im Fenster* 91

Chapter VI: *Das kleine Welttheater* 121

Chapter VII: *Jupiter und Semele* 133

Chapter VIII: "Knabengeschichte" ("Dämmerung und nächtliches Gewitter") 141

Chapter IX: *Andreas oder die Vereinigten* 155

Chapter X: *Der Turm* 271

Conclusion 253

Bibliography 265

Index 281

In memory of both my grandmothers,
Laura E. Frink and Helen M. Hiller,
without whose rare example I might
never have become an educated woman.

INTRODUCTION

Gesehen mit diesen Augen sind die Tiere die eigentlichen Hieroglyphen, sind sie lebendige geheimnisvolle Chiffren, mit denen Gott unaussprechliche Dinge in die Welt geschrieben hat. Glücklich der Dichter, daß auch er diese göttlichen Chiffren in seine Schrift verweben darf. (P, 2:87)[1]

1 Hofmannsthal's works have been quoted from the standard edition: Hugo von Hofmannsthal, *Gesammelte Werke in Einzelausgaben,* ed. Herbert Steiner, 15 vols. (Frankfurt S. Fischer, 1945-73). The abbreviations used throughout the paper refer to this edition and are listed below. Because the pagination of the reprinted volumes differs from that of the original edition, the copyright date is given first below, followed by the date of the reprint to which reference is made.
    A, *Aufzeichnungen,* 1959, 1973
    D, 1, *Dramen,* vol. 1, 1953, 1974
    D, 2, *Dramen,* vol. 2, 1954, 1966
    D, 3, *Dramen,* vol. 3, 1957, 1969
    D, 4, *Dramen,* vol. 4, 1958, 1970
    E, *Erzählungen,* 1945, 1968
    GLD, *Gedichte und lyrische Dramen,* 1946, 1970
    L, 1, *Lustspiele,* vol. 1, 1947, 1959
    L, 2, *Lustspiele,* vol. 2, 1948, 1965
    L, 3, *Lustspiele,* vol. 3, 1956, 1968
    L, 4, *Lustspiele,* vol. 4, 1956, 1973
    P, 1, *Prosa,* vol. 1, 1950, 1956
    P, 2, *Prosa,* vol. 2, 1951, 1959
    P, 3, *Prosa,* vol. 3, 1953, 1964
    P, 4, *Prosa,* vol. 4, 1955, 1966

The abbreviation SW refers to the new critical edition, Hugo von Hofmannsthal, *Sämtliche Werke, kritische Ausgabe,* ed. Heinz Burger et al, 38 vols. (Frankfurt: S. Fischer, 1975ff.):

References to two volumes of Hofmannsthal's correspondence have also been abbreviated throughout the paper. "B, 1" refers to: Hugo von Hof-

In his "Gespräch über Gedichte" Hofmannsthal repudiates the stale term "symbol," preferring instead to speak of animals as "Chiffren, welche aufzulösen die Sprache ohnmächtig ist" (P, 2:87). His emphasis on the inadequacy of language with respect to animals clearly demonstrates their intimate connection with the problem of poetic creativity. The poet, recognizing the inadequacy of his chosen medium, language, to deal with animals in the same manner as it serves to define and conceptualize the other elements of his universe, simply follows his creator's example, incorporating them into his work. This paper will examine various aspects of the relationship between animal and man, particularly the poet, attempting wherever possible to decode these animal ciphers.

I have chosen to substitute the word "symbol" for Hofmannsthal's preferred term "cipher" in order to de-emphasize the mysterious incomprehensible quality of these images I intend to decipher. But we must now consider what we mean by symbol. Hofmannsthal himself offers little enlightenment, for his definition of the symbol as "das sinnliche Bild für geistige Wahrheit, die der ratio unerreichbar ist" (P, 4:49), only underscores the irrational nature of poetic imagery. He does, to be sure, make the distinction fundamental to most definitions of symbolism between the sensory quality of the symbol as contrasted with the intangible nature of the thing represented. But his attempt to define symbolism in terms of animal sacrifice in the "Gespräch über Gedichte" merely confuses the issue, for instead of explaining the essence or function of symbolism, he explains how it originates. Furthermore, he approaches symbolism not in the comparatively simple form of a symbolic object, but as a symbolic act, that of animal sacrifice.

Let us consider briefly Goethe's concept of symbolism as a point of orientation:

> Die Symbolik verwandelt die Erscheinung in Idee, die Idee in ein Bild, und so, daß die Idee im Bild immer unendlich wirksam und unerreichbar bleibt und, selbst in allen Sprachen ausgesprochen, doch unaussprechlich bliebe.

mannsthal, *Briefe, 1890-1901* (Berlin: S. Fischer, 1935). "B, 2" refers to: Hugo von Hofmannsthal, *Briefe, 1900-1909* (Vienna: Bermann-Fischer, 1937).

> Das ist die wahre Symbolik, wo das Besondere das Allgemeinere repräsentiert, nicht als Traum und Schatten, sondern als lebendig-augenblickliche Offenbarung des Unerforschlichen.[2]

Like Hofmannsthal, Goethe stresses that language alone is incapable of exhausting all the possibilities of expression incorporated in the symbol. Further similarities between Goethe's and Hofmannsthal's concepts of symbolism have been observed by Karl Pestalozzi, who determines that Goethe compresses several isolated experiences into one symbol which reveals their common traits. He quotes Goethe's statement: "Nichts ist drinnen, nichts ist draußen/ Denn was innen, das ist außen" and continues:

> Das Symbol schlägt zwischen innen und außen eine Brücke. Hofmannsthals Symbolauffassung scheint sich von derjenigen Goethes vorerst kaum zu unterscheiden. "Daß wir und die Welt nichts Verschiedenes sind" (P, 2:105) ist auch seine Voraussetzung. Aber was er drinnen und draußen sieht, ist nicht mehr eine gesetzmäßige Natur, das Symbolisierte ist das regellos strömende, alles umgreifende "Leben."[3]

Pestalozzi's distinction between the lawfully ordered nature which formed the backdrop of Goethe's symbolism and the unstructured flux at the basis of Hofmannsthal's symbolism provides an important clue. Hans-Jürgen Schings in his interpretation of "Das Märchen der 672. Nacht" explains the dependence of classical-idealist symbolism on natural philosophy: "Nur auf der Grundlage der Identität von Idee und Erscheinung, von Allgemeinem und Besonderem, von Absolutem und Endlichem gewährt sich jene Identität von Bild und Bedeutung ..."[4] By Hofmannsthal's time, the classical faith in a lawful cosmic order has weakened. His experience of the identity of phenomenon and idea, of the specific and the general no longer rests on the world view of a rational universe, but rather on a personal mystical union with nature, unique to one individual at one point in

---

2 *Goethes Werke,* Hamburg ed. in 14 vols., ed. Erich Trunz (Hamburg: Christian Wegner; Munich: C. H. Beck, 1966-73), 12:470-71.

3 *Sprachskepsis und Sprachmagie im Werk des jungen Hofmannsthal,* Zürcher Beiträge zur deutschen Sprach- und Stilgeschichte, no. 6 (Zurich: Atlantis, 1958), pp. 36-37.

4 "Allegorie des Lebens, zum Formproblem von Hofmannsthals 'Märchen der 672. Nacht'," *Zeitschrift für deutsche Philologie* 86 (1967), 554.

time.[5] His description of this ecstatic union of the individual with the cosmos in the Chandos letter concludes with an affirmation of the symbolic significance of natural phenomena as generated by the mystical experience.[6]

> Mir erschien damals in einer Art von andauernder Trunkenheit das ganze Dasein als eine große Einheit: geistige und körperliche Welt schien mir keinen Gegensatz zu bilden, ... in allem fühlte ich Natur ... Das eine war wie das andere; keines gab dem andern weder an traumhaft überirdischer Natur, noch an leiblicher Gewalt nach, und so gings fort durch die ganze Breite des Lebens, rechter und linker Hand; überall war ich mitten drinnen, ... Oder es ahnte mir, alles wäre Gleichnis und jede Kreatur ein Schlüssel der andern, und ich fühlte mich wohl den, der imstande wäre, eine nach der andern bei der Krone zu packen und mit ihr so viele der andern aufzusperren, als sie aufsperren könnte. (P, 2:10-11)

Because Hofmannsthal's experience of the unity of image and idea depends upon the union of the individual with the universe, that irrational state Chandos describes as "andauernde Trunkenheit," his symbols lack the unambiguous significance and lucidity of Goethe's. Wolfram Mauser explains that Hofmannsthal's symbols, originating as momentary flashes of insight, do not always point toward general

---

5 See Karl J. Naef, *Hugo von Hofmannsthals Wesen und Werk* (Zurich: Max Niehans, 1938), p. 30: "Im Allheitsempfinden hat die ganze Hofmannsthalsche Bild und Gleichniswelt ihren Ursprung. ... In sämtlichen Dingen der Welt hat er irgendeinmal gewohnt, ... Das Resultat ist ein überbordender Gleichnis- und Sinnbildreichtum..."

6 Throughout this discussion we have used the terms "mystical" and "mysticism" in their broadest sense to refer to the individual's ecstatic, non-rational sense of oneness with the universe. Manfred Hoppe has more precisely defined two forms which this experience may take. In the state which he calls "Magie" and describes as "coercitiv" the ego actively pursues unification with the universe. In the state he calls "Mystik" and characterizes as "inducierend" — that state described in the Chandos letter — the ego remains passive, overcome involuntarily by the sensation of unity with the cosmos. In our discussion of the mystical experience as the basis for much of Hofmannsthal's symbolism, we have treated both of these active and passive states as belonging to that experience, leaving aside the distinction between "Magie" and "Mystik." See Hoppe, *Literatentum, Magie und Mystik im Frühwerk Hugo von Hofmannsthals,* Quellen und Forschungen zur Sprach- und Literaturgeschichte der germanischen Völker, n. s., vol. 28 (152) (Berlin: de Gruyter, 1968), pp. 117-18.

truths, but rather remain bound to specific objects, insights and experiences. They are characterized by:

> ... bestimmende Merkmale magischen Welterlebens, die darin bestehen, daß aus intuitiver und plötzlicher Erleuchtung und nur für Augenblicke währender Erhellung große elementare Zusammenhänge ahnbar werden, daß dieses Erleben unter Schauer und Erschütterung vor sich geht und auf geheimnisvolle Weise Verzauberung und Verwandlung bewirkt.[7]

This statement of the origin of Hofmannsthal's symbols in the ecstatic suspension of his individuality in an intuitive fleeting unification with the cosmos explains the equation of the tower symbol with Sigismund's selfhood in *Der Turm* or how the underworld of the Bergkönigin becomes synonymous with Elis' subconscious in *Das Bergwerk zu Falun*. Margit Resch has analyzed Hofmannsthal's concept of the symbolic experience and concludes (like Mauser) that this feeling of oneness with the universe and with all species of life frequently occurs in a dream-like state in which the poet loses awareness of space and time; past, present and future flow together; memories come to life in the here and now; and light or illumination may accompany this sensation. Although such experiences are of central importance throughout Hofmannsthal's work, they can neither be forcibly evoked by the poet nor scientifically analyzed by the literary critic.[8] She applies her understanding of symbolic experiences

---

7 *Bild und Gebärde in der Sprache Hofmannsthals.* Österreichische Akademie der Wissenschaften, philosophisch-historische Klasse, Sitzungsberichte, vol. 238 (Vienna: Hermann Böhlau, 1961), p. 11.
While Mauser emphasizes the fleeting, intuitive nature of the mystical experiences, a more recent critic states that Hofmannsthal shared with the French symbolists the fundamental belief in a "transcendent world beyond empirical reality." The poet "can reveal his insight into this realm by means of correspondences" which, however, do not precisely equate symbols from reality with mystical, profound, undefinable experiences or insights, for the poet communicates "through suggestion, evocation, and through the creation of dream-like states rather than by description or direct statement." (Steven P. Sondrup, "Three Notes on Symbolism by Hugo von Hofmannsthal," *Modern Austrian Literature*, 9 (1976), 1-5.

8 *Das Symbol als Prozess bei Hugo von Hofmannsthal.* Hochschulschriften Literaturwissenschaft, 48 (Königstein: Forum Academicum, 1980), pp. 115-17.

such as those described in the Chandos letter (see above) to a study of the fragment, "Das Märchen von der verschleierten Frau."

However, this discussion of the symbolic experience brings us no closer to an understanding of Hofmannsthal's animal images, for it is precisely in the area of animal symbolism that the scheme breaks apart, for animals are perhaps the only phenomena which resist or defy mystical union with the individual. Although this thesis must be developed through the next several chapters, one example may be anticipated here for the sake of clarification. In "Das Märchen der 672. Nacht" we read that the merchant's son experiences through the art objects ornamenting his secluded existence a sort of ecstatic union with and complete possession of the world of nature:

> Er erkannte in den Ornamenten, die sich verschlingen, ein verzaubertes Bild der verschlungenen Wunder der Welt. ... Er fand die Farben der Blumen und Blätter, die Farben der Felle wilder Tiere und der Gesichter der Völker, die Farbe der Edelsteine, ... Er war für lange Zeit trunken von dieser großen, tiefsinnigen Schönheit, die ihm gehörte ... (E, p. 8; SW 28:15-16)

Trusting his mystical identity with nature as presented in these art forms, the merchant's son is lulled into the belief that he possesses not merely the art image of reality, but the world itself. The objects enumerated above reappear to menace him in his journey through the city: the flowers and leaves ensnare him in the greenhouse, the jewels dropped under the horse contribute to cause his death, and the yellowish faces of the soldiers withstand his gesture of compassion. The pattern of resistance to him causes Schings to speak of the story as the "Widerlegung eines falschen Symbolismus," a repudiation of precisely that symbolism arising from the ecstatic trance uniting the individual with the cosmos.[9] But the process of resistance to or rejection of his advances culminates in the fatal kick of the ugly cavalry horse, resulting in the young man's death. Again and again the animals in Hofmannsthal's work resist assimilation into the harmonious flux in which individual consciousness is suspended in blissful oblivious oneness with the universe.

Judging in terms of Hofmannsthal's statement, "Alles, was ist, ist, Sein und Bedeuten ist eins, folglich ist alles Seiende Symbol" (A,

---

9 "Allegorie des Lebens," p. 555.

p. 106), the horse is not a symbol at all. Seen from the point of view of the merchant's son, its "meaning" within the context of the story is the place it occupies as part of the whole fabric of nature presented in the art objects which he admires. Yet its "being" within the "Märchen" is its function as source of the deadly blow. In this case, being and meaning are obviously not identical.

Since neither Goethe's nor Hofmannsthal's definition of the symbol affords a valid framework for the discussion of animal imagery, let us adopt as a working hypothesis the fairly general definition formulated by Alfred North Whitehead:

> The human mind is functioning symbolically when some components of its experience elicit consciousness, beliefs, emotions, and usages, respecting other components of its experience. The former set of components are the 'symbols' and the latter set constitute the 'meaning' of the symbols.[10]

A definition by Carl G. Jung supplements this general one, stating more emphatically the intuitive or unconscious aspect of the symbol:

> ... a word or an image is symbolic when it implies something more than its obvious and immediate meaning. It has a wider "unconscious aspect" that is never precisely defined or fully explained. ... As the mind explores the symbol, it is led to ideas that lie beyond the grasp of reason. ... Because there are innumerable things beyond the range of human understanding, we constantly use symbolic terms to represent concepts that we cannot define or fully comprehend. ... A symbol always stands for something more than its obvious and immediate meaning. Symbols, moreover, are natural and spontaneous products.[11]

Literary symbols are most successful when the consciousness or emotion they elicit in the mind of the reader corresponds closely to that elicited in the mind of the author. Such is the case when the author draws his symbols from literary, artistic, religious or cultural tradition (choosing, for example, the lamb as a symbol of Christ or the dog as a symbol of faithfulness), or when the symbol's effectiveness is based on some fundamental human experience. The shared

---

10 *Symbolism, Its Meaning and Effect,* Barbour-Page Lectures, University of Virginia, 1927 (New York: Capricorn, 1959), pp. 7-8.
11 *Man and his Symbols* (Garden City, N.J.: Doubleday, 1964), pp. 20 and 55.

human experience may not lend itself to brief verbal expression, yet the perceptive reader intuitively grasps the implication of the symbol, realizing, for instance, that the "damned spot" staining Lady Macbeth's hand signifies her guilt or that the snowfall in Robert Frost's "Stopping by the Woods on a Snowy Evening" creates a foreboding of death. These examples function as a sort of imagistic shorthand, as hieroglyphs or ciphers whose meaning, contrary to Hofmannsthal's assertion, can be decoded or re-expressed through language. They go beyond the simplistic substitution of one object for another which Hofmannsthal rejects as a form of symbolism in the "Gespräch über Gedichte," for that which is represented by the symbol is not one object, but an entire experience.

> The true symbol does not, then, stand for something. It is the precipitate of the poet's symbolic experience and the medium for evoking a symbolic experience in the reader. Its value as a symbol depends entirely upon its power to evoke the symbolic experience.[12]

The symbol may fail to evoke the desired symbolic experience in the mind of the reader for one of several reasons. Eckhart Krämer, who utilizes the term "Chiffre" in his dissertation on Hofmannsthal's imagery, cites the "Gespräch über Gedichte" (1903) as proof that the "irresolvable, complex irrational cipher" commonly regarded as symptomatic of modern poetry originated not with the advent of expressionism around 1910 as is generally assumed, but several years earlier with Hofmannsthal.[13] He discovers the basis for the development of increasingly difficult incomprehensible poetic imagery in the loss of communal spirit and shared experiences, a loss which has deprived the poet of beliefs, emotions and consciousness shared with his reader and has limited his self-expression to personal images of his own unique and frequently inaccessible experience of the world — Goerg Trakl is a case in point.

Second, the symbol may be a means of concealing rather than communicating a belief, sensation or concept.

---

12 Penrith Goff, "Hugo von Hofmannsthal: the Symbol as Experience," *Kentucky Foreign Language Quarterly* 7 (1960), 199.
13 "Die Metaphorik in Hofmannsthals Lyrik und ihr Verhältnis zum modernen Gedicht" Diss. Marburg/Lahn 1963, pp. 183, 197.

> In matters of social or individual behavior [symbolism] may be the abdication of language and even of rational thinking in favor of primordial rituals, demonstrative actions, and sinister obscurantism. ... The symbol as a mode of expression is peculiarly germane to primitive societies and is closely associated with elemental experiences.[14]

Symbolism enables the author to place a protective distance between himself and a represented experience, alluding to it without recalling it to the conscious mind, a healing process not unlike the catharsis of classical tragedy.[15] Symbolism makes possible a mode of existence Hofmannsthal expressed in one of his favorite adages, "Il faut glisser ne pas appuyer la vie" (A, p. 120).[16]

Third, an author may unconsciously weave symbols into his work, images which do not form an integral part of the story, but allude unintentionally to events in the author's life. Charles Dickens, for example, describes in *Great Expectations* a blacking factory among the sights presented to a visitor to London. In such a blacking factory (which is devoid of any significance in the novel) he was forced to work as a child to help pay the creditors of his father, who had been thrown into debtor's prison. Although he was apparently unable to confront and resolve the painful childhood memory in his conscious mind, its intrusion into the novel suggests a subconscious effort to come to grips with a shameful experience. In the following examination of Hofmannsthal's animal imagery, we shall have occasion to discuss comparable instances of unconscious symbolism.

Now that we have defined what we mean by symbol and have illuminated its more significant aspects, it will be useful as a second preliminary to our investigation to consider Hofmannsthal's knowledge of animals. At first glance, one might suppose Hofmannsthal no more intimately acquainted with them than such aesthetes of his early work as the merchant's son, who know nature only through art. Hermann Bahr's characterization of the refined, sensitive untroubled

---

14 Helmut Rehder, "Introduction" to *Literary Symbolism, A Symposium*, ed. Helmut Rehder (Austin: University of Texas, 1965), p. 3.
15 Cf. Lessing's treatment of aristotelian tragedy in the seventy-fifth section of his *Hamburgische Dramaturgie*.
16 Richard Exner identifies the source of the proverb in *Hugo von Hofmannsthals "Lebenslied," eine Studie* (Heidelberg: Winter, 1964), pp. 91-92.

young Loris hardly seems consistent with a firsthand knowledge of the brutal and stark reality of the animal kingdom. Bahr writes:

> Von den suchenden Qualen weiß er nichts, von den Martern der ungestillten Begierde, die rathlos irrt und sich nicht verstehen kann. In ihm ist kein Ringen und Stürmen und Drängen, kein Zwist von unverträglichen Motiven, kein Haß zwischen erworbenen Wünschen und geerbten Instincten; in ihm ist alles zu heiterer Einheit ausgesöhnt.[17]

Hofmannsthal sometimes equates knowledge of animal life with an awareness of reality. When Fortunio in *Der weiße Fächer* fails to distinguish the cry of a rabbit caught by a weasel from a birdcall, his grandmother exclaims, "Was hast du mit deinen Bubenjahren angefangen, Fortunio, daß du das nicht kennst!" (GLD, p. 231; SW, 3: 160). Although one might assume that Hofmannsthal, who had spent his youth becoming thoroughly familiar with the world of literature and art, would be similarly ignorant of animal habits, quite the reverse is true. His entire work attests to a profound interest in animals. Instead of contenting himself with the mention of those birds common to world literature, he names in addition: blackbird, magpie, sparrow-hawk, vulture, goatsucker, crane and partridge. He supplemented his firsthand observation of animals with zoological texts such as *Die Spiele der Thiere* and Brehm's ten-volume *Allgemeine Kunde des Tierreichs*.[18]

In spite of such evidence, Hofmannsthal's animal symbolism has thus far received inadequate critical attention. Werner Volke summarizes the events of his year of military service without commenting upon Hofmannsthal's strange relationship to his horse and its reflection in his letters and early creative work.[19] Where animal image-

---

17 *Studien zur Kritik der Moderne* (Frankfurt: Ruiten & Loening, 1894), p. 128.
18 I am indebted to Dr. Rudolf Hirsch for the mention of these two works belonging to Hofmannsthal's library: Karl Groos, *Die Spiele der Thiere* (Jena: Gustav Fischer, 1896) and Alfred Edmund Brehm, *Brehms Tierleben, Allgemeine Kunde des Tierreichs,* 10 vols., 2d. ed. (Leipzig: Verlag des Bibliographischen Instituts, 1876-79). In a drama sketch from 1893, Hofmannsthal noted: "Brehms Thierleben lesen" (SW, 3:253).
19 *Hugo von Hofmannsthal in Selbstzeugnissen und Bilddokumenten* (Hamburg: Rowohlt, 1967), pp. 51-59.

ry has of necessity aroused the curiosity of the critics (in "Lebenslied" and the *Andreas* novel) a cursory treatment of the pertinent images has often resulted in erroneous conclusions about the broader scope of animal symbolism. Thus Exner concludes that the eagle appears more frequently than any other animal in Hofmannsthal's work,[20] neglecting the far more numerous occurrences of dog and horse, which, because of their presence in the writer's urban surroundings, figure more often in his work. An earlier critic of "Lebenslied" fallaciously assumes that all of Hofmannsthal's animal images "haben einen vorgegebenen literarischen, mythologischen oder biblischen Bezug."[21] Others have misconstrued Hofmannsthal as an animal lover; Werner Metzeler writes of a "mystischer Selbstidentifizierung" with animals."[22] Likewise Karl Gautschi assumes Hofmannsthal's benevolent attitude toward animals and doubts that Andreas is actually guilty of those misdeeds — the crippling and murder of a cat and dog — which weigh upon his conscience.[23] More recent studies of the *Andreas* novel have proven more perceptive and fruitful. David H. Miles provides an especially productive analysis of the dog and horse symbols in the ninth chapter of his book, *Hofmannsthal's Novel Andreas; Memory and Self*.[24] Clement Gerald Chapple concerns himself in his dissertation with the function of animal imagery as a structural principle.[25]

Although vital groundwork for an investigation of the topic has been laid by the above critics, none has applied an examination of animal symbolism to the interpretation of Hofmannsthal's major works. This study, therefore, intends an analysis of significant animal images to serve as a tool for the interpretation of selected poems,

20 *Hugo von Hofmannsthals "Lebenslied,"* p. 83.
21 Paul Gerhard Klussmann, "Hofmannsthals Lebenslied," in: *Hugo von Hofmannsthal*, ed. Sibylle Bauer, Wege der Forschung, vol. 183 (Darmstadt: Wissenschaftliche Buchgesellschaft, 1968), p. 252.
22 *Ursprung und Krise von Hofmannsthals Mystik* (Munich: Wilh. Gottl. Korn, 1956), p. 57.
23 "Hugo von Hofmannsthals Romanfragment 'Andreas' "Diss. Zurich 1965, pp. 26 ff.
24 (Princeton, N.J.: Princeton University, 1972).
25 "Themes and Symbols in Hofmannsthal's *"Andreas."* Diss. Harvard University 1967.

narratives and dramas. It is not my aim to establish an annotated catalog of the innumerable references to animals to be found in the oeuvre, but rather to proceed from a consideration of the significance of certain animals in folklore, mythology, art and literature to a discussion of their function in those works where animal imagery plays a central role. Instances of comparable animal imagery in other literary works, whether possible sources of influence on Hofmannsthal or merely parallels to his conceptions, will be noted wherever relevant.

I shall begin with a brief description of those events in Hofmannsthal's life bearing directly on his relationship to animals and move to the analysis of selected works in chronological order. By devoting one chapter to each of the works considered, I hope to achieve a coherent interpretation of those chosen for study. It will be necessary to return frequently to the recurring images, such as horse and dog, effecting a cumulative interpretation of their significance throughout the work.

I have limited this study to those works in which animal symbolism plays a crucial role, texts which can scarcely be adequately interpreted without reference to animal imagery. I have omitted from extensive examination most of Hofmannsthal's translations and adaptations, for dealing with such works necessitates inquiring after the use of animal symbolism in the sources themselves. Nonetheless I have included *Der Turm*, certainly far from a mere adaptation of Calderon's *La vida es sueño*, because its 1925 version combines two themes central to Hofmannsthal's animal imagery: man's mistreatment of animals, and his search for valid criteria distinguishing man from beast. Animal symbols in those works not treated in an entire chapter have, however, been cited where they illuminate similar images in one of the works treated at length. Works from each period of Hofmannsthal's life and from each literary genre have been included to provide the broadest possible scope for the investigation.

CHAPTER I

MILITARY SERVICE: "DIE TÜCKE DES PFERDES UND DES EIGENEN KÖRPERS

Hofmannsthal's earliest noteworthy comments on animals occur during his period of military service. In September of 1894 he entered the service in Göding in Moravia; maneuvers in May 1896 took him to Tlumacz and in July 1898 to Czortkow, both in the province of Galicia. The shared existence of humans and animals in the army caused him to reflect on the physical needs common to both. In his diary he notes, "Viel Stalldienst. Um 4 Uhr früh aufstehen. Die Dragoner und die Pferde wie tot im Stroh schlafend" (A, p. 110). He writes his mother that his living quarters smell of "Wachtmeister und Hundefett, in unserem Vorzimmer nach Franz und nach nicht zimmerreinen Terriers..." (B, 1:132). Another letter concludes: "Die Hunde schlafen, der Franz schläft, der B. schläft, die Offiziere und Pferde schlafen " (B, 1:133).

His father bought Hofmannsthal a chestnut mare (Fuchs) which at first delighted the young officer. He strove to improve his riding, considering good horsemanship indispensable to a true gentleman: "Ich möchte sehr berühmt werden; ich möchte gut reiten können; gut italienisch, gehen und reden und ein wirklicher gentleman sein."[1] Letters from the summer of 1895 refer often to his pleasure in outdoor activity and in physical exercise, which he considered a good alternative to the indoor life of a Viennese writer. He had responded a year earlier to Richard Dehmel's intimations that he might be an aesthete or a decadent by writing, "Ich arbeite mässig, schlafe viel, reite und fechte täglich..."[2]

---

1 Hugo von Hofmannsthal and Edgar Karg von Bebenburg, *Briefwechsel* (Frankfurt: S. Fischer, 1966), p. 22.
2 "Hugo von Hofmannsthal − Richard Dehmel: Briefwechsel 1893−1919," ed. Martin Stern. *Hofmannsthal-Blätter*, Heft 21/22 (1979), p. 15.

In spite of his enjoyment of riding, Hofmannsthal failed to master his horse completely; in a conversation with Helene von Nostitz years later he describes his "merkwürdiges Verhältnis" to this "wildes, unheimliches Pferd," his chestnut mare, which at least once broke from his control and endangered his very life.[3] It was through the struggle with his rebellious horse that Hofmannsthal became acquainted with physical danger, as we shall see in examining the events surrounding the composition of the poem, "Ein Traum von großer Magie." Furthermore, his troubling experiences with this horse gave rise to several instances of unconscious symbolism (in the Dickensian sense); Andreas' horse in the unfinished novel is a "Fuchs," as is the unruly horse which Sigismund intuitively masters in *Der Turm*.

His mare defied his authority not only through disobedience; she had an "unartiges und verbittertes Temperament." Hofmannsthal describes her "sogenannte Rassigkeit, ... eine mit dem ganzen Temperament zusammenhängende sexuell-geistige Störung" (B, 1:165). Because of her delicate hooves, the mare could seldom be ridden over hard ground. Hofmannsthal confronted her difficult temperament and physical infirmities with feelings of inadequacy and helplessness. His loss of self-assurance is evident in the tone of a letter to his parents describing the mare's latest injury:

> Dieser leichte Sturz ist nicht der Rede wert, wird bei Veränderung des Stalles und ruhiger rationeller Behandlung höchstwahrscheinlich baldigst verschwinden und brauchte gar nicht erwähnt zu werden. Auch ich selber würde das Pferd herrichten können, wenn mich nicht manchmal eine so merkwürdige Ratlosigkeit erfassen würde, genau wie bei den mathematischen Kompositionen im Gymnasium. (B, 1:160)

Toward the end of his military service in Göding he worries that the mare is still lame, but writes resigniedly, "Ich hab' mir so unsinnig viel Gedanken und Sorgen darüber gemacht, dass ich's jetzt aufgebe" (B, 1:177).

The depiction of ill or lame horses figures predominantly in Hofmannsthal's "Soldatengeschichte," drawing on his military experi-

---

[3] Hugo von Hofmannsthal and Helene von Nostitz, *Briefwechsel* (Frankfurt: S. Fischer, 1965), p. 162.

ences from the summer of 1895 (SW, 29:50-62). The story's protagonist, Schwendar, looks after disabled horses. Suffering from childhood memories of an aunt's drowning and his mother's death, he undergoes a quasi-religious experience which comforts and encourages him. The transformation in his character is portrayed through the confidence and self-assurance with which he now enters the stalls. Horses which suddenly appear lame also constitute important elements of the plots of "Reitergeschichte" and the unfinished *Andreas* novel.

With his chestnut mare in Göding, then, Hofmannsthal experienced the danger of being unable to control a horse, and the helplessness of being unable to cure its lameness. Furthermore, as the following quotation demonstrates, these experiences gave him new insight into the power of money:

> Im Leben gefangen sein.
>
> Die Elemente. Der beschwerliche Staub, die mühseligen Steine, die traurigen Strassen, die harten Dämme, die Tücke des Pferdes und des eigenen Körpers.
>
> Leben und sich ausleben nur im Kampf mit den widerstrebenden Mächten. So lehrt mich mein Pferd den Wert des Vermögens, der Unabhängigkeit. (A, pp. 126-27)

Hofmannsthal came to realize the power of money to shield his sensitivity from the desolate ugliness of his surroundings. The merchant's son, Claudio, and Titian's pupils use wealth in the same manner to distance themselves from the contemplation of depressing or menacing surroundings: they retreat into the cocoon of aesthetic pleasure. Although "Lebenslied" celebrates the triumph of such a mode of existence, the frequent intrusion of threatening reality, usually in the form of death, into the other early works demonstrates Hofmannsthal's awareness of the fragility of this privileged life style. The same insight is revealed in his letters: "Ich glaube: das schöne Leben verarmt einen. Wenn man immer so leben könnte, wie man will, würde man alle Kraft verlieren" (B, 1:185). In another letter he writes:

> Das Leben, das wir in Wien führen, ist nicht gut. Wenigstens sollte es unterbrochen werden, auch hie und da durch sehr unscheinbare Reisen, durch den Aufenthalt in kleinen unschönen Städten und am Land. Wir leben in

geistiger Beziehung wie die Cocotten, die nur französischen Salat und Gefrorenes essen.[4]

The year of military service also taught Hofmannsthal that his creative fantasy as well as money could serve as a bulwark against menacing reality. He confides to his journal:

> 22.VI. [1895] Nachtübung. Der Dragoner Schmidt stärker als ich. Das Benehmen der Pferde in der Nacht. ... 23 ... An den Dragoner Schmidt gedacht. Eine phantastische Komödie, des Starken und des Schwachen, Verträumten, dem Unmittelbarkeit fehlt und der zuletzt doch quasi der Stärkere bleibt. (A, p. 122)

The weaker combattant is doubtless Hofmannsthal himself; by writing a fantasy comedy he intends to make good his lack of physical strength. Dragoon Schmidt may be superior to him in body, but Hofmannsthal defeats him through his creative imagination. Psychology defines this attempt to outweigh feelings of inferiority in one area through higher accomplishments in another as compensation, to which Hofmannsthal owes in part the composition of "Ein Traum von großer Magie" as we shall see later.

It would be unfair to contend that Hofmannsthal reacted to the threat of hostile reality only with a desire to shield himself through wealth or to prove his own worth through his art. As his letters show, he deems suffering an ennobling experience: "Das Leben ist für uns alle unsagbar schwer, tückisch und grenzenlos übelwollend: im Ertragen liegt alles Schöne und Wertvolle."[5] He realizes that the crude existence in the remote villages where he has served has given him a deeper contact with his fellow creatures: "Vorher geht man in Gedanken leichtfertig mit den Wesen um wie mit Marionetten (Scheinhaftes Leben.)" (A, p. 127).

He counters his experience of physical inferiority and of the inability to master his horse by increased poetic creativity. His dominance through the power of the word remains uncontested. "Magie," as he calls this power, shall animate the desolate villages, illuminate the chaos of soldiers and horses sleeping side by side.

---

4   Hugo von Hofmannsthal and Richard Beer-Hofmann, *Briefwechsel*, ed. Eugene Weber (Frankfurt: S. Fischer), 1972, p. 59.
5   Hofmannsthal and Karg von Bebenburg, *Briefwechsel*, p. 52.

Lebensweg; führt zu immer stärkerer Magie. Magie: Fähigkeit, Verhältnisse mit Zauberblick zu ergreifen, Gabe, das Chaos durch Liebe zu beleben. Chaos als totes dumpfes Hinlungern der Dinge im Halblicht. (A, p. 124)

Chaos is the wooded thicket his horse bolts toward, chaos is the labyrinth of stairs and passageways in "Das Märchen," chaos is the wretched village in the "Reitergeschichte." Silence, the absence of language, darkens the irrational forbidding chaos. Dead silence fills the unnamed village where Lerch's hopes are betrayed; the forest animals flee silently before the hunter in *Das kleine Welttheater;* Sigismund imprisoned in the tower is capable only of disjointed sentence fragments, his speech reduced to an animal-like cry. Animals lead man into the chaotic wordless realm or they confront him there. Through intellect and language man attempts to assert his superiority over the mute creature. The clash of these opposing spheres: that of commanding "magic" language and that of chaos forms the core of "Das Märchen der 672. Nacht" and of the "Reitergeschichte."

One of Hofmannsthal's earlier sketches deals with the same clash of opposing spheres and reflects the influence of his period of military service. Between December 1894 and July 1895 he attempted an adaptation of the "Geschichte von den Prinzen Amgiad und Assad" from the *Arabian Nights*.[6] Although his notes are too fragmentary to be coherently interpreted, they are interesting as evidence of his earliest concern with animal imagery. On May 30, 1895, he writes:

> Der andere: er sieht das Leben fortwährend harmonisch, aber wie hinter einer Glasscheibe, unerreichbar: ... Fortwährend verwirrt ihn, daß dieselben Abenteuer in der Vorstellung und in der Realität so gar nicht zusammenzuhängen scheinen ... er sieht gleichsam mit einem halben Auge übers Leben hinaus, wie einer der träumt und dem die reale Welt hineinspielt, weil er nicht tief genug schläft.
>
> Straße vor der Begegnung der beiden Prinzen mit ihrem Großvater, dem Zauberer und Kaiser Timur: die im Leben gefangenen Wesen: viele Hunde,

---

6 For a discussion of the source of this tale see Wolfgang Köhler, *Hugo von Hofmannsthal und "Tausendundeine Nacht,"* Europäische Hochschulschriften, series 1, Deutsche Literatur und Germanistik, vol. 77 (Bern: Lang, 1972), pp. 96-102 and Hanna B. Lewis, "The Arabian Nights and the Young Hofmannsthal," *German Life and Letters* 37 (1984), 188.

die sich balgen, Kinder; ... kranke Tiere (mit ihren besonderen Krankheiten: Dummkoller etc.) (A, p. 113; SW, 29:40-41)

This episode, not found in the *Arabian Nights,* demonstrates the confrontation of fantasy and reality through the encounter with unhealthy or repulsive animals. Animals usually present themselves to the human imagination as healthy normal creatures, the horse proud and noble as in the French romantic paintings of Géricault and Delacroix, the dog faithful and affectionate, like Bauschan in Thomas Mann's "Herr und Hund." Hofmannsthal, on the other hand, frequently portrays animals as ugly, diseased, and without the usual tie to man.

The quarreling dogs recur in "Reitergeschichte," but Hofmannsthal has already made their meaning clear: they are trapped in the material existence, outside the harmonious dream world and beyond the magical pale of art. Marta Karlweis reports that Hofmannsthal was by no means fond of dogs:

> Daß man ihm Gefühl zeige, liebte er nicht, Zärtlichkeit erweisen sah ich ihn nicht einmal einem Kinde oder einem Hund. Hunde mochte er nicht leiden, Kinder machten ihn scheu.[7]

Hofmannsthal's letters and journal offer ample proof that he found dogs distasteful; in one letter he muses "daß so viele Lebende für mich dumpf und tot sind, ärger wie Hunde."[8]

His dislike of the dog is certainly not an exceptional case; expressions such as "auf dem Hund sein," "ein Hundesleben führen" and "auf den Hund kommen" imply contempt for the dog.[9] Freud dis-

---

7 "Erinnerungen an Hofmannsthal," in: *Hugo von Hofmannsthal: der Dichter im Spiegel der Freunde*, ed. Helmut A Fiechtner, 2d ed., (Bern: Franck, 1963), p. 254.

8 Hofmannsthal and Karg von Bebenburg, *Briefwechsel,* p. 100.

9 Karl-Heinz Fingerhut in his study of Franz Kafka's animal imagery, describes as follows the influence of Jewish tradition in Kafka's use of the dog symbol:
"Beeinflußt von der jüdischen Tradition sieht Kafka in diesem Tier nicht positiv den treuen Freund und Begleiter des Menschen, sondern ... das devot-aufdringliche Wesen, das mit hartnäckiger Neugier und Sinnlichkeit alles beschnüffelt, umläuft und beschmutzt und deshalb ein Bild verachtenswerten Daseins ist."

tinguishes two traits making the dog repugnant to man, "daß es ein Geruchstier ist, das sich vor Exkrementen nicht scheut, und daß es sich seiner sexuellen Funktionen nicht schämt."[10] Hofmannsthal occasionally refers to such aspects of the dog's behavior. A servant in *Christinas Heimreise,* annoyed by a man whose dog is nosing around her baggage, complains: "Es geht nicht, mein Herr. Wenn Ihr Hund sich unartig aufführt, so haben wir alle Dorfhunde hinter unserem Gepäck her. Das wäre eine saubere Wirtschaft" (L, 1:403). Pierre in *Das gerettete Venedig* returns to his mistress, Aquilina, but tells her disgustedly,

> Freu dich nicht.
> Es sind gemeine Seelen, die zurück
> wie Hunde gehn zu ihrem Ausgespie'nen.
> (D, 2:165; SW, 4:69)

Freud explains that the dog, devoid of that shame which must be painstakingly taught to children, reminds man of past, more primitive stages of his development and is therefore repugnant to him. Marta Karlweis has commented on Hofmannsthal's dislike of both dog and child; indeed he mentions them together remarkably often. In "Terzinen über Vergänglichkeit" the poet finds it "grauenvoll"

> ... daß mein eignes Ich, durch nichts gehemmt,
> Herüberglitt aus einem kleinen Kind
> Mir wie ein Hund unheimlich stumm und fremd.
> (GLD, p. 17)

Schwendar in the "Soldatengeschichte" mentioned earlier likewise confronts memories of his earlier self, a figure (Gestalt) "die ihm fremd war wie ein fremdes Kind, ja unverständlich wie ein Hund" (SW 29, 52). In a post-war letter, Hofmannsthal connects dog and child in the description of a grisly incident:

(Die Funktion der Tierfiguren im Werke Franz Kafkas, Abhandlungen zur Kunst-Musik- und Literaturwissenschaft, vol. 89 [Bonn: Bouvier, 1969], p. 215.)

10 *Gesammelte Werke,* 18 vols. (London: Imago, 1940-68), 14:459.

Hier geht alles de mal en pis, unlängst haben Leute ein kleines Kind erschlagen und weggeworfen, und andere haben das Fleisch gegessen unter dem Vorwand, sie hätten es für einen Hund gehalten.[11]

As a cavalry officer in Göding he observes "Zehn oder zwölf Kinder von Wachtmeistern, zwei bis sieben Jahre alt, und fünfzehn Hunde, alle häßlich ..." (B, 1:164).[12] In Tlumacz he finds everything hideous, "die Menschen, die Pferde, die Hunde, auch die Kinder."[13] The dyer's wife in "Die Frau ohne Schatten" marvels at the dual nature of a child, at once debased and sublime: "Schmutzig ist ein kleines Kind und sie müssen es dem Haushund darreichen, um es rein zu lecken; und dennoch ist es schön wie die aufgehende Sonne" (E, p. 337; SW, 28:168).[14]

We may conclude that Hofmannsthal regards the dog, like the child, as a relic of more primitive stages of man's development and a reminder of his corporeal nature.

The physical attributes of any creature become more salient when it is ill; disease deprives it of personality and mobility and distorts its interaction with its surroundings and with man. Accordingly the infirmities of the quarreling dogs (assuming them to be included among the "kranke Tiere" in the story of Amgiad and Assad) underscore their bestial sensual nature and negate any connotations of loyalty, affection or devotion to its master which the reader is accustomed to associate with the dog.

A horse appearing in the same story also falls ill:

> Der Prinz Amgiad mit der Leiche seines Bruders am Weg zu Timur. Er muß ein größeres Pferd nehmen, um den Leichnam zu tragen. Erlebnisse mit diesem Pferd, seine Krankheit.

---

11 Hugo von Hofmannsthal and Carl J. Burckhardt, *Briefwechsel* (Frankfurt: S. Fischer, 1956), p. 24.
12 Also given in: Hugo von Hofmannsthal and Leopold von Andrian, *Briefwechsel* (Frankfurt: S. Fischer, 1968), p. 54.
13 Ibid., p. 63.
14 These utterances contrast sharply with Hofmannsthal's esteem of the child as one step toward the individual's assimilation into society: in "Ad me ipsum" he writes: "Der Weg zum Sozialen als Weg zum Höheren Selbst: ... a) durch die Tat b) durch das Werk c) durch das Kind" (A, p. 217).

Brüderlichkeit aller Tiere in einer großen Mulde erkannt. Gespenstisch sieht er in allen Tieren sich selbst. Auch die Unterschiede von Klein und Groß werden ihm plötzlich sehr nichtig... (A, p. 113; SW, 29:41-42)

Superstition holds that a horse drawing a hearse or carrying a corpse may become saddened or even ill through compassion with the dead person.[15] It seems possible that the horse's sickness leads Amgiad to the realization that all creatures, human and animal, are made of mortal stuff. If such is the case, his experiences with the horse supplement the recognition of the dogs as "die im Leben gefangenen Wesen:" both confront the prince with incontrovertible evidence of his corporeal and therefore mortal existence.

Hofmannsthal seems to vacillate between presenting this awareness of shared physical mortality through the prince's identification with all animals ("Brüderlichkeit aller Tiere in einer großen Mulde erkannt") and through his sudden recognition of their distinct and separate being as external to his own, an insight prepared in the encounter between the princes and the dogs and diseased animals. In later works the same theme — the material existence common to man and beast alike — will be expressed, as in the "Reitergeschichte" through the encounter with animals clearly set apart from man and which obtrude upon his consciousness through their depravity or suffering; the dissolution of individuality in an *unio mystica* encompassing animals as well as all other creatures of the universe is symptomatic of the earliest attempts, "Amgiad und Assad" and "Das Märchen der 672. Nacht."

In a letter Hofmannsthal gives the following synopsis of his story:

... Der Lebensweg führt eigentlich zur immer stärkeren Magie, wie das in den Prinzen Amgiad und Assad so schön ist. Denn schließlich in einem welligen gelbbraunen Land werden ihnen eine Menge Hunde und kranker Pferde höchst wunderbar ... (B, 1:158; SW, 29:286)

As well as prefiguring major themes of his later work, the tale mirrors the sum of Hofmannsthal's experience in military service: on the road toward increasing literary productivity he, like the princes, en-

---

15 Hans Bächthold-Stäubli, ed. *Handwörterbuch des deutschen Aberglaubens*, 10 vols. (Berlin: de Gruyter, 1927-43), 6, col. 1907.

counters a world of hostile, hideous reality crystallized into the ugly dogs and children he observes in Göding and into a sick horse which teaches him the limits of his capabilities. Neither the power of money to alleviate the desolation of his surroundings nor the power of language to conjure up a world of art suffices to ban the awareness of physical needs and infirmities common to man as well as animal.

CHAPTER II

"EIN TRAUM VON GROSSER MAGIE"

One aspect of this poem pertinent to our topic has gone unnoticed by most of Hofmannsthal's critics and deserves attention here. The dogs and horses appearing in the third stanza have been interpreted only in the most general terms as symbols of life or reality:

> So sind die verschiedenen Tiere im "Lebenslied" und im "Traum von großer Magie" nicht unter dem Begriff der Tiermetaphorik zu vereinen oder sonst in eine tradierte Symbolik zu stellen, sondern sie verkörpern das in dichterische Anschauung gefaßte Leben, das gerade in seiner sprachlichen Erscheinungsform, d.h. so wie die Worte ausgewählt und zusammengestellt werden, das ausdrücken will, was jenseits der Worte liegt.[1]

The significance of these animals within the poem is not readily apparent, they hardly seem an integral part of the text, dominated by the sublime vision of the *Magier*,[2] and in fact the dogs and horses do not appear in any of the preparatory sketches for the poem.

1 Jürgen Schwalbe, *Sprache und Gebärde im Werk Hugo von Hofmannsthals*, Studien zur deutschen Sprache und Literatur, vol. 2 (Freiburg, Breisgau: Klaus Schwartz, 1971), p. 66. Hans Steffen concurs in stating simply: "im Bild der Jagd wird das Leben als Bewegung sichtbar." See: "Das sich selbst erlebende Ich. Hugo von Hofmannsthals 'Ein Traum von großer Magie'," *Jahrbuch der deutschen Schillergesellschaft* 18 (1974): 511. Erny Wampach gives a sound text-immanent analysis of the poem based on its "Entstehungsgeschichte," but mentions no specific incidents; rather she concludes that the poem deals with Hofmannsthal's turn away from the study of law to a literary career. "Ein Traum von großer Magie," in *Mélanges de linguistique et de littérature offerts au Professeur Henri Draye à l'occasion de son émeritat*, eds. Jacques Lerot and Rudolf Kern, Université de Louvain, Recueil de travaux d'histoire et de philosophie, 14 (Louvain: Bibliothèque de l'université, 1978), pp. 241-55.
2 The words "Magier" and "Magie" will be retained in our discussion for the English terms "magician" and "magic" inappropriately connote side-show sleight of hand.

In a conversation with Helene von Nostitz in 1906, Hofmannsthal informs us that the poem was written immediately following a wild horseback ride in the summer of 1895.[3] It will be useful to our interpretation of "Ein Traum von großer Magie" to quote at length from Frau von Nostitz' account of Hofmannsthal's conversation:

> Dieses Gedicht habe ich in einem großen Glücksgefühl geschrieben. Ich war lange krank gewesen, und mußte beim Militär dienen. Ich besaß ein wildes unheimliches Pferd. Es war ein merkwürdiges Verhältnis zwischen uns. Es war wie ein Dämon, dieses Pferd. Eines Tages ging es durch, wir flogen durch die Wälder. Es war schön, denn die Sonnenstrahlen schossen durch die Baumstämme und flimmerten um uns. Ich wußte, daß wir dem sicheren Tode entgegenritten, denn vor uns lag ein Walddickicht mit harten aneinander gepreßten Stämmen. Da, plötzlich besann sich das Pferd und trabte, langsamer werdend, in eine andere Richtung. Wir kamen in ein freundliches Dorf. Ein schönes böhmisches Mädchen trat mir entgegen, den Körper nur mit einem losen Hemde bekleidet. Zum ersten Male nach langen Wochen fühlte ich Hunger; ich bat sie um ein Glas Milch und trank es aus. Dann saß ich noch eine Weile. Der Mond ging auf, und in seinem Schein ritt ich nach Hause. Ich habe ein solches Glücksgefühl wie in den Stunden niemals empfunden.[4]

This event apparently became for Hofmannsthal one of the symbolic experiences described in our opening chapter. Although at first glance it appears to lack their chief criterion, a sensation of mystical union with the cosmos, this unio mystica is hinted at by the word "Glücksgefühl" which begins and ends the passage, and found expression in "Ein Traum von großer Magie," the poetic crystallization of this event. Because of its traumatic impact on the young Hofmannsthal, the incident is interwoven through the poem, "Reitergeschichte," *Andreas* and *Der Turm,* works in which the rider's mastery of his horse is of critical importance. Yet our understanding of the symbolic significance of mastering or failing to master a horse is by no means automatic. The power of the horseback riding symbol to evoke in us those connotations Hofmannsthal intended as its impact remains questionable. Because it will become a major source of Hofmannsthal's horse imagery, we must discuss it in detail.

---

3 Particulars of the composition and dating of the poem are given in SW, 1:251-52.
4 Hofmannsthal and Helene von Nostitz, *Briefwechsel,* p. 162; SW, 1:252.

In this account Hofmannsthal confesses his complete incapability as an equestrian, for even the beginning rider must be able to turn and stop his mount. We do not learn whether he lacked the strength to do so after his long illness, or whether the indolence and boredom of military service had lamed his will. In any case, it was the horse which turned away from the thicket and thus saved its rider. The incident was in all likelihood not an isolated event, for even the slightest rebellion against human control, if not immediately quashed, incites the horse to repeated attempts at revolt. In fact, Hofmannsthal confesses to his friend Leopold von Andrian that during his service in Göding the ongoing struggle with his defiant horse even disturbed his sleep.[5]

The speaker in the passage just quoted splits into rider and narrator, into the man in acute physical danger and the story-teller creating an impression for his audience. Of course the ambivalent point of view may be explained by equating the rider with Hofmannsthal of 1895 who underwent the dangerous experience and the narrator with the Hofmannsthal of 1906 recalling the event for his friends, but closer examination suggests a different interpretation. The storyteller seems oblivious to his precarious circumstances, he remarks upon the beauty of the wild ride and the play of light and shadow.[6] By contrast the rider is frightened by the knowledge that the horse may at any moment throw him against the hard, densely clustered tree trunks. As soon as the horse slows to a trot, the speaker's two points of view merge again into one voice. Now the entire scene smiles benignly on him, the village is "freundlich," the girl "schön." After the exhausting deadly fright, Hofmannsthal feels only the elemental bodily sensations; his life has reduced itself to the instinct for

---

5   Hofmannsthal and Leopold von Andrian, *Briefwechsel*, p. 121.
6   David Miles considers this play of light and shadow one of the characteristics of the mythic experience, "grounded in an imagery of chiaroscuro." He points out that the contrast of darkness and light is a common feature of several decisive scenes in the *Andreas* novel and functions as a "dynamic blend of opposites" symbolizing the "coincidentia oppositorum," an essential component of myth (*Hofmannsthal's Novel Andreas*, p. 160). In the description of Hofmannsthal's wild ride in Göding the contrast seems to point out the divergence of an awareness of the beauty of nature and life — sun — and the consciousness of deadly peril — the dark thicket of trees.

self-preservation; he is aware only of hunger and of a latent eroticism embodied in the girl wearing nothing but a loose garment. His intense happiness springs from a renewed lust for life, doubly precious to him now because barely preserved.

Just as Hofmannsthal's confidence in his poetic creativity provided an imaginary triumph over Dragoon Schmidt, the viewpoint of the storyteller, superimposed on that of the endangered rider, spreads a glow of success over his account of the wild ride. Indeed the intrusion of the experience into Hofmannsthal's conversation years later reveals an attempt to come to grips with it, and to endow it in his memory with a tinge of victory, of superiority over the very real physical circumstances of his plight.

The rider's control over his horse depends not on brute physical strength, but upon force of will. Faulkner characterizes the horse as that "which you control only through your ability to keep the animal from realizing that actually you cannot, that actually it is the stronger."[7] Thus it is hardly surprising that expert horsemanship develops in Hofmannsthal's writing into a symbol of absolute control over external circumstances by force of will, a capability attributed to Baron Rofrano in the "Reitergeschichte" and to Sigismund in *Der Turm*.[8]

This unquestioned dominance over one's self and surroundings may reveal itself just as convincingly through gesture as through language. Such is the case in "Die Beiden," whose second stanza reads as follows:

> So leicht und fest war seine Hand:
> Er ritt auf einem jungen Pferde,
> Und mit nachlässiger Gebärde
> Erzwang er, daß es zitternd stand.

A girl approaches the youth, her gait "leicht und sicher," and hands him a goblet of wine:

---

7 William Faulkner, *Absalom, Absalom!*, The Modern Library (New York: Random House, 1964), p. 53.
8 Cf. Rolf Tarot's remarks on riding and the power of gesture regarding Sigismund and "Die Beiden," *Hugo von Hofmannsthal, Daseinsformen und dichterische Struktur* (Tübingen: Niemeyer, 1970), pp. 200-201.

> Jedoch, wenn er aus ihrer Hand
> Den leichten Becher nehmen sollte,
> So war es beiden allzu schwer:
> Denn beide bebten sie so sehr,
> Daß keine Hand die and're fand
> Und dunkler Wein am Boden rollte.
> (GLD, p. 11; SW, 1:50)

This poem may be compared to Hofmannsthal's meeting with the Bohemian girl who brought him a glass of milk after his wild ride in Göding. But Hofmannsthal, in contrast to the youth in the poem, lacked the critical self-assurance expressed here through gesture. The girl's light sure movement "suggests her inner quiet, completeness, her total harmony with her surroundings. Similarly, the young man is *leicht* in that he is in total control of *his* world."[9] He rides a young horse, probably spirited and not altogether tame, yet a "nachlässige Gebärde" suffices to halt it, it trembles before his superior strength of will, which lends authority to even a spontaneous gesture.[10] Baron Rofrano in a like manner raises "mit einer nachlässigen, beinahe gezierten Bewegung den Arm" to shoot Anton Lerch (E, p. 61; SW, 28:48). Andrew O. Jaszi views the self-assurance expressed through the youth's commanding gesture as more significant than the action itself: "der ganze Nachdruck ist nicht auf die Handlung als Folge eines Wunsches gelegt, sondern auf die Handlung als Verkörperung eines Gefühls. ..."[11]

Because of the preponderant role of gesture — non-language — in mastering the horse, control over the horse becomes an opposite pole

---

9   Michael Porter, " 'Leicht' und 'Schwer' in the Poetry of Hugo von Hofmannsthal," *Monatshefte* 65 (1973), 245.

10 My interpretation of mastery over the horse as evidence of a superior strength of will differs from the interpretation offered by Mary E. Gilbert. She sees in the relationship of rider to horse not a tension between will and instinct, but a balance of the two. She regards the youth in "Die Beiden" as "a symbol of pre-existential life, that transitory condition when the balance between the instinctual and the spiritual aspects of the person is as yet undisturbed, when the being is at one with himself and the world." See her article, "The Image of the Horse in Hofmannsthal's Poetic Works," *Modern Austrian Literature* 7 (1974), 62.

11 "Ausdruck und Leben in Hugo von Hofmannsthals 'Die Beiden,' " in: *Hugo von Hofmannsthal*, ed. Sibylle Bauer, p. 220.

or counterweight to the power wielded through the word. Not a word is spoken in "Die Beiden," and Hofmannsthal's brush with death must have taught him the inutility of language, and thus of his highest accomplishment, poetic creativity, in the battle of wills with his daemonic horse. We shall return to this theme shortly in connection with "Ein Traum von großer Magie."

Although one might assume Hofmannsthal's experience with his runaway mare to be the starting point of this opposition between horse and language, his conception connects with literary precedents: Goethe shares the concept of language as a counter force to the horse. In the eighth chapter of the second book of the *Wanderjahre,* Wilhelm visits Felix in the "pädagogische Provinz." In keeping with Felix' desire to learn to ride as quickly as possible in order to return to Hersilie, he is given the task of caring for horses. Wilhelm asks the overseer what additional instruction is given those pupils tending horses to prevent them from assuming the animal traits of their charges. He is informed "daß gerade mit dieser gewaltsam und rauh scheinenden Bestimmung die zarteste von der Welt verknüpft sei: Sprachübung und Sprachbildung."[12] The overseer explains the necessity of language instruction because pupils come to the province from several countries; to prevent each nationality from forming a closed group, all pupils speak the same language for a month's time, then change to another. Goethe concerns himself with language as a means of social traffic; a common language ties the individual to a group or the group to the whole community. The rough life tending horses, on the other hand, coarsens the boys' nature; language instruction serves to counteract the inclination to violence and aggression fostered by their existence among animals.

To be sure Hofmannsthal's early work deals less with speech as a communal tie — its function in the *Wanderjahre* — than with language as the poet's chosen medium, as his means for producing that ecstatic union with the universe from which his art springs. These experiences isolate the entranced poet instead of bringing him closer to his fellow man:

---

12 *Goethes Werke,* 8:246.

> Die Magie sucht das Moment der Mitteilung aus der Sprache völlig auszumerzen. Sie verunmöglicht jedes Gespräch und bleibt immer monologisch, da sie die Wahrheit durch Schönheit und nicht durch Wirklichkeit zu erreichen sucht. ... Indem sie das Ich mit dem Kosmos zu vereinigen vorgibt, löst sie es aus der menschlichen Gesellschaft heraus.[13]

Amgiad, sensible of the "Brüderlichkeit aller Tiere," remains in this enchanted union with the cosmos. Any awareness of reality vanishes in this state. The euphoria created in the expansion of self to encompass the the entire world denies the necessity of any bridge, such as speech, to span the gap between one individual and the next, denies in fact any distinction or separation between one individual and the rest of the universe. But the horse destroys these mystical epiphanies. The horse becomes ill and useless to man, the horse bolts and endangers its rider's life, the horse obliges his owner to consider his financial responsibilities and the horse forces its rider to acknowledge the fragility of his own body. The monologue glorifying the beauty of the world ceases as soon as the poet is brought to the realization that his individuality has not dissolved, that he must survive or perish according to the fate of his body. Hofmannsthal's wild ride contains the seed of this new awareness of his own limitations: the narrator describing the beauty of the sun's rays in the forest has partaken of the mystical union with the cosmos; upon realizing that his horse may cast him against the hard tree trunks he returns to the individual consciousness.

Now that we have established the significance of the events leading up to the composition of the poem, we may proceed to examine the text itself. The poet says very little about the animals:

> Und früher liefen schon geschirrte Pferde
> Hindurch und Hunde eine ganze Schar
> An meinem Bett vorbei. (GLD, p. 20; SW I, 52)

We notice first that no people accompany the horse and dogs. Yet the fact that the horses are saddled or harnessed points to human ownership. Have the horses somehow escaped from human control like Hofmannsthal's rebellious mare in Göding? Or have the horses and dogs somehow become separated from a hunt? In the poem "Le-

---

13 Pestalozzi, *Sprachskepsis und Sprachmagie*, pp. 106-8.

ben, Traum und Tod" the poet's boat glides past verdant shores "Feucht im Abendrot,/ Stiller Pferde Tränke,/ Herrenloser Pferde .../ Leise treibt das Boot" (GLD, p. 510). These horses, just as free of any master as those in "Ein Traum von großer Magie" are nonetheless not disturbing to the reader, for they show no evidence of human ownership. Rather they seem to exist in a natural state anterior to man's domination. Furthermore they remain quiet, drinking or grazing silently as part of the peaceful landscape, in sharp contrast to the horses of "Ein Traum von großer Magie" which run through a park or garden where they do not belong.

The pack of dogs accompanying the horses suggests disorder and confusion. Stray dogs often appear during times of war or pestilence, as in the "Reitergeschichte" and in the prophecy to King Basilius in *Der Turm*. Their presence points to the breakdown of moral and social order, to the disintegration of a human community which ordinarily feeds and tends the dogs attached to it.

A further disquieting effect is the dreamer's unprotected situation. The four doors of the "Pavillon" where he is sleeping are of glass and, in addition, they stand open, affording no protective enclosure around the bed, normally a secure place of refuge.[14] The intrusion of these animals into the sleeper's proximity may be a reminiscence of Hofmannsthal's experience in the military; he observes cavalrymen sleeping in the straw beside their horses (A, p. 110). Speaking in general terms, the pavilion surrounds although it does not enclose the imaginary world of the dream and the dreamer, a fragile sphere threatened by the violent incursion of chaos embodied in the horses and dogs.

The position of the horses and dogs within the text must not be overlooked. They appear fleetingly in the third stanza, introduced by

14 Hanna B. Lewis finds several parallels between "Ein Traum von großer Magie" and Coleridge's "Kubla Khan," among them the poem's setting. She compares the pavilion with its open door to Coleridge's "pleasure dome" which he would build in the air; "It is a structure of the poet's imagination." "Hofmannsthal, Shelley and Keats," *German Life and Letters*, n. s., 27 (1974): 221. Symbolically the physical threat posed to the pavilion by the running animals may be equated by the threat to the poet's imaginary world presented by the self knowledge gained in Hofmannsthal's encounters with animals.

the word "und" as an observation of no particular importance. It becomes obvious that the events of these first three stanzas, forming a sort of prologue to the poem, are not related in the order of their occurrence. If we rearrange the stanzas according to the sequence of events, they belong in the following order:

> Und früher liefen schon geschirrte Pferde
> Hindurch und Hunde eine ganze Schar
> An meinem Bett vorbei. ...
>
> Durch offene Glastüren ging die Luft.
> Ich schlief im Pavillon zu ebner Erde,
> Und durch vier offene Türen ging die Luft –
>
> Viel königlicher als ein Perlenband
> Und kühn wie junges Meer im Morgenduft,
> So war ein großer Traum – wie ich ihn fand.

To what purpose does Hofmannsthal distort the order of these stanzas? And what is this apparently incoherent prologue supposed to convey to the reader?

If the poet had followed the above order of the stanzas quoted and had introduced the animals at the very beginning of the poem, they would have carried a great deal more importance in the text as a whole. Bearing in mind that the dogs and horses represent a loss or defiance of human control, hostile elements which poetic *Magie* is powerless to master, it becomes clear that Hofmannsthal intentionally diminishes their significance by giving them only a modest place in the third stanza. Just as the dream which followed their appearance left a more vivid impression on the dreamer's memory, the vision of the omniscient *Magier* is intended to outweigh the fleeting incursion of chaos into the world of creative fantasy.

The final line of the third stanza affords a second explanation for the altered sequence of these first three stanzas. This line forms the transition from the prologue to the vision of the *Magier:*

> Und früher liefen schon geschirrte Pferde
> Hindurch und Hunde eine ganze Schar
> An meinem Bett vorbei. Doch die Gebärde
>
> Des Magiers – des Ersten, Großen – war
> Auf einmal zwischen mir und einer Wand:
> Sein stolzes Nicken, königliches Haar.
> (GLD, p. 20; SW, 1:52)

The animals disappear immediately upon the entrance of the *Magier,* as if his lordly gesture dismissed them. If they came at the very beginning of the poem, two stanzas would stand between their appearance and that of the *Magier;* they would have to leave the scene by themselves. As the poem stands, they are driven away by the *Magier's* commanding gesture, a movement which announces the transition from the half sleeping state of the prologue to the creative state personified in the *Magier.* Returning for a moment to the experience which gave rise to the poem, we may also interpret the situation of the animals immediately preceding the *Magier;* according to its biographical significance: Hofmannsthal overcame the defeat of his intellect and will power represented by his defiant horse through recourse to *Magie,* to the world of fantasy created by language; in short he compensated for his shortcomings as a horseman by a triumph of poetic creativity: "Ein Traum von großer Magie."

It is significant that the narrator does not immediately hear the *Magier's* voice, but becomes aware of his presence through his movements. For this aspect of the *Magier's* power surpasses that of the poet: the poet's language does not suffice to master the horses and dogs, to shield his bed, the dream world of poetic fantasy, from their intrusion, or to make them disappear. The *Magier,* by contrast, is master of the necessary commanding gesture. He is characterized through his movements: he nods, bows, sits, draws the depth toward him, and springs over cliffs.

His movements demonstrate his liberation from any physical constraints, limitations that Hofmannsthal found particularly trying during his experiences with animals. The speaker remains earthbound, he sleeps "im Pavillon zu ebner Erde." The *Magier,* on the other hand, frees himself from the pull of gravity; in his notes Hofmannsthal pictures godlike creativity "auf der höchsten Terrasse" (A, p. 125). Earth is the animal realm, plane of "die im Leben gefangenen Wesen" which Hofmannsthal connects with "der beschwerliche Staub, die mühseligen Steine" (A, p. 126). The physical material quality of this sphere, the earth, dogs and horses, contrasts with the sphere of the *Magier,* where the elements appear in their purest form, where water is transformed into opals and rings, where eyes resemble living jewels, where consciousness of the body dissolves: the *Magier* senses "traumhaft aller Menschen Los,/ So wie er seine eignen Glieder fühlte."[15] He is scarcely aware of his body, it is a mere shell he could cast off without suffering, as the Madman in *Das kleine Welttheater* maintains.

The dissolution of the body corresponds to the disintegration of individual consciousness; the *Magier* partakes of the fate of all mankind, like the poet who writes:

> Ganz vergessener Völker Müdigkeiten
> Kann ich nicht abtun von meinen Lidern, ...
> (GLD, p. 19; SW, 1:54)

The suspension of time and space, a state in which nothing appears large or small, nothing near or far, seems a prerequisite for that mystical union with the universe from which springs the poet's art:

> ... er leidet an dem einzelnen so sehr als an der Masse. ... Denn ihm sind Menschen und Dinge und Gedanken und Träume völlig eins. ... Er kann nichts auslassen. Keinem Wesen, keinem Ding, keinem Phantom, keiner Spukgeburt eines menschlichen Hirns darf er seine Augen verschließen. ... In ihm muß und will alles zusammenkommen. ... Aus Tier und Mensch und Traum und Ding, aus Groß und Klein, aus Erhabenem und Nichtigem [schafft er] die Welt der Bezüge. (P, 2:244-45)

At the same time, however, the mystical state protects the poet from the suffering attendant on experiencing reality as an individual. The *Magier*, and through identifying with him the dreamer-speaker of the poem, renounces individual consciousness and thereby assures his invulnerability: only individuals are capable of suffering. The *Magier*, by contrast, springs like a lion over the highest cliffs, defying the gravity which chains the individual body to earth, to its material existence. The image of the majestic lion presents the final triumph

---

15 Werner Derungs erroneously interprets these lines as evidence that the *Magier* loses his omnipresent world consciousness and becomes limited to individual bodily existence: "Nun fühlt er 'seine eignen Glieder' wie etwas Fremdes, nämlich wie 'aller Menschen Los.' Der Genius des Raumes hat sich zum körperhaften Individuum eingeschränkt. Noch weiß er um das 'Überall' aber schon bedrohen Begriffe wie 'nah und fern,' 'Klein und groß' seine aperspektivische Sicht." "Form und Weltbild der Gedichte Hugo von Hofmannsthals in ihrer Entwicklung," Diss. Freiburg, Switzerland, 1960, pp. 119-20.

over those earthbound creatures, dog and horse, and over the threat or defiance they oppose to the physical existence of the individual.

CHAPTER III

DAS MÄRCHEN DER 672. NACHT

The majority of Hofmannsthal's critics regard the "Märchen der 672. Nacht" as a moral fable; its subject is, in the words of Richard Alewyn, "die Fragwürdigkeit des schönen Lebens und seine Überwindung."[1] Werner Volke likewise interprets the story's message as follows:

> Das schöne Leben ist Lebensflucht und niemand entflieht dem Leben ungestraft. – Die Erzählung bannt ... das Grauen vor der Gemeinheit des rohen Lebens. Sie ist die verdichtete Erfahrung des Gödinger Jahres.[2]

The tale has stimulated numerous interpretations (particularly since its publication in the critical edition in 1975) ranging from the biographical to the Freudian. Eugene Weber identifies Oscar Wilde with the story's protagonist, and makes a convincing comparison be-

---

1 *Über Hugo von Hofmannsthal,* 4th ed. Kleine Vandenhoeck Reihe, nos. 57, 57a, 57b (Göttingen: Vandenhoeck & Ruprecht, 1967), p. 170. Alewyn's interpretation of the tale is shared by Wolfgang Köhler, *Hugo von Hofmannsthal und "Tausendundeine Nacht,"* pp. 72-77; Hans-Jürgen Schings, "Allegorie des Lebens," pp. 434-35; Manfred Schunicht, "Die frühen Erzählungen Hugo von Hofmannsthals," *Germanisch-Romanische Monatsschrift,* n.s. 15 (1965), 276; and by Bernhard Böschenstein, "Der junge Hofmannsthal heute," *Etudes Germaniques* 24 (1974), 163. Marcel Brion departs from such interpretations in his essay, "Hofmannsthal und die Erfahrung des Labyrinths," describing the tale as "eine Kette übernatürlicher Ursächlichkeiten, determinierter Zufälle." He places little emphasis on the catastrophe as punishment for the protagonist's retreat from reality into the world of art. (In *Hugo von Hofmannsthal,* ed. Sibylle Bauer, p. 212.) Jens Rieckmann also recognizes a conflict between the realms of art and reality, and suggests that the tale expresses Hofmannsthal's fear, "daß die Gewinnung einer festumrissenen Identität, Voraussetzung für die Menschwerdung des Künstlers, gleichbedeutend mit dem Verlust künstlerischer Produktivität sein könne." "Von der menschlichen Unzulänglichkeit: zu Hofmannsthal's 'Das Märchen der 672. Nacht'," *German Quarterly* 54 (1981), 299.
2. *Hugo von Hofmannsthal in Selbstzeugnissen und Bilddokumenten,* p. 59.

tween the merchant's son and Wilde's Dorian Gray, who also avoids reality by immersing himself in the contemplation of beautiful art.[3] Hofmannsthal complicated the question of the tale's significance by dedicating the story to Richard Beer-Hofmann and identifying him with its protagonist:

> Von dir erzählt diese Geschichte − ich wünsche, du nähmest sie als dir gegeben, geschenkt, gewidmet hin; mögen die Götter die Vorbedeutung, die man sonst Träumen zuschreibt, in ihr Gegenteil verkehren und den Dichter für ein langes Leben und mir den ausgezeichneten Freund zu meiner Freude erhalten.[4]

Yet in a letter to his father, Hofmannsthal denies that his story has any didactic intent: "Mir ist nicht eingefallen, mit der Geschichte etwas anderes zu 'meinen', als mit jeder Lokalnotiz in den Tagesblättern gemeint ist"; he hopes to have expressed "die Märchenhaftigkeit des Alltäglichen, ... das Absichtlich-Unabsichtliche, das Traumhafte" (B, 1:169; SW, 28:208). His denial of a moralistic purpose in the story does not, however, altogether contradict the warning in its dedication to Beer-Hofmann, for the dream-like atmosphere he hopes to have reproduced includes the significance of dreams as omens which he maintains in his dedication. The two differing statements of purpose may be reconciled by concluding that Hofmannsthal intended to warn his reader, as well as his friend, of the price exacted for flight from reality, but wished to clothe his message in the ambience of the dream.

Hofmannsthal frequently utilizes dreams, like memory, to place a certain distance between the events of a story and its protagonist, or the reader. Comforted by the thought that what he has read is only a dream, the reader accepts it more easily. Shakespeare secures the good will of his audience in this manner in *The Tempest* and *A Midsummer Night's Dream.* Furthermore, since the dream makes no claim to plausibility, fantasy, such as the vision of the *Magier,* can be presented as a dream without arousing the reader's critical faculties. Terrifying events are less likely to shock when they appear as a mere

---

[3] "Hofmannsthal and Oscar Wilde," *Hofmannsthal-Forschungen* 1 (1971): 99-106.
[4] Hofmannsthal and Beer-Hofmann, *Briefwechsel,* p. 222, note 60.

dream; the young lord's hunting dream in *Das kleine Welttheater* reveals the dark side of his character, but without destroying him. Painful experiences may be better overcome if recalled only as dreams; thus Sigismund survives his disastrous entrance at court by convincing himself it was nothing but a dream.

The Märchen's title purposely removes it from the sphere of reality and places it in the fantasy world of the *Arabian Nights*.[5] As with the "Traum von großer Magie," the title informs the reader that what will be narrated may seem improbable, inexplicable, or irrational. Hofmannsthal noted that both dreams and fairy tales could reveal associations or relationships hidden from the conscious mind:

> Das unablässig Märchenhafte im Leben: wir leben durch (sogar bewußtes) Verwechseln, unablässige Analogien, durch das Gewinnen der Idee. ... Das Zukünftige als ein schon Vorhandenes.
> Stufenleiter: Traum − wachender Halbtraum − Vernunft: − inneres Märchen − dichterisches Gebilde.[6]

In this series of mental activities, "Vernunft" intrudes between the dream, where inhibitions are absent, and the resulting creative work. We have already suggested that "Vernunft" (the poet's need to triumph over a deeply unsettling experience) rearranged the position of the dogs and horses at the beginning of "Ein Traum von großer Magie," and it will be useful to look for the same sort of transformation in the progression from unconscious to conscious, from dream or experience to "dichterisches Gebilde" here.

5 Hanna B. Lewis cites Hofmannsthal's introduction to a 1908 Insel Verlag edition of *Die Erzählungen aus tausendundein Nächten* as evidence that the term "Kaufmannssohn" as well as the story's title refers purposely to that source. ("The *Arabian Nights* and the Young Hofmannsthal," pp. 187-89). Wolfgang Köhler compares the events in the story to possible sources in the *Arabian Nights: Hofmannsthal und "Tausendundeine Nacht,"* pp. 72-77. For a discussion of the possible significance of the number 672 see: Jürg Matthes, "Überlegungen zur Verwendung der Zahlen in Hofmannsthals Erzählungen −, 'Die 672. Nacht'," *Germanisch-Romanische Monatsschrift* 32 (1982), 202-204, and also Heinz Rölleke, "Nochmals zum Rätsel der 672. Nacht bei Hofmannsthal," *Germanisch-Romanische Monatsschrift* 33 (1983), 344-45.
6 " 'Meine Träume'. Aspekte einer Aufzeichnung Hofmannsthals," ed. Rudolf Hirsch, *Hofmannsthal-Blätter* Heft 23/24 (1980/81), 3.

If we expand the concept of dream in Hofmannsthal's work to include reality presented as a dream, we remark that animals appear with uncommon frequency in dream-like states: the horses in the "Märchen," the degenerate dogs in "Reitergeschichte," the forest animals in *Das kleine Welttheater,* and the dog and cat tortured by the young Andreas in the novel, to cite a some of the most significant examples. The reason for the coincidence of animals and dream in Hofmannsthal's case may be that both function symbolically. We have ascertained that dog and horse represent whole complexes of emotion or experience: the dog's shameless physicality and sexuality were alleged to be reminiscent of earlier human states, and the horse was interpreted as a rebellious counter-force opposing the domination of the poet's world through his creative use of language, through "Magie." Just as various elements of feeling and experience are concentrated in the horse and dog images, the dream brings together the dreamer's repressed thoughts, unresolved doubts, and memories and combines these diverse components in an often incomprehensible series of events. Freud explains that while the conscious mind formulates its thoughts through language, the subconscious and the dream work primarily through visual images.[7] Accordingly, that which cannot be expressed through language may nonetheless be incorporated into a dream image as well as a symbol. In both cases the emotion, experience or thought reaches the mind in an acceptable form. Because the formulation of such phenomena through language forces people to abstract them and fit their content into words, it necessitates their entry into the conscious mind and may cause severe trauma. Veiled in symbolism or dreams, on the other hand, these emotions and events assume a harmless shape which we can accept subconsciously. The dream-like quality of "Das Märchen der 672. Nacht" will form the basis for our interpretation of the tale.[8] Accordingly, we will explore whether several details and events have

---

7 *Gesammelte Werke,* 2/3: 41-42.
8 Dorrit Cohn interprets the story through Freudian analysis as a "punishment dream" in " 'Als Traum erzählt': the Case for a Freudian Reading of Hofmannsthal's 'Märchen der 672. Nacht'," *Deutsche Vierteljahresschrift* 54 (1980), 284-305. Her perceptions contribute much to our understanding of Oedipal overtones in the story.

symbolic meaning which may be masked by reason or ego to facilitate their acceptance by the conscious mind. Indeed, the horse which kills the young man seems so alien to all that has appeared in the first half of the story that we must establish a basic understanding of the tale before probing the horse's possibly symbolic role within it.

The hero of the story, called simply "der Kaufmannssohn" has withdrawn from society at the age of twenty-five to a peaceful and secluded existence.[9] The fact that the young man continues to be designated by his father's occupation confirms that the merchant's son has not yet made the transition from son of his father to father of his own children. About his father we learn only that the merchant's love of the treasures in his warehouse, his unfeeling surrogate children, filled his son with anger. At the age when one would expect the young man to marry and establish his own family, he withdraws from his friends and busies himself with a book of legends about a great king, undoubtedly Alexander the Great, retreating from adulthood into a childlike fantasy. His relationship to his servants is also that of a child. His housekeeper is dear to him because she reminds him of his childhood, "die er sehnsüchtig liebte" (E, p. 9; SW, 28:16). Both his mother and his wet nurse, who was the daughter of this woman, have died. Dorrit Cohn has suggested that the pair of older servants function as surrogate parents, the manservant caring for him as an ideal father.[10]

The younger servant girl, most menacing of the four figures, is fifteen, the age of puberty, but bitter and uncommunicative. After she has attempted to kill herself by jumping from a window, the merchant's son visits her in the evening in her bedroom, but she turns away from him so abruptly that her weight falls on her injured shoulder and she faints. Her hostile reaction to his solicitude appears puzzling. Later in a greenhouse he confronts a four year old girl who reminds him of his servant, and strokes her short, fine hair:

---

9 Hermann Broch points to the name "Kaufmannssohn" as typical of the Oriental fairy tale which deals in standard figures rather than individuals: "seine Gestalten sind keine ich-getragenen, ich-tragenden Charaktere, sondern rein visuell erfaßte Typen." *Hofmannsthal und seine Zeit* (Munich: R. Piper, 1964), p. 175.

10 "Als Traum erzählt..." pp. 290-91.

> Aber augenblicklich erinnerte er sich an das Haar des Mädchens in seinem Hause, das er einmal berührt hatte, als sie totenblaß, mit geschlossenen Augen, in ihrem Bette lag, und gleich lief ihm wieder ein Schauer den Rücken hinab und seine Hände fuhren zurück. (E, p. 21; SW, 28:25)

Had he touched his servant's hair as she lay in bed after her fall, or does he remember a different incident which accounts for her hostility to him after her injury? We have only to think of Madonna Dianora to realize that hair connotes sexual intimacy; the description of the four-year old's hair as short and fine shows that she does not yet belong to that stage of life where intimacy might be appropriate, and differentiates her from the fifteen year old servant whom she otherwise resembles. Given the paucity of direct information, we can only conclude that any personal relationship attempted with the fifteen year old girl was troubled and inconclusive.

His older servant girl arouses his interest only once, when she appears from the depths of a mirror carrying two statues of Indian deities. Both details remove her from reality and create distance between her and the merchant's son who watches her. The statues' mouths with snakes brush her cheeks; snakes suggest the danger which forbids or inhibits intimacy. Her beauty fills him with longing but not with desire (E, p. 14; SW, 28:20) for he is unprepared for and perhaps incapable of physical love. The horse kicks him in the groin, the seat of his undeveloped sexuality.

Hofmannsthal makes it quite clear that the merchant's son's shortcomings in the relationship to his two younger servants are in large measure sexual. He feels "wie die beiden Mädchen in das öde gleichsam lustlose Leben hineinleben"; he senses the joyless sterility of their lives. He feels the eyes of both girls upon him:

> die der Größeren mit einer unbestimmten, ihn quälenden Forderung, die der Kleineren mit einer ungeduldigen, dann wieder höhnischen Aufmerksamkeit, die ihn noch mehr quälte. (E, p. 13; SW, 28:19)

The older girl torments him with the challenge of her ready sexuality, while the younger girl already recognizes his impotence and scorns him for it.

Since so many critics have sought autobiographical significance in the story, it is interesting to note that the merchant's son's inadequacy when confronted with these demands was apparently not foreign to Hofmannsthal himself. His confidant Arthur Schnitzler noted in his diary:

> Loris: "Ich habe manchmal eine theoretische Angst, daß sich gar keine Sehnsucht nach den Weibern in mir regen wird. Ich habe das mit zehn, elf Jahren durchgemacht, sinnliche Erregungen, etc. Im übrigen, Eure Schriften machen mir Angst vor dem Weibe.[11]

His description of the older servant girl carrying Indian deities whose snakes brush her cheeks incorporates exactly this kind of "Angst vor dem Weibe."

To return to the merchant's son, it is through his servants that he experiences what Hofmannsthal describes as "die Unentrinnbarkeit des Lebens"; he senses their lives more intensely than his own (E, pp. 12, 13; SW, 28:18). In "Ein Traum von großer Magie" the Magier's participation in all human fate was part of his glory; in the tale of the merchant's son, by contrast, vicarious experience of the lives of others is proven detrimental to direct awareness of one's own existence. Indeed the observation that the youth's servants circle him like dogs may suggest that they regard him as already lifeless, as carrion. Further, the image communicates the servants' function as embodiments of the inescapable material existence of mankind, for it is through them that the youth recognizes such biological changes as sexual maturity, senility and death. Amgiad and Assad, Anton Lerch and Hofmannsthal himself[12] confront in the encounter with quarreling diseased dogs the realization of man's imprisonment in his physical being.[13]

The merchant's son combats such intimations of the common mortality binding him to his servants with the study of art objects in which all life, plant and animal, is represented as a harmonious unity:

---

11 Arthur Schnitzler, "Hugo von Hofmannsthal. Charakteristik aus den Tagebüchern," ed. Norbert Altenhofer and Wolfram Mauser, *Hofmannsthal-Forschungen* 3 (1975): 17.
12 See the letter to Andrian dated August 7, 1895, *Briefwechsel*, p. 54.
13 Schings speaks of the "unheimliche in den Tod treibende Kraft der Diener" and remarks quite correctly that for Hofmannsthal dogs are "die Geschöpfe des niederen, unerlösten Lebens par excellence". "Allegorie des Lebens," p. 547 and note 23.

Er erkannte in den Ornamenten, die sich verschlingen, ein verzaubertes Bild der verschlungenen Wunder der Welt. Er fand die Formen der Tiere und die Formen der Blumen und das Übergehen der Blumen in die Tiere; die Delphine, die Löwen und die Tulpen, die Perlen und den Akanthus; ... (E, p. 8; SW, 28:15).

Threatening aspects of reality, such as death, are completely assimilated into the entirety represented in these objects. Although the young man does not distinguish between art and nature, believing in the possession of his treasures to possess life itself, the choice of nouns in the above passage reveals that the decoration of these art works is drawn from artistic convention rather than from nature; dolphins and acanthus leaves appear more commonly in architecture or sculpture than in our environs. In fact, Eugene Weber has discovered that the source for this series of plants and animals is literary; Oscar Wilde's Dorian Gray contemplates "ecclesiastical vestments decorated with acanthus leaves ... lions ... tulips and dolphins."[14]

The dolphin, a creature friendly to humans and supposedly a bearer of good fortune, appears frequently in Hofmannsthal's work.[15] Classical myth relates that Arion, who first composed the dithyramb and enchanted the animals with his music, was once attacked by pirates on the high seas. He sprang into the ocean and was rescued by a dolphin attracted to his music, who then carried him to Taimoron. Hofmannsthal probably read this legend in the *Gesta Romanorum*.[16] He alludes to it in *Der Abenteurer und die Sängerin*. Vittoria jokingly wishes that sailors might capture Cesarino and sell

---

14 "Hofmannsthal and Oscar Wilde," *Hofmannsthal-Forschungen* 1 (1971): 104. In fact the acanthus, lions, tulips and dolphins are interspersed with other ornamental plants and animals in several different vestments which Dorian Gray admires. See Oscar Wilde, *The Picture of Dorian Gray* (London: Oxford University Press, 1974), pp. 139-40.

15 See the treatment of the dolphin and the legend of Arion in Exner, *Hofmannsthals "Lebenslied,"* pp. 108-109; and Mauser, *Bild und Gebärde in der Sprache Hofmannsthals*, p. 36.

16 "How Amon was saved from death by a dolphin" appears as Tale CXLVII in *Gesta Romanorum*, trans. Charles Swan, revised and corrected by Wynnard Hooper (New York: Dover, 1959), pp. 254-55. Hooper expresses his certainty that the story is that of Arion.

him in a faraway land. Cesarino retorts: "Gut, dann spräng ich/ ins Wasser und es käme ein Delphin/ und trüge mich auf seinem Rücken fort!" (D, 1:262). In his "Verse auf ein kleines Kind" the poet wishes the child "den freundlichen guten Delphin" as playmate (GLD, p. 31; SW 1:79).

Elsewhere in Hofmannsthal's work dolphins figure in sculpture or in architecture whose excess of ornamentation suggests decadence; "Drei Delphine gießen murmelnd/ Fluthen in ein Muschelbecken" in the "Prolog zu dem Buch 'Anatol' " (GLD, p. 43; SW 1:24). Andreas waits undecidedly outside a door with a bronze knocker for Zorzi to introduce him to Nina.

The dolphins in "Das Märchen der 672. Nacht" connect with both spheres of meaning, with the dolphins joyously expressing their lust for life and with the stylized renditions of dolphins in art. The art objects treasured by the merchant's son purport to depict the fullness of life, yet they present not nature itself, but "ein verzaubertes Bild" in which the laws of nature are ignored: the shapes of flowers and animals flow into one another in an indistinct continuum which is neither nature nor reality.

Lions are intermingled with the dolphins, tulips, pearls and acanthus leaves in these designs and, like the dolphins, they have a multi-faceted significance. Hofmannsthal esteems the lion for its sure gait, its strong voice and its keen gaze. The lion's movements demonstrate absolute control over its physical and mental being: the *Magier* springs like a lion from one cliff to the next. "With a voice like a lion" the dyer Barak cries out for the unborn children he has dreamt of (E, p. 333; SW, 28:165). The child king coming to save Poland in *Der Turm* is supposed to be a strong handsome lad "und aus den Augen schauen wie ein junger Löwe" (D, 4:178). The comparison of a fictitious character to a lion attributes to him its strength, courage and self-assurance.

In spite of its ferocity, the lion is considered a loyal friend to man; the story of Androcles who drew the thorn from the lion's paw or of Iwein, "le chevalier au lion," come readily to mind. Hofmannsthal describes in detail Prince Eugene of Savoy's faithful African lion which died in the same hour as its beloved master (P, 3:316-17; SW, 28:103).

Like the dolphin, the lion often serves as an architectural ornament. The merchant's son imagines that he watches death slowly crossing a bridge supported by winged lions. When lions appear as guardians of an entrance or as supports beneath the columns their strength and boldness are usually presented in somewhat abstracted or stylized form.[17] The transition from jungle to architectural ornament deprives the lion of some of his nobility and fierceness, thus Baron Weidenstamm in *Der Abenteurer und die Sängerin* commands: "Schaff mir Löwen,/ die Blumensträuße aus den Rachen werfen!" (D, 1:171). Like the dolphins in the prologue to *Anatol* which merely spout water instead of jumping playfully through the waves, the lions in the poem "Mein Garten" have lost their vitality and no longer roar, but only dream:

> Schön ist mein Garten mit den goldnen Bäumen,
> Den Blättern, die mit Silbersauseln zittern,
> Dem Diamantentau, den Wappengittern,
> Dem Klang des Gong, bei dem die Löwen träumen,
> Die ehernen ... (GLD, p. 500; SW, 1:20)

It is characteristic of Hofmannsthal's aesthetes (the merchant's son and Fortunio in *Der Weiße Fächer* are two examples) that they lack firsthand knowledge of animal and plant life, becoming acquainted with nature only through art. Hofmannsthal too drew his knowledge of animals not indigenous to his surroundings from artistic tradition or natural history rather than his own observations. The borrowing of the juxtaposition of dolphins and lions with tulips and acanthus from *Dorian Gray* demonstrates his succeptibility to suggestion from literary sources. It has become obvious from the letters and notes giving an account of his military service, however, that he was thoroughly familiar with such common animals as dogs, birds, and horses. One might therefore assume that the representation of these animals in art or literature seldom influenced their significance

---

17 One thinks of the scarcely recognizable lions ringing the fountain in the court of the Alhambra, or of those supporting the chancel in the cathedrals of Siena and Pisa, or of those by the door of St. Zeno in Verona which Hofmannsthal himself mentions (P, 3:350). These animal forms have all been subordinated to their practical function in the structure as water fountains or supports.

in his imagery. The validity of this hypothesis, however, must first be tested against the evidence to be presented in the next several chapters. We shall continue to ask which images are an outgrowth of Hofmannsthal's own experiences with animals and which derive from or correspond to literary and artistic tradition.

Because the merchant's son experiences life only indirectly, through his four servants, through the legends of Alexander the Great, or through art, he overlooks reality. In much the same way Amgiad and Assad prefer art to life itself and consequently pass over the significant experiences. In the following description of their reunion after a lengthy separation, Hofmannsthal equates that preference, typical of the merchant's son as well, with what he calls "das Kernlose des Lebens" (A, p. 114).

> Es ist möglich, daß in dem Gemach des Prinzen Assad eine wundervolle ornamentale Tapete, das Leben der Tiere der Wälder darstellend, hängt, und daß die beiden so lange getrennten Brüder von diesem Kunstwerk reden, statt von vielen anderen Dingen, teils aus allzugroßer Ergriffenheit, teils auch weil sie verlernt haben, im Reden eine Erleichterung des Daseins zu suchen. (A, p. 112; SW, 29:39)

Since Hofmannsthal regards knowledge of animal life (the subject of the brothers' wonderful carpet) as symptomatic of an awareness of reality, the preoccupation with the artistic representation of animal life comes to signify a superficial or pseudo acquaintance with reality. The tragic guilt of the merchant's son arises not from his ignorance of life, but rather from the mistaken belief that in knowing the depiction of plant and animal life through art, he knows life itself.

The merchant's son's lack of direct experience of reality is typified by the lack of spoken communication in the story. Even its first half is almost entirely devoid of speech. The young man speaks little ("wenig") to his servants, the manservant devines his wishes "schweigend," and the master senses that his servants observe him often "ohne ein Wort zu reden." The only direct quotations in the first part of the story are the two self-fulfilling proverbs, "Wo du sterben sollst, dahin tragen dich deine Füße" and "Wenn das Haus fertig ist, kommt der Tod." The absence of speech emphasizes the lack of genuine human contact between the young man and his servants; they do nothing to refute the image he has projected on them.

Real confusion arises from written communication; a mysterious letter accuses the manservant of an unspecified crime, but it is unsigned and the writer does not identify himself. Nonetheless, the letter motivates the merchant's son to actively confront reality and abandon the fantasy he has lived in to date.[18] It is worth noting that letters (in Hofmannsthal's oeuvre as in Kleist's) may be a source of deceit and confusion. Zdenka in *Arabella* can imitate her sister's handwriting to mislead Matteo, and Maria in *Andreas* complains that her hand is bewitched when Mariquita writes in her stead; such a mistake over the provenance of a letter leads to the first meeting between Andreas and Sacramozo.

Whereas in the first half of the story, the merchant's son perceives his surroundings as a harmonious unity unbroken by dissonant voices of his servants, in the second half, the lack of spoken communication points more clearly to the total isolation which is death. The author of the "Briefe des Zurückgekehrten" emphasizes silence as a forewarning of death. He imagines himself dying in one of several unremarkable places, all filled with deadly quiet: "stiller tückischer Rand eines gelben Sumpfes, stiller Platz im Wald, stiller Hang unwegsamer grauer Klippen" (P, 2:297). The jeweler wraps the purchases of the merchant's son "ohne mehr ein Wort zu sprechen" (E, p. 19; SW, 28:24). The child in the greenhouse braces herself against his knees "ohne ein Wort zu reden" (E, p. 21; SW, 28:25). When she bolts the door, the young man tries to call for help, "aber er fürchtete sich vor seiner eigenen Stimme" (E, p. 19; SW, 28:26). Later soldiers behind a barred window call out to him, but he fails to understand what they want of him. Finally he awakens from a troubled sleep fatally wounded "und wollte schreien, weil er noch immer allein war, aber die Stimme versagte ihm (E, p. 28; SW, 28:30). His totally silent, isolated and uncomprehending state is, as Hofmannsthal intended, utterly dreamlike.

---

18 Bernhard Dotzler points out that while the first half of the story is almost purely descriptive, the second half is narrative; while the first half is timeless, the second abounds in adverbs of time, changes of scene, and events which advance the plot. "Beschreibung eines Briefes; zum handlungsauslösenden Moment in Hugo von Hofmannsthal's 'Märchen der 672. Nacht,' *Hofmannsthal-Forschungen* 8 (1985), 49-55.

With the young man's entry into his native city, nature and art, which seemed to blend in the unified vision of beauty presented in his objets d'art, separate into distinct and contrasting spheres. When the jeweler offers to show him some antique saddle ornaments, he declines, replying, "daß er sich als Sohn eines Kaufmannes nie mit Pferden abgegeben habe, ja nicht einmal zu reiten verstehe und weder an alten noch an neuen Sätteln Gefallen finde ..." (E, p. 19; SW, 28: 24). Although he earlier regarded nature and art as components of the harmonious entirety of life, he is no longer able to do so. He makes a distinction between the ornaments as works of art (for the jeweler presents them to him as such) and their function in everyday life, of which he knows nothing. His confession of ignorance of everything regarding horses shows him to be unprepared for the later confrontation with the cavalry horses and heightens the reader's awareness of his vulnerability.

Furthermore, the youth admits that he does not belong to the nobility and as the son of a merchant has never had anything to do with horses. Hofmannsthal apparently esteems good horsemanship as an innate capability of the landed gentry, a facility which no amount of training can compensate for. We recall that Hofmannsthal's great grandfather was raised to the nobility in 1835, but the family rose through business prosperity and never belonged to the ancient lineage of aristocracy. Hofmannsthal himself lacked the instinctive untaught mastery over the horse he values so highly in Sigismund. Quite possibly he found his shortcomings as a rider embarrassing and came to conceive of horsemanship as an inherited facility of the aristocracy, as the merchant's son does here. Andreas von Ferschengelder, a member of the "Bagatelladel," similarly suffers from his incompetence as a rider.

Later the merchant's son enters a greenhouse where the roles of art and nature appear reversed. In the controlled climate of the greenhouse, artificial flowers, out of place among the natural plants, remind him of "heimtückische Masken mit zugewachsenen Augenlöchern" (E, p. 22; SW, 28:26). The artificiality of a mask contradicts the biological process of growth implied in the comparison. This incident, like the youth's preference for seclusion and his suggested impotence, recall certain passages in Huysmans' *A Rebours,* which appeared in 1884.[19] Des Esseintes, the novel's protagonist, so exaggerates his aestheticism that he collects real flowers whose grotesque shape or repulsive color resemble those of artificial flowers. Some "avaient le ton rose vif des cicatrices qui se ferment ou la teinte brune des croûtes qui se forment. ..."[20] Like the merchant's son, Des Esseintes is so disturbed by the flowers that he must flee from them.

In his increasing distress and confusion the merchant's son begins to long for the security of his bed, and for the legendary world of Alexander the Great, whose bed was supported by griffins and winged bulls. The griffin, with the body of a lion and the head of an eagle, symbolizes the boldness and strength of Alexander, whom the merchant's son wishes to emulate. These animals, like the lion and dolphins decorating his treasures, are once again part of a work of art. They do not, however, represent a unification of nature and art, for they are only imaginary creatures and belong to the fantasy world in which the young man hopes to escape from his real peril.

Once confronted with a reality contradictory to his tranquil dream image of life, the merchant's son seeks to buy his freedom from his menacing surroundings. Wishing to take leave of the jeweler, he thinks to appease him by buying a chain for his servant girl. Similarly, he tries to ingratiate himself with the child in the greenhouse by giving her silver coins, which she throws on the ground. Touched by the misery of the last soldier in the courtyard, he attempts to cheer him with a gift of money.

Hofmannsthal's other early works as well deal with aesthetes' attempts to use their wealth to shield themselves from depressing reality or to beautify their ugly surroundings. Titian's wealth erects a protective barrier between his students and the nearby plague-infested city, where animals and madmen live side by side. Claudio and Andrea enjoy financial prosperity, indeed wealth is a prerequisite of

---

19 J.D. Workman suggests parallels between the story and Huysmans' novel: "Hofmannsthal's 'Märchen der 672. Nacht'," *Monatshefte* 53 (1961): 306. *A Rebours* is also one of Dorian Gray's favorite books.

20 J. K. Huysmans, *A Rebours* (Paris: Editions Fasquelle, 1968), p. 125.

their self-indulgent life styles. Claudio takes the mysterious figures in his garden for beggars and orders them shut out so that the sight of their poverty might not disturb his reflections on his failure to participate actively in the fate of his fellow man. The blazed face of the last cavalry horse brings a similar instance to the mind of the merchant's son. He recalls that many years ago a poor man pursued by an angry mob sought refuge in his father's shop. The intruder forced him, like Claudio, to perceive that wealth, regardless of its efficacy as a shield from want and discomfort, fails to eradicate them completely.

Hofmannsthal's letters and notes show that he used money in a similar fashion to protect himself from the unpleasant side of reality.[21] At the same time he struggled throughout his life against a fear of financial need, which would have put an end to the shelter wealth could erect around him. He writes his parents that he must have inherited something of his maternal grandfather's uneasy fearfulness, a trait corresponding to the merchant's son dread of the inescapability of life, "nämlich manchmal gewinnen äußere widrige Umstände eine unbegrenzte Macht über mich, gegen die ich hilflos bin wie gegen einen Alpdruck." He continues to discuss his exaggeratedly apprehensive misconceptions of the relationship of his father's income to the family's style of living:

> In schlechten Stunden überkommt mich eine kleinliche und nutzlose Ungeduld und Angst, jedes zerrissene Kleidungsstück ängstigt mich, und ich verliere vollständig den Kopf. So ähnlich ist es mit dem Pferd. (B, 1:159-60)

His mare had recently gone lame and Hofmannsthal worried about her care. About the same time he notes: "Leben und sich ausleben nur im Kampf mit den widerstrebenden Mächten. So lehrt mich mein Pferd den Wert des Vermögens, der Unabhängigkeit" (A, p. 127). More than any other experience, the worry over his horse taught him that wealth was no more powerful a weapon than *Magie* in his struggle against the opposing forces of reality. It is therefore by no means coincidental that financial concerns connected with a horse play such a significant role in the "Reitergeschichte" and in the *Andreas* novel.

---

21 See the letter to his father dated Spring, 1903, B, 2:105-6.

Money guarantees personal freedom of movement. Later Hofmannsthal notes in a book on the development of technology: "Mit dieser Complexität Steigen der Macht des Geldes, als der Freiheit, in der alles ausruht."[22] After the war, obliged to sell his works of art to liberate himself from his depressing situation, he writes that financial need forces him to live like a chained dog.[23] Anyone lacking the means to live comfortably is reduced to the animal level of existence, forced to consider daily how to obtain material necessities.

Apparently the father of the protagonist of "Das Märchen der 672. Nacht" also used his wealth to distance himself from the oppressive contemplation of poverty and ugliness, for he is described as loving his art treasures, the "schönen, gefühllosen Kinder seines Suchens und Sorgens" (E, p. 16; SW, 28:21-22). He shares this fondness for inanimate objects with the poet's grandfather:

> Die zärtliche Liebe meines väterlichen Großvaters zu seinen kleinen Besitztümern: den Bildern, die er auf dem Mailänder Markt zusammengekauft hatte, chinesischen Vasen, alten Stoffen, Schnitzereien, dem ganzen Inhalt des Glaskastens. Er war der Erwerber dieses ganzen Gewebes von Gefühlen, Begierden, Zärtlichkeiten, Behaglichkeiten. (A, pp. 136-37)

The fact that the art treasures are devoid of feeling excludes the possibility that they might affect their owner; the merchant seems to have cut himself off from all human sympathy, like his son, who could not tolerate the constant presence of a woman; even if her beauty pleased his aesthetic sense, she would oblige him to enter a human relationship. It is characteristic of his desire to avoid entanglements that the young man seeks to buy a flower whose scent would substitute for the gratification to be gained in a love affair with his servant. When he purchases something, such as a flower, he transforms an abstract estimation of its worth into monetary terms, thus simplifying his relationship to the object in a manner not possible in human contact.

This childlike aesthete who seeks either to escape from reality into the world of fantasy or to shield himself from it through the

---

22 Quoted by Michael Hamburger, "Hofmannsthals Bibliothek, ein Bericht," *Euphorion* 55 (1961), 32.
23 Hofmannsthal and Burckhardt, *Briefwechsel*, p. 39.

careful use of wealth stumbles upon one situation, the misery and dejection of the soldiers tending their horses, which defies his power to do either. The scene focuses on the ugly ill-tempered horses altogether unlike the proud charges of Alexander the Great on which the young man's fantasy has dwelt. The horses do not stand weary and submissive before their masters, as befitting strenuously exercised cavalry mounts, rather their rolling eyes and distended nostrils suggest excessive strength and uncontrollable wildness, as if they were really demons, as Hofmannsthal describes his mare.

The soldiers' position, kneeling to wash the hooves of these powerful horses, indicates their degradation and submission to the beasts' unnatural strength. In contrast to the human heads swaying weakly as if in a strong wind, the horses' heads move threateningly of their own volition.

Hofmannsthal described a similar scene in an unfinished "Soldatengeschichte" written about the same time as the "Märchen." There a tailor too feeble-minded to serve as a soldier is assigned to tend horses and can be observed kneeling for hours "unter dem Leib der ihm anvertrauten Pferde ... mit lautloser Emsigkeit darin verloren, ihre Hufe mit einem kleinen Lappen so heftig zu reiben bis sie glänzten wie poliertes Horn" (SW, 29:53). In this fragment Hofmannsthal experimentally sketched out animal images derived from his military experience which were to be used later in other works; the diseased horses reappear in *Andreas*. The tailor's worthless industry in polishing the horses' hooves makes him a pathetic and foolish figure, and it is worth noting that his activity is "lautlos," he does not reason or communicate. The soldiers of the "Märchen" must also perform this inane, degrading task; their lives are debased, deprived of purpose and sunk below the norm of human existence.

The memory of the poor man seeking refuge in his father's shop which the merchant's son connects with the face of the last horse allows two interpretations. Superstition holds that death may appear as a horse man attempts to bribe; thus the merchant's son tries to give money to the soldier caring for the last horse.[24] The dead may

---

24 Jürg Matthes also connects money with death, interpreting the seven gold coins the soldiers later steal from the merchant's son as an "obolus" paid for transportation into the underworld. "Überlegungen zur Verwendung der Zahlen..." p. 210.

appear as an animal, a degrading form appropriate to those who have died a violent death,[25] such as the poor man, who may have been beaten to death by the angry crowd. Although we do not learn what became of him, it seems unlikely that the merchant, reluctant to show any human sympathy, would have protected or assisted him. The refusal to welcome a stranger into one's house has always been considered a serious transgression; Goethe reminds us in *Faust II* how Zeus and Hermes flooded an entire region as punishment for its inhabitants' refusal to take them in, sparing only Philemon and Baucis, who showed proper hospitality. The merchant's refusal to grant the poor man refuge may have led to the latter's death; he then appears in animal form to punish the son for his father's refusal to admit into his sheltered surroundings a figure symbolizing poverty and fear.

The common error of father and son is their attempt to avoid or withdraw from all human relationships. The emphasis on social involvement in "Ad me ipsum" proves that Hofmannsthal believed such avoidance of participation in human affairs to be wrong. Wealth makes possible self protection from the encroachments of human relationships and from the contemplation of disquieting poverty, ugliness, or crime. The fact that the merchant's son draws his hand out of his pocket just before handing money to the soldier may signal his realization that such attempts at flight from reality or such substitutes of money for personal involvement are futile. After he is fatally wounded, the soldiers steal his money, his means of self-preservation, and consequently he sinks into bestiality; his facial expression, teeth and gums exposed, resembles that of the last horse.

While this reading of the story is fully consonant with that of Alewyn and his followers, a second, concurrent interpretation can be derived from the spatial symbolism, with which Hofmannsthal takes noticeable pains. The merchant's son walks into the city along a dried up river bed, presumably the same river along whose banks he sought to buy a flower whose odor would gratify his sense of possession as a substitute for his older servant girl. But instead of fresh flowers he sees only dusty potted plants in the windows of houses where many prostitutes live (SW, 28:22). In contrast to the usual

---

[25] *Handwörterbuch des deutschen Aberglaubens,* vol. 6, col. 1615.

connotations of fertility and vitality associated with water and flowers, every element of this scene contributes to an impression of sterility somehow linked to sexual relationships.

The dried up river bed suggests artistic or spiritual sterility as well. It contrasts most sharply with the water imagery associated with the *Magier* in "Ein Traum von großer Magie." The whole "Traum von großer Magie" is described as "kühn wie junges Meer im Morgenduft," the *Magier* himself stands against a background of "dunklem Meer," his hands move "Im Boden so, als ob es Wasser wär," and the very act of creativity is depicted as giving form and harmony to "dünnem Quellenwasser" (GLD, p. 20; SW, 1:52). The dry, dusty scene which the merchant's son enters in the city suggests that in spite of his intense interest in art objects, he lacks all creative (artistic) as well as procreative power.

He continues on his way and enters "eine ganz öde, totenstille Sackgasse, die in einer fast turmhohen, steilen Treppe endigte (E, p. 17; SW, 28:22). Considering the dream-like atmosphere Hofmannsthal purposely created in the story, it is appropriate to apply Freudian dream analysis to this passage. Hofmannsthal seems to have read several of Freud's works as they appeared,[26] and remarked in 1922 that his psychological discoveries had given Freud a key to the human character which had before belonged exclusively to the poet (A, p. 289). Thus it is logical to inquire what light Freud's insights may cast on Hofmannsthal's symbolism.

To return to the merchant's son and his ascent of the steep high stairway — Freud comments: "Die Stiege und was ihr analog ist (Treppen, Leitern) stellt ein sicheres Koitussymbol dar."[27] A later follower of Freud elaborates:

Das Emporsteigen auf einer Stiege, häufig ein Symbol für coitus (Hinaufgehen, wobei man außer Atem kommt), entpuppt sich oft in einem tieferen

---

26 See Michael Hamburger, "Hofmannsthal's Bibliothek," pp. 26-27 for a list of Freud's works found in Hofmannsthal's library. Hofmannsthal's knowledge of Freud has also been well documented by Mary Gilbert in her article, "The Image of the Horse in Hofmannsthal's Poetic Works," p. 75, note 22.
27 *Gesammelte Werke* 2/3: 360, note 1. Hofmannsthal again uses the stairway as a scene for intercourse in *Elektra*, where Elektra has cursed the children which servants "hündisch auf der Treppe/ im Blute glitschend, hier in diesem Haus/ empfangen und geboren haben" (D, 2:13).

> Zusammenhang als das Bemühen, von den Widerwärtigkeiten des Lebens zu irgendeinem den anderen Leuten (=Gedanken) unzugänglichen Zufluchtsort (einsamer Dachkammer usw.) zu gelangen und nun sieht man ein, daß diese tiefere Bedeutung sich unbeschadet der ersten einstellt, denn auch der Coitus ist, wie jeder Rauschzustand, nur ein Spezialfall der Flucht vor dem äußeren Leben, eine der Formen des seligen Vergessens.[28]

The merchant's son's search for a secure refuge from life's unpleasantness is demonstrated by his withdrawal from society and, when he is trapped in the city, by his longing for his bed. The figure of the mother embodies both goals of his ascent, coitus and the place of refuge. On the one hand, as the first and apparently only significant woman in the young man's life, she becomes his first love, who guarantees him blissful oblivion in the ecstasy of incestuous lovemaking. On the other hand, her womb, suggested by the bed for which the young man longs so desperately, offered the first place of refuge from the inescapability of life. Elis Fröbom longs for just such refuge and oblivion in the underground realm of the Mountain Queen:

> ...könnt ich mich in die dunkle Erde
> Einwühlen. Ging es nur, mir sollt es schmecken,
> Als kröch ich in den Mutterleib zurück, ...
> (GLD, p. 342)

Michael Hamburger comments upon the "Mutterfixierung" intimated in these lines and discerns similar "Freudian implications" in the other early dramas, *Der Kaiser und die Hexe* and *Der Tor und der Tod*. Because conjugal love signifies for Hofmannsthal a vital step in the integration of the individual into society, Hamburger continues, such deviations as that of a blacksmith's wife in the "Idylle" or the regression to mother love implied in the early plays can not be countenanced.[29] The same holds true, of course, for the "Märchen." The

---

28 Herbert Silberer, *Probleme der Mystik und ihrer Symbolik* (Vienna: Heller, 1914), p. 159. Hofmannsthal quotes Silberer's work in "Ad me ipsum" (A, p. 215; see also Herbert Steiner's note, A, p. 378-79). Alewyn cites Silberer's book as one of the sources for *Andreas: Über Hugo von Hofmannsthal*, p. 135.

29 *Hugo von Hofmannsthal, Zwei Studien*, Schriften zur Literatur, vol. 6 (Göttingen: Sachse & Pohl, 1964), pp. 56-57. See also Hugo Wyss, comments on *Das Bergwerk zu Falun* in *Die Frau in der Dichtung Hofmannsthals* (Zurich: Niehans, 1954), pp. 42-44.

merchant's son's longing for a return to childhood or to the womb corresponds to his inclination to avoid human involvement and commitment, that is, to avoid integration into society, and parallels his desire to escape to the imaginary world of Alexander the Great or to the harmonious unity of nature and art presented in his treasured objects. His regressive Oedipal tendencies, his indulgence in fantasy, and his use of money to preserve his detachment from his surroundings all comprise one pattern of avoiding unpleasant reality.

In his flight from the hideous, menacing regions of his native city, he encounters many hindrances, the locked door to the greenhouse, the walled-in passageway, and the deep ditch he must cross by means of a narrow board. Like a series of those "unablässige Analogien" Hofmannsthal considered characteristic of both dream and fairy tale, these hindrances repeat in ironic form elements from the young man's fantasy of dying "wie ein auf der Jagd verirrter König" (E, p. 11; SW, 28:16). Instead of the forest of "wundersamen Bäumen" among which he envisaged meeting his fate, he flees from the tangle of macabre plants in the greenhouse. Instead of watching death approach his palace across a bridge borne by winged lions, he sees himself as he crawls along the narrow board suspended precariously high above a ditch. The Freudian interpretation of dreams places a special meaning on such obstacles as these and the locked doors and gates which substantiates the thesis that an unnatural desire lies at the root of his dilemma:

> Die Traumpsychologie hat in Erfahrung gebracht, daß Hemmungen im Traum Willenskonflikten des Träumers entsprechen, genau wie dies bei krankhaften Hemmungen des Neurotikers der Fall ist. Die Angst entwickelt sich, wenn sich ein verdrängter Trieb ausleben will, dem ein anderer Wille, etwa jener unserer Gesittung, verbietend sich entgegenstellt. Das gehemmte Ausleben erzeugt Angst statt Lust. Angst mag deshalb auch eine Libido mit negativem Vorzeichen heißen.[30]

These obstacles then, may signify moral inhibitions standing between the young man and the incestuous desire for his mother.

The interpretation of the passage through the city as a dream of Oedipal desire casts new light on the ugly horse which sends the merchant's son to his death. Freud regards animals occurring in dreams

---

30 Herbert Silberer, *Probleme der Mystik und ihrer Symbolik*, p. 36.

as frequent substitutes for the father. According to him, the child transfers his fear of the father, who opposes his love for his mother, to one of the animal species common to the child's environs. The cavalry horse, viewed as a representative of the father, strikes a blow at the young man's groin, or castrates him as punishment for the illicit longing for his mother.[31] In his "Analyse der Phobie eines fünfjährigen Knaben" (which first appeared in 1909) Freud describes a neurotic child's projection of his fear of his father onto draft horses. After once wishing his hated father dead, the child actually sees a horse fall dead and draw up his legs in death writhings.[32] The boy subsequently shows an intense fear of such leg motions, which he nonetheless imitates at times. It is interesting to note that the merchant's son moves his legs in the same fashion when felled by the horse's hoof: "seine Knie zogen sich in die Höhe, und mit den Fersen schlug er immerfort auf den Boden" (E, p. 27; SW, 28:29).

Although the problem of incest occupies a central role in Freudian psychopathology out of proportion to its role in normal human life, a consideration of Hofmannsthal's work justifies applying Freud's insights into the Oedipus complex to his art. The father-son conflict forms the major theme of *Der Turm* and of his adaptation of the Oedipus myth. His translation of a little known French play, *Poil de Carotte,* by Jules Renard, also treats the relationship between a son and his parents. The same problem reappears as the focal point of the fragments "Knabengeschichte" and the *Andreas* novel. The fact that Hofmannsthal completed his adaptations of sources dealing with the father-son conflict while his original compositions on the same subject remained unfinished suggests that the problem touched him so deeply as to preclude objective impartial treatment. *Der Turm,* to be sure, achieved a final stage version, but the class struggle has replaced the father-son conflict as the main theme of the play. Hermann Broch, who interprets Hofmannsthal's works as an indictment of the "aesthetisierende Bürgerlichkeit" in which he was brought up, finds in them no hint about "das Vater-Sohn Verhältnis, das für Hof-

---

31 Dorrit Cohn concurs, stating that the youth's "father executes (castrates) the son for the love he bears the mother." "Als Traum erzählt...", p. 301.
32 *Gesammelte Werke* 7:285.

mannsthal unzweifelhaft ein konkretes Erlebnis gewesen ist."[33] In contrast, a more recent critic, Wolf Wucherpfennig, finds in Hofmannsthal's correspondence with his parents, in "Age of Innocence," and particularly in the "Märchen" evidence of a deep seated conflict between his parents' pressure to achieve professional and financial success and Hofmannsthal's own existence as a poet.[34] His insight enables us to weave together several themes in our interpretation of the story.

Hofmannsthal's dedication of the story to Beer-Hofmann, his emphasis on its dream-like quality, and his insistence in the letter to his father that it means nothing more than any human interest item in a daily newspaper (B, 1:169-70) may be intended to diminish the impact of our and his father's understanding of the horse's kick. As he noted, "Vernunft" has intruded between the dream and the work of art ("dichterisches Gebilde") to censor the impact of conscious recognition of unconscious Angst. Although within the dream or fairy tale the son has been castrated by his father as punishment for his Oedipal desire, and for his refusal to progress beyond the Oedipal phase into adult relationships, inhibitions have caused the ego to repress this awareness, to cloak it in the disguise of symbolism. The role of money as the youth attempts to buy off the jeweler, the child in the greenhouse, and the soldier washing the hooves of the last horse links the tale with its author's complex of emotions surrounding financial success and the protection it offers from ugliness, danger, and malaise. The horse's fatal kick refutes the young man's faith in the power of money and thus parallels Hofmannsthal's experiences with his lame, defiant mare in Göding, experiences which taught him, as he writes ironically in a letter for his father, "den Wert des Vermögens," i.e., that wealth is in fact useless in such circumstances. And finally, the protagonist's failure to make the transition from basking in the harmonious whole of life represented in his objets d'art to a personal relationship with individuals such as his servants is typified by the lack of spoken communication throughout the story. These failures prevent the merchant's son from becoming a

33 *Hofmannsthal und seine Zeit*, pp. 104-105.
34 "Das junge Wien und seine Väter. Bahr und der junge Hofmannsthal im gesellschaftlichen Zusammenhang," *Hofmannsthal-Forschungen* 7 (1983), 162.

father, from progressing to adulthood and maturity, a failure for which his symbolic dream father punishes him with castration and death.

CHAPTER IV

"REITERGESCHICHTE"

Like the "Märchen," "Reitergeschichte" draws on Hofmannsthal's experiences in military service, this time on cavalry maneuvers in Czortkow (in Galicia, now Poland) in summer, 1898. Because the similarity of material links this story to the earlier "Märchen," it seems useful to discuss them in sequence, leaving aside for the moment the lyrical dramas written during the intervening years.

Although the atmosphere pervading "Reitergeschichte" is entirely different from that of the "Märchen," its plot merely varies the model of the earlier story: a man briefly steps outside of his secure existence and enters a village, where he encounters the inescapable reality of life, again presented in animal form. Lerch of course is no fugitive from life, but in his visions of the future he does lose touch with actuality, a contact which the merchant's son constantly avoids. Finally both protagonists are unable to return to the secure existence depicted in the early pages of both stories.

The beginning and end of "Reitergeschichte" present Anton Lerch as member of the victorious Austrian squadron, they frame the middle portion, which contains the main action. Our discussion of the story accordingly falls into three parts: Lerch as part of the squadron, his deviations (the meeting with Vuic and the ride through the village), and finally his attempt to return to the squadron.

The subject of "Reitergeschichte" is a fictitious episode in the Austrian campaign against rebellious Italian forces in the environs of Milan in 1848. The narrator begins by contrasting the bold, often destructive deeds of the Austrian squadron with the harmony of the landscape lying peacefully under bright skies; the trees appear freshly washed, the villas and churches gleam in the sun. The Austrians encounter little resistance in their path; a herd of cattle falls into their hands, and they later drive "einen Trupp ungleichmäßig bewaffneter Menschen wie die Wachteln vor sich her" (E, p. 49; SW, 28:39). In comparing the enemy to quail, a commonly hunted game bird, Hofmannsthal stresses their helplessness and emphasizes that they are easy and welcome prey to the Austrian troops.

After a few similar easy skirmishes, the arrogance of the victors comes to the fore: the squadron's commander yields to the temptation to parade through the defenseless city. His troops, their faces caked with blood-spattered dust, march past ancient world-famous churches "vom trabenden Pferde herab funkelnden Auges auf alles dies hervorblickend" (E, p. 51; SW, 28:40-41).

Only after the triumphal march through Milan is the reader's attention shifted from the whole squadron to sergeant Anton Lerch, who turns out from the marching column to look for a woman he thinks he recognizes. Lerch, focus of the rest of the story, differs greatly from the aesthete protagonists of the early work (Amgiad and Assad, the merchant's son, Andrea, Claudio, and Titian's pupils). Unlike these, Lerch has never separated himself from the mainstream of life, shows no interest in art, seldom reflects on himself, and lacks one vital pre-requisite of the aesthetic existence, namely, money. Among Hofmannsthal's creations he may be ranked with Gotthelf, Baron Ochs von Lerchenau, Olivier, and Euseb (in the fragment "Knabengeschichte"). After "Reitergeschichte" these aggressive unrefined men no longer appear as protagonists (with the exception of Euseb, who is the main figure in an unfinished short story) but as opponents of milder, more sensitive youths, so that contrasting pairs may be established: Ochs-Octavian, Gotthelf-Andreas, Olivier-Sigismund; even Euseb becomes the opponent of his own better self. Frequently the rivals appear as contrasting aspects of the same personality: Ochs and Octavian are distant relatives, Andreas proves his inner kinship with Gotthelf by identifying with him. The opposition between Lerch and the squadron's commander, Baron Rofrano, flares up only at the end of "Reitergeschichte."

These coarse male figures are further connected through their ironic appellations: Gotthelf serves the devil rather than God, Euseb "the pious" sins against reverence for nature by torturing animals. The name Olivier, whose source is the thief and marauder Olivier in *Simplicissimus*,[1] is also suggestive of the French "olivier" meaning

---

[1] According to Michael Hamburger, *Hofmannsthal, Zwei Studien*, p. 103.

olive tree, whose branch is the emblem of peace. The fact that Hofmannsthal actually knew a sergeant Lerch during his military service may explain why the ironic overtones of his name have received no mention in Hofmannsthal scholarship.[2]

The significance of the sergeant's name holds the key to the irony. The lark (for Lerch approximates Lerche) flies uncommonly high, and symbolizes high ideals in Shelley's "To A Skylark." In *Der Abenteurer und die Sängerin* Hofmannsthal uses the lark as a metaphor for the joy of creating music; Vittoria describes the aging musician thus:

> ...hier saß einst Musik,
> so süß wie in der Brust von jungen Lerchen,
> die überladen mit Triumph aufsteigen
> und manchmal tot vor Lust zur Erde fallen. (D, 1:240)

By contrast Anton Lerch is completely absorbed in daily occurrences. Baron Ochs von Lerchenau, whose name harks back to that of sergeant Lerch, demonstrates their kinship through his equally coarse nature. Baron Rofrano, Anton Lerch's opponent, bears the same noble name as young Octavian, who is pitted against Ochs von Lerchenau.

Focusing our attention on this for Hofmannsthal atypical protagonist, we observe that Lerch is scarcely portrayed as an individual, rather, as the title states, as a rider.[3] The horse is his essential complement; together with his horse he becomes part of the total unit, of the squadron. The soldiers' arrogant triumph over Milan's inhabitants rests, in fact, on their superior position as riders, for they look down upon the city from the vantage point of their trotting horses.

---

2 Hofmannsthal writes his father a letter that if a presumptive buyer does not purchase his mare, she must be fetched from the care of "eines Wachtmeisters Lerch von der III. Eskadron" (B, 1:167).

3 Ulrich Heimrath interprets the story's denouement as justified by Lerch's failure to realize his true self and its connection with the outer world. The gesture with which he seeks to ward off his *Doppelgänger* is evidence of his refusal to accept his self. Heimrath considers the title a formula for Lerch's tragic flaw: he remains a "Reiter," anonymous and undeveloped as an individual. Hugo von Hofmannsthals 'Reitergeschichte,' eine Interpretation, *Wirkendes Wort* 21 (1971): 317-18.

As Lerch glimpses the face of a woman he believes he recognizes, he senses that his horse has lodged a stone in a front hoof. Both coincidences cause him to turn out from the marching column and halt his horse before the woman's house. The lameness of his horse, quite welcome to Lerch at this moment, has already separated rider and steed from the squadron, for the animal is no longer able to sustain the marching tempo. Lerch is by no means helpless, as was the young Hofmannsthal, in dealing with the animal's disability. Nor does the horse rest its weight oppressively on him while he bends to examine the hoof, as did the unnaturally powerful horses of the "Märchen."

As soon as Lerch dismounts, he ceases to function as a member of the total unit and becomes an unattachable individual separate from the ordered and disciplined framework of the squadron of which his horse is so much a part.[4] Since the horse is a social animal easily accustomed to routine, it dutifully observes military order and discipline. At the end of the story, the restlessness of the squadron's horses, particularly those standing next to the strange horses the soldiers have captured, indicates the general slackening of order and obedience among the troops. Lerch speaks briefly with the woman, who is, as he suspected, a former acquaintance, but, as he feels his horse pulling uneasily at the bridle, then loudly whinnying after its companions, he mounts again and returns to his post. His willingness to be directed by his horse proves that Lerch's membership in the army depends not on loyalty or devotion to duty; rather, as his later daydreams show, he is primarily concerned with physical comfort. Lerch enjoys a harmonious relationship with his horse, not, like Prince Amgiad, because he loses himself in brotherly feelings for all fellow creatures, but because his horse's impulses and movements correspond to those of its rider. Together horse and rider form a single unit: the warrior.

The meeting with Vuic begins to disrupt this soldier figure, a change signalled by the fact that Lerch dismounts. He is uncertain of his claim on this woman; only the consciousness of the squadron's

---

4 Compare Mary E. Gilbert's perceptive essay, "Hugo von Hofmannsthals 'Reitergeschichte,' Versuch einer Interpretation." *Der Deutschunterricht* 8, no. 3 (1956), 105. Alewyn concurs with her interpretation of the horse's function (*Über Hugo von Hofmannsthal*, p. 83).

collective triumphs gives him the courage to declare that her house will be his quarters. The comment upon his statement, "das ausgesprochene Wort aber machte seine Gewalt geltend" (E, p. 53; SW, 28:42), has led critics to place considerable emphasis on the power of Lerch's spoken word.[5] In fact, however, the lack of spoken communication in the story heightens the reader's awareness of Lerch's total isolation from human society.[6] It parallels the deathly silence pervading the labyrinthine city of the "Märchen." Further, both utterances directly quoted in the story derive their validity from acts of violence with which they are immediately reinforced: Rofrano's command is followed by the pistol shot which kills Lerch, and the sergeant exercises his domination over Vuic by placing his heavy hand upon her neck and forcing her head forward. The entire "Reitergeschichte" depicts a world of crude inarticulate sensuality; the scarcity of spoken dialogue and the multiplicity of animal imagery are complementary indications that we are entering the realm of chaos, where the word and reason have no power.

The gesture with which Lerch forces Vuic to bow her head is motivated by the pretense of waving away a fly crawling over a comb in her hair. The fly, with its connotations of filth and decay, suggests that despite her rather luxurious surroundings, Vuic is not above Lerch, but part of the same animal sphere as he. In his letters from Czortkow in the summer of 1898 Hofmannsthal complains of the flies which attack his neck (B, 1:250,253). Because the insistent pest leaves man no peace, the fly sometimes connotes unrest, as in Sartre's *Les Mouches,* where the Erinnyes, classical representations of guilt,

---

5   Pestalozzi finds in this "magischen Zauberwort des Wachtmeisters" one of the two focal points of the story, point of departure for Lerch's daydreams of the future. These daydreams are shattered by the second focal point and only other direct quote of the story. Baron Rofrano's curt command. *(Sprachskepsis und Sprachmagie,* p. 114). Alewyn concurs in this estimation of the importance of the spoken word, maintaining that like the emperor in *Der Kaiser und die Hexe* and like Elis Froböm, Lerch "[hat] sich durch ein einziges ungedacht ausgesprochenes Wort wie durch ein Verlöbnis einer dämonischen Macht ausgeliefert" (*Über Hugo von Hofmannsthal,* p. 82).
6   Thus Michael Lakin, "Hofmannsthal's Reitergeschichte and Kafka's Ein Landarzt," *Modern Austrian Literature* 3, (1970), 46.

pursue Orestes as flies. Hofmannsthal in his dramatic sketch *Pentheus* uses a similar image:

> Pentheus von einer ungeheuren Angst und Verzagtheit überfallen. Ihm scheint eine furchtbare Fliege vor den Augen, um die Schläfen zu schwirren. (D, 2:523)

Both Vuic and Lerch show signs of inner unrest. Vuic's laughter is "verlegen," for she already has a portly man as her companion. Lerch is intimidated by her dress and living quarters, with their evidence of prosperity and comfort. The fly, with its connotations of uncleanliness, diminishes somewhat the impression created by the piece of bisque statuary and by the wide bed visible to Lerch.

The meeting with Vuic excites the sergeant's sensuality; her behavior "[treibt] ihm das Blut in den starken Hals und unter die Augen" (E, p. 53; SW, 28:41). He indulges in daydreams centering around "das schöne breite Bett und die feine weiße Haut der Vuic;" her stout companion plays a significant role in Lerch's fantasies as purveyor of tobacco, capons, gossip, and other amenities of the idle civilian existence so attractive to Lerch. He is beset by "ein Durst nach unerwartetem Erwerb, nach Gratifikationen, nach plötzlich in die Tasche fallenden Dukaten" (E, p. 54; SW, 28:42-43), the means of realizing his daydreams.

The thirst for booty leads the sergeant to turn aside for the second time from the squadron he has accompanied throughout the afternoon, and to investigate a village with a crumbling steeple lying in a hollow a bit off the road. In the village he experiences (as did Amgiad and Assad) "das Trügerische des Lebens" (A, p. 114; SW, 29:42). Like the merchant's son in his native city he stumbles upon "die Unentrinnbarkeit des Lebens" in the many obstacles opposing his search for sudden riches.

Alewyn has remarked that the ride through the village presents an exact reversal of the noonday ride through Milan.[7] Immediately upon entering the village, Lerch must pull his horse up sharply as it is in danger of slipping on what appears to be grease. The connection between a horse's hesitant or unsure tread and premonitions of

---

7 *Über Hugo von Hofmannsthal*, p. 82.

danger is self-evident.[8] Perhaps more significant is Hofmannsthal's similar experience during his military service in Tlumacz. Hofmannsthal gives the following description of the terrain of his ride there:

> Steile Abhänge, gleich daneben versumpfte Wiesen, tiefe Einschnitte mit lehmigen rutschigen Rändern, hohe Zäune, und aus jeder elenden Lehmhütte fahren die elenden verwilderten Bauernköter zwischen die Pferde. Ich bin einmal vom Pferd gerutscht, aber absichtlich, weil es auf beiden Vorderfüßen gelegen ist und auf dem glitschigen Boden nicht hätte mit dem Reiter aufstehen können ... (B, 1:202-3; SW, 28:219)

In weaving this experience into his writing, Hofmannsthal changes the scene to a village, where the narrow streets concentrate and magnify the wretchedness of Lerch's surroundings.

In contrast to the sound of trumpets and marching horses filling Milan, the village remains deathly still, "kein Kind, kein Vogel, kein Lufthauch" (E, p. 55; SW, 28:43). Lerch sees "hie und da eine faule, halbnackte Gestalt auf einer Bettstatt lungern oder schleppend, wie mit ausgerenkten Hüften, durchs Zimmer gehen" (E, p. 55; SW, 28:43).[9] The "schönen Unbekannten" in Milan with their bare arms suggest amorous adventures, but the semi-nakedness of the villagers stresses only the seriousness of their disease, which leaves them unable to clothe themselves. Vuic's bed enticed the sergeant to erotic fantasies, but in these beds the diseased villagers suffer and die. Lerch noticed a stiffness in the horse's gait in Milan when he glimpsed Vuic's face; here a woman appears as he turns to look at his horse's rear hooves for an explanation of its uneasy gait. Vuic's negligee excited Lerch's imagination; the woman in the village is likewise only half clothed, but her attire is soiled and ragged. She is so much a part of the animal world that she shows no fear of walking directly in front of the horse. The greasy knot of her hair moved slightly by the

---

8 *Handwörterbuch des deutschen Aberglaubens*, vol. 6, col. 1620.
9 These figures share the awkward gait characteristic of Maria in the *Andreas* novel. Because of her schizophrenia, she can not walk normally, but only as if her lower body were wound in chains. The doctor in *Der Turm* recognizes a comparable inner struggle in Julian's gait: "heroischen Ehrgeiz, in den Hüften verhalten von ohnmächtigem, gigantisch mit sich zerfallenem Willen" (D, 4:44). Whether the village inhabitant suffers a similar disunity of self can not be determined from the brief description.

horse's breath is perhaps intended as a reminiscence of the fly on Vuic's comb. The suggestion of uncleanliness and corruption links the two women.

The fact that the horse, by his hesitant step, allows the sergeant time to contemplate the shabbily clothed woman gives rise to the suspicion that Hofmannsthal somehow connects the horse with the erotic encounter.[10] The description of his wild ride in Göding ended with the encounter with the Bohemian girl. Since the horse carries the lover to his mistress, it is an appropriate bearer of erotic connotations. One thinks of Felix in the *Wanderjahre,* who wants to learn to ride as quickly as possible so as to return to Hersilie. Hofmannsthal's use of horses and horseback riding to describe the relations between men and women forms an integral part of the imagery of *Die Frau im Fenster* and the *Andreas* novel. We must withhold our conclusions about the significance of the image, however, until we have examined *Die Frau im Fenster* and *Das kleine Welttheater*, where the very act of not riding becomes symbolic.

Lerch's brown horse falters at the sight of two bleeding rats locked in combat; the one beneath cries out in pain as the pair rolls into the street. The presence of the rats suggests that the disease infecting the village may be bubonic plague.[11] The plague represents the moral disarray brought on by war, as in Kleist's *Robert Guiskard.* In addition, plague signifies, as in Hofmannsthal's "Erlebnis des Marschalls von Bassompierre" the ascendancy of irrational forces and the accompanying breakdown of human order.

The rats' angry struggle reflects the human situation, the harshness and degradation of death in the midst of disease, corruption, and poverty. The rats in the Chandos letter similarly reflect the state of mankind. Chandos imagines the death agonies of rats he has or-

10 Michael Lakin observes a comparable association of horses with the eroticism in Kafka's story, "Ein Landarzt," in which the doctor's maid, Rosa, is pursued by a groom who appears with the demonic horse. Later the horses slow their pace, preventing the doctor from reaching home in time to save Rosa from the groom's attack. In Kafka's story, as in Hofmannsthal's work, the horse is linked particularly with violent sexual encounters. See Lakin's article, "Hofmannsthal's Reitergeschichte and Kafka's Ein Landarzt," p. 44.
11 In 1894 it was discovered that the plague was transmitted to humans from fleas harbored by rats.

dered poisoned in one of his dairies. Although he is not actually present, his imagination is so intensely occupied with the rats' struggle that he visualizes the entire scene:

> ... das Gellen der Todesschreie, die sich an modrigen Mauern brachen; diese ineinander geknäulten Krämpfe der Ohnmacht, durcheinander hinjagenden Verzweiflungen; das wahnwitzige Suchen der Ausgänge, der kalte Blick der Wut, wenn zwei einander an der verstopften Ritze begegnen. (P, 2:15)

He associates the rat's plight directly with the human condition as recorded in history and literature, with Livius, with the burning of Carthage, and with the death of Niobe. He feels not sympathy for the dying rats, but a oneness with their suffering, "ein Hinüberfließen in jene Geschöpfe oder ein Fühlen, daß ein Fluidum des Lebens und des Todes, des Traumes und Wachens für einen Augenblick in sie hinübergeflossen ist ..." (P, 2:15). The rats in "Reitergeschichte" evoke an awareness of man's plight in their deadly struggle, a parallel of which Lerch seems to take no notice, only his horse balks at the sight of them.

Elsewhere in Hofmannsthal's work rats evoke disgust and revulsion. The soul in *Das Salzburger große Welttheater* refuses the beggar's role, complaining:

> Da hause ich unter einer Brücke und zehre von dem, was Ratten nicht mehr wollen. Da schrei ich in Herzensangst, ... — da bleck ich die Zähne in Verzweiflung. (D, 3:268; SW, 10: 18-19)

The quarter where the dyer Barak lives in "Frau ohne Schatten" is described as follows: "Da wohnten die ärmsten Leute, die Kesselflicker, die Lumpensammler, die Fallensteller, in dichten Klumpen beisammen wie die Ratten" (E, p. 337; SW, 28:167). The conspirators in *Das gerettete Venedig* repeatedly compare their existence of that of rats in order to emphasize their captivity in the Venetian social structure; Jaffier describes thus his denigration at the hands of his father-in-law:

> ... Unter seinem Blick
> in seinem Vorsaal stand ich, rings umstellt
> von Wänden, wie ein Tier, wie eine Ratte,
> die nicht ihr Loch kann finden, sich zu bergen.
> (D, 2:91; SW, 4:17)

The rats of the "Reitergeschichte" share the fate of man in time of war: they consume their last strength in battle against their own kind. The comparison of humans to rats, here implied rather than stated, signifies the utter denigration of the most base sort of human existence.

The brown horse balks at the sight of the rats, and Lerch is obliged to urge him on forcefully. The horse's movements no longer coincide with his own wishes. Since turning aside from the squadron where horse and rider functioned together as part of the whole unit, the sergeant's libidinous urges, the desire for money and an easy civilian life with Vuic, come into ever stronger conflict with his horse, the bearer of his military ego, who is eager to return to the secure order of the squadron.[12] The reader learns nothing firsthand about Lerch's reaction to the diseased villagers, to the half-clothed woman, to the rats or dogs. Everything is expressed indirectly through his horse's progress or lack of it.[13] Lerch must use increasing force to urge his mount on: first leg pressure and then his spurs.

The appearance of the pack of degenerate dogs is rooted in Hofmannsthal's actual experience. In a letter from Göding he describes a garden where he often sits:

> Und auf dem Rasen sind ... 15 Hunde, alle häßlich, Mischungen von Terriers und Bauernkötern, übermäßig dicke Hunde, läufige Hündinnen, ganz junge schon groß mit weichen ungeschickten Gliedern, falsche Hunde, verprügelte und demoralisierte, auch stumpfsinnige, alle schmutzig, mit häßlichen Augen, und wundervollen weißen Zähnen. Darin lagen alle Mächte des Lebens und seine ganze erstickende Beschränktheit, daß es von sich selbst hypnotisiert ist. (SW, 28:219)

There are three salient aspects of this description. The dogs are utterly degenerate, no longer bred by humans but rapidly reproducing

---

12 See William R. Donop's comments on the horse as embodiment of Lerch's military ego in "Archetypal Vision in Hofmannsthal's *Reitergeschichte*," *German Life and Letters*, n.s., 22 (1969): 128.

13 Peter Mollenhauer analyzes verbs of perception in this context and concludes that the village depicts the misery and deprivation which Lerch, like professional soldiers in general, would rather not perceive. See "Wahrnehmung und Wirklichkeitsbewußtsein in Hofmannsthals *Reitergeschichte*," *German Quarterly* 50 (1977): 283-97.

mongrels. Their sexuality is emphasized: even the young females have already born litters. Finally, the relationship between man and dog consists only of hostility and distrust: some dogs have been mistreated, others demoralized. Therefore their eyes are ugly and no longer reveal any fondness for man.

Hofmannsthal considers the eyes of the mute animal a clue to its character: "In der Tat hat der tierische Blick etwas Vages, das ergreifend und schauerlich ist," he writes in "Versuch über Victor Hugo" (P, 1:353). To Edgar Karg von Bebenburg he writes that all the innumerable things in life express something: "das Hoch-sein der Berge, das Groß-sein des Meeres, das Dunkel-sein der Nacht, die Art wie Pferde dreinschauen, wie unsere Hände gebaut sind."[14] Elis Fröbom describes the gaze of a Javanese girl: "ihr Reden/Verstand ich so, wie ich ein Tier versteh;/In ihren Augen war was Bittendes,/Wie Hunde bitten..." (GLD, p. 335). Because the animal's regard replaces human speech as an organ of expression, Hofmannsthal's emphasis on the animal's eyes simultaneously underscores the inarticulate, non-rational, non-human aspects of the creature.

In "Reitergeschichte" as in the letter from Göding, Hofmannsthal stresses the weakness, ugliness, and disease among these dogs who represent the powers of life. Alewyn, concurring with our interpretation of the dogs in "Amgiad und Assad" and in "Ein Traum von großer Magie" as representative of gross corporality, speaks of the "schamlosen Kreatürlichkeit der Tiere."[15] Benno von Wiese contrasts the pack of hideous dogs with the orderly triumphant squadron and concludes that the dogs show "die beschränkte, verdammte und zum Tode verurteilte Kreatur in allen Spielarten."[16] Because the dog is one of the commonest and most significant of Hofmannsthal's animal symbols, it is useful to investigate its meaning in his other works. We have already ascertained that the dog is frequently connected with mute physicality.

Elsewhere we find evidence that Hofmannsthal portrays the dog in its traditional role as watchdog and guard. Cerberus, a dog with

---

14 Hofmannsthal and Karg von Bebenburg, *Briefwechsel*, p. 81.
15 *Über Hugo von Hofmannsthal*, p. 82.
16 "Hugo von Hofmannsthal, 'Reitergeschichte,' " in: *Die Deutsche Novelle von Goethe bis Kafka*, part 1 (Düsseldorf: August Bagel, 1956), p. 82.

many snake-covered heads, guarded the entrance to the underworld, according to classical mythology. He fawned on the newly arrived shades, but should one try to escape, Cerberus attacked and devoured him. He was merciless in the fulfillment of duty; even the Furies were powerless against him, and his eyes never closed. Hofmannsthal's "dogs of fate" exercise a similar function: Oedipus sends his father the following message:

> ... Sag ihm, ich haus im Walde —
> Sag ihm, die Hunde des Geschicks, die niemals
> ihr Auge schließen, sind mir auf den Fersen.
> (D, 2:534; SW, 8:119)

Elektra is almost canine in her unrelenting pursuit of revenge; she warns Klytemnästra: "ich bin wie ein Hund an deiner Ferse" (D, 2:23, 531). In a poem entitled "Brief" the poet asks,

> Hast du nicht deiner Sinne dumpfe Flur,
> Darüber des Lebens Göttin dich,
> Die wilde, jagt,
> Mit großen schwarzen Hunden,
> Leben, Traum und Tod,
> Drei großen schwarzen Hunden?
> (GLD, pp. 513-14)

Like the degenerate curs in Göding, these dogs represent the "Mächte des Lebens," giving man no respite from their inexorable chase.[17]

In addition to his role as guardian of the underworld and as dog of fate, the dog appears in classical literature, as in Hofmannsthal's work, as guardian of the home. It is his office to decide who belongs to the house and to warn its inhabitants of any approaching stranger. His instinctive perspicacity, enabling him to recognize a familiar human even after a long absence or when returning in disguise, surpasses human perception. Orestes scolds Elektra: "Die Hunde auf dem Hof erkennen mich,/ und meine Schwester nicht?" (D, 2:62). Argos, Odysseus' dog, is the only one to recognize the wanderer, who

---

17 Erwin Kobel reminds us that in Greek drama the Eumenides were often represented by or compared to dogs. See his *Hugo von Hofmannsthal* (Berlin: de Gruyter, 1970), p. 189.

returns home as a beggar after an absence of twenty years.[18] Hofmannsthal compares the poet to this "princely pilgrim" whom the servants force beneath the staircase "wo nachts der Platz der Hunde ist." The poet lives "gestoßen von der letzten Magd und gewiesen zu den Hunden; und ohne Amt in diesem Haus, ohne Dienst, ohne Recht, ohne Pflicht, als nur zu lungern und zu liegen ... und ein ungeheures Leiden, ungeheures Genießen zu durchleben" (P, 2:243). The poet, then, is obliged to seek his material in life itself, even in the physical existence he shares with animals, and to remain open to all sense impressions.

Hofmannsthal develops the dog's function as guardian to such a point that the feeling of belonging to a home coincides with man's relationship to the dog guarding the home. Elis describes the pleasure of belonging to a home:

> Und wo der Hund dann herkommt, sich an dir
> Zu wärmen, weil er weiß, du bist vom Haus:
> Nicht fremd und flüchtig, wie das wilde Wasser ...
> (GLD, p. 414)

When Elis first came to Dahlsjö's house, the family dog, sensing the discontent in the stranger, behaved in an unfriendly manner; Elis recalls:

> Der Unstete bin ich, der Heimatlose, ...
> Der lang sein Brot an Eurem Tische brach
> Und keinem wagte ins Gesicht zu schaun,
> Im Innern grauenvolle Zwiesprach führend,
> Der Finstre, dem der Hofhund winselnd auswich ...
> (GLD, p. 417)

Hofmannsthal frequently underscores the animal's ability to see through human secrets. Just as Odysseus' dog Argos recognizes his master despite his outward appearance, the dog has an infallible instinct for sensing the frame of mind of everyone he meets. Animals "wittern das, was über menschliches Begreifen hinausgeht" he writes (P, 1:353). One who has been ostracized by his fellow man will likewise be shunned by dogs. Faninal in the *Rosenkavalier* feels so disgraced by the behavior of Ochs von Lerchenau that he laments:

---

18 Homer, *Odyssey* 17. 290 ff. See also P, 3:93.

"Kein Hund nimmt mehr ein Stückl Brot von mir" (L, 1:376). The heroine of *Silvia im Stern* so delights one of her suitors that he exclaims:

> Die unschuldigen Kinder auf der Straße lassen sich mit mir ein, der wütende Hund, der mir begegnet, kuscht vor mir. Jetzt hab ich mich wieder. (L, 2:345)

We have previously mentioned those traits characteristic of both child and dog: both are sensual creatures showing traces of earlier stages in human development. In addition Hofmannsthal suspected that both dog and child penetrated man's social mask and read his innermost secrets. Self-assurance, however, like that vouchsafed Elis and Silvia's suitor, wins mastery over the dog — as over the horse.

Summarizing now the conclusions to be drawn from this excursus on dogs, we have derived several insights applicable to "Reitergeschichte." The animal, having no power of verbal expression, expresses itself through its gaze. The classical representation of Cerberus or the Eumenides as dogs corresponds to Hofmannsthal's "dogs of fate" or presentation of the "Mächte des Lebens" in canine form. The watchdog's recognition of those belonging to a certain house imparts a feeling of security to those accepted, while marking as strangers those who have no place within the home.

If we study "Reitergeschichte" in the light of these conclusions, we perceive in the appearance and attitude of the pack of dogs an all encompassing breakdown of human society. These dogs do not watch over any house, indeed they are unsuited for such a post, for they are diseased, half starved, and the young dogs can neither bark nor bite. Nor does any connection exist between dog and man; they pay no attention to Lerch, nor do they alert the villagers to his presence.

The white female dog with drooping nipples is doubtless a representation of sexuality; she occupies the lowest level among the females, Vuic and the shabbily dressed village woman, who have appeared so far. In Hofmannsthal's imagination, the dog is an appropriate symbol of woman, because it unites loyalty, devotion, and sensuality in the animal figure.[19] The empress' nurse in *Die Frau ohne*

---

19 Men are, to be sure, compared to dogs, but such comparisons rest principal-

Schatten watches "der Hündin gleich" at the threshold of her mistress and because of devotion to her remains "die Hündin" in the emperor's palace.

Frequently the women Hofmannsthal compares to dogs have been mistreated or deserted by men. Ariadne points to the cave where she lived after Theseus abandoned her, saying: "Da innen lag die arme Hündin/ An' Boden gedrückt" (L, 3:64). Sobeide begs her former lover Ganem to take her into his house, pleading:

> ich hab sonst kein Daheim als die Streu
> zur Seite deinem Hund, ... (D, p. 137)

Elis Fröbom tells how he mistreated the Javanese girl who was his mistress:

> Der arme Hund, das Mädchen, wollt ich sagen,
> Von Java ... einmal stieß ich so nach ihr,
> Wie man nach Hunden stößt ... (GLD, p. 335)

The brutality of an aggressive male is directed against any weaker creature, be it woman or dog. Such mistreated women often persist, doglike, in loyalty to the men who abuse them.

Hofmannsthal emphasizes the sensuality linking the women in "Reitergeschichte" to the white dog by mentioning her light fur, an echo of Vuic's fine white skin. This trait shared by woman and dog deprives the former of any non-physical powers of attraction; in Lerch's consciousness she exists only through her physical attributes; that is, as a sex object. Furthermore, Hofmannsthal seems to attribute sexual desire to both woman and dog. He narrates the following incident from the life of Madame de La Vallière, former mistress of Louis XIV. The king

> ... hatte ein schönes Epagneulhündchen ... Da nahm der König auf Antrieb der Montespan [seiner jetzigen Mätresse] das Hündchen und warf es der Duchesse de la Vallière zu und sagte: "Da, Madame! Da ist Gesellschaft für Euch!" (P, 2:108)

ly on loyalty, sensuality plays no part. In *Das gerettete Venedig* Senator Dolfin begs Aquilina to keep him in place of the lapdog she had just lost. She asks, "Herr, wodurch/wollt ihr an einen solchen Freund erinnern?" Dolfin replies: "Durch meine Treue." Aquilina: "Pfui, die Blasphemie!/Die quoll aus seinem muntern stummen Aug" (D, 2:160).

Although the linking of woman to dog places the woman in a disadvantageous light, it says a great deal about the character of the author and his figures. Like Elis, Lerch would be inclined to mistreat a woman. His bowing Vuic's head forward demonstrates that he seeks in the relationship to a woman further gratification of his aggression, which is not extinguished by his military career.

The close association of Vuic to the white female raises the question whether the other dogs can be interpreted in a similar manner. William Donop, cognizant of the similarity between Vuic and the white dog, goes on to identify the bloated whippet with Vuic's portly companion, the greedy dog with inflamed eyes with Lerch, and the degenerate dachshund with Baron Rofrano on the basis of his weary melancholy eyes.[20] His attempt to establish these further parallels seems scarcely justified by the slight details provided in the text. Furthermore, his strict concept of the symbol as an equation of two things contradicts Hofmannsthal's statement in "Das Gespräch über Gedichte" that poetic symbolism never merely substitutes one thing for another. The effective symbol admits of several interpretations within its context, without establishing a direct equation. The other dogs in the "Reitergeschichte" seem not substitutes for other figures in the story, but rather serve to illuminate certain conditions of human existence.

The white female dog is probably mother of the two younger weak dogs, yet she demonstrates no motherly care for them, trying instead to bury the bone only to save herself from starvation. Her selfishness and greed characterize Lerch as well; in wartime the desire for self-preservation precludes any more tender sentiments such as love of family. The young dogs appear to have soft bones, sagging skin, and to be incapable of biting or barking, thus they are unfit for life itself. Near starvation appears to have caused bloating in the tawny whippet. The next dog suffers an eye ailment; the organ which is intended to reveal his character to man displays nothing but disease, indicative of the corrupted degenerate man-dog relationship in the village. The dachshund alone remains aloof from the quarrel of the other dogs. He looks upon the scene with weary eyes, as if warning

20 "Archetypal Vision in Hofmannsthal's *Reitergeschichte,*" p. 130.

Lerch against the war whose effects (destruction and famine) shorten his painful life.

The dogs taken together as embodying the "Mächte des Lebens" demonstrate those powers to be sexual urges, greed, selfishness, hunger, disease, and death. Unlike the merchant's son, Lerch does not fall at the initial confrontation with creatures foreign to his nature, rather he meets certain aspects of himself externalized in the dogs. As they surround him, he makes no greater attempt than did the merchant's son to establish contact with them; the young aesthete tried to buy his liberation, Lerch tries to secure his through brute force. His pistol fails to function, he is unable to combat these forces, he can only flee from them, and accordingly spurs on his horse.

But the way is blocked again, this time by a cow being led to the slaughterhouse. The cow, reminiscent of the herd of cattle easily captured by the Austrian soldiers earlier in the day, shies away from the fresh hide of a black calf, draws "mit geblähten Nüstern den rötlichen Sonnendunst des Abends in sich" and snatches a mouthful of hay Lerch has fastened to his saddle to feed his horse.

In *Elektra* Hofmannsthal makes use of an image remarkably similar to that of "Reitergeschichte." Elektra explains to her sister that anyone who is not a mere animal is incapable of forgetting significant events:

> Das Vieh schläft ein, von halbgefressner Beute
> die Lefze noch behängt, das Vieh vergißt sich
> und fängt zu käuen an, indes der Tod
> schon würgend auf ihm sitzt,
> ....
> ich bin kein Vieh, ich *kann nicht*
> *vergessen!* (D, 2:20-21)

In this utter ignorance of approaching death, Lerch resembles the cow. He too is concerned only with stilling the moment's hunger, with seizing booty, just as the cow before him snatches a last mouthful of hay, unaware that death will render futile all attempts at self preservation.[21]

21 Volker O. Durr writes that the cow's snatching at the hay can well be equated to Lerch's seizure of the gray horse and relates the unawareness of his im-

The cow's appetite for life is visually presented through her drawing in the air through distended nostrils. The same image occurs in the prologue to *Die Frau im Fenster,* where the poet narrates his dream of a voyage:

> Und unaufhörlich, wenn bei mir im Schiff
> Der Stier mit vorgestreckten Nüstern brüllte,
> So spürte ich, wie auf den fernen Triften
> Im dunkelsten Gebirg' die jungen Kühe
> Sich auf die Knie erhoben, völlig dann
> Auf ihre Füße sprangen und durchs Dunkel
> Hinliefen und die Luft der Nacht einsogen.
> (GLD, p. 131; SW, 3:125)

Here the hunger for life becomes inseparable from sexual desire; a combination recurring in the poem "Vor Tag:"

> ... Nun streckt
> Die junge Kuh im Stall die starken Nüstern
> Nach kühlem Frühduft. (GLD, p. 9; SW, 1:106)

The heifer's instincts are not explicitly stated, but she forms part of the background in the poem for the image of the young man returning at dawn from a woman's bed. The cow, then, connotes the life drive and its attendant themes, sexual desire and fertility.

The air which the cow in "Reitergeschichte" so eagerly inhales, however, is filled with the bloody vapors of war, war which lays waste the productive fertility she represents. In her hunger for life and her instinctive fear of death she embodies the life drive controlling the human who, like Anton Lerch, has sunk to the level of mute, unsuspecting beast.

After Lerch finally makes his way past the cow, his horse laboriously passes centipedes and woodlice, as if these tiny living things filled a vast, slowly traversed space. Because one must look to the ground to perceive these creatures, their mention signals intensive preoccupation with the details of one's physical existence. Ariadne,

---

pending death to that of the cow. See: "Der Tod des Wachtmeisters Anton Lerch und die Revolution von 1849; Zu Hofmannsthals *Reitergeschichte,*" *German Quarterly* 45 (1972), 42.

reflecting upon the transformation wrought by Bacchus, points to the cave where she lived:

> Da innen lag die arme Hündin
> An' Boden gedrückt, auf kalten Nesseln
> Mit Wurm und Assel ... (L, 3:64)

Theseus' abandonment of her has reduced Ariadne to an animal existence. Similarly, the woodlice plaguing Sigismund in his tower prison contribute to his degradation in captivity (D, 4:25).

Lerch misjudges spatial relationships, feeling that his horse labors past these tiny insects, and temporal measurement eludes him as well. Inwardly disoriented, he does not immediately recognize his Doppelgänger. Only his horse's "schwere rohrende Atem" draws his attention to the apparition. According to superstition, horses perceive ghosts and other spirits more readily than do their human masters.[22] The brown horse balks instinctively as he did before the rats, and Lerch must force him to go on.

The Doppelgänger's appearance demonstrates that Lerch's experiences in the village have alienated him from his former self. In two of Hofmannsthal's poems the main figures experience alienation from previous more innocent selves who then appear, as a child in "Erlebnis" and in a mirror in "Vor Tag." At a distance Lerch first recognizes not himself as rider, but the brown horse with white forelegs, next the uniform of his own regiment, and finally himself. Unaccustomed to self contemplation, he has no image of himself save that of the cavalryman, the unit formed of horse and rider.

This encounter concludes the second or middle portion of the novella; these first two thirds of the "Reitergeschichte" have followed the basic outline of the "Märchen." Like the merchant's son, Lerch left the familiar surroundings of his squadron and ventured alone into the village. Just as the merchant's son's experiences in his native city mirrored in distorted form his proverb about meeting death like a king lost on a hunt, Lerch's encounters in the village mirrored in distorted form the squadron's ride through Milan. In contrast to the splendid Milanese churches, the village church boasted only a dilapidated belltower. Instead of Vuic's alluring presence,

---

22 *Handwörterbuch des deutschen Aberglaubens*, vol. 6, col. 1620.

Lerch met only the slovenly village woman. While the merchant's son's face in death revealed that he had sunk into bestiality, resembling the face of the last horse, Lerch's failure to recognize his own double shows that he has undergone an equally profound transformation.

Lerch's return to the squadron, with which the last third of the novella begins, happens so quickly that he has no time for reflection. He gallops toward enemy soldiers in a wood, a chaotic scene reminiscent of Hofmannsthal's dangerous gallop through the woods in Göding. The ensuing battle seems to reunite his military ego and his libidinous desires, extremes which had become polarized in the village. Once again the movements of the brown horse correspond to the intentions of his rider. The killing of the enemy officer, in fact, seems predominantly the deed of horse rather than rider: the saber which enters the officer's mouth compresses in its tip the furious energy of the galloping horse.[23]

The gray horse whose bridle Lerch seizes just as the dying officer's fingers let it fall symbolizes Lerch's hopes of a better future. The horse is "young, handsome, vain" and lifts its feet "delicately as a deer" over its dying master. Lerch's brown horse, as we have observed, binds him to military service and provides the means of recognizing himself, or more precisely, his *Doppelgänger,* as cavalryman. He hopes that the gray horse will lend his appearance something of its grace and nobility before he returns to claim Vuic. The color of his brown horse may be associated with the earth and the bondage of corporeal existence. The gray horse, on the other hand, connotes light and supernatural powers. Further, the gray horse contributes to the foreshadowing of Lerch's death, for it often appears as death's mount, as in Theodor Storm's *Der Schimmelreiter.* In the book of Revelations the personification of death rides a pale horse. The *Dop-*

[23] Wolfgang Mauser comments on this co-operation of horse and rider as evidence that Lerch's internal conflicts, revealed through his horse's hesitant gait in the village, have now been resolved: "So wie sich im Dorf der konflikthaft erfahrene Zustand des Reiters lähmend auf das Pferd übertragen hatte, so erfährt der Wachtmeister auch das sieghaft-erfüllende Ereignis als gemeinsamen Vorgang." *Hugo von Hofmannsthal: Konfliktbewältigung und Werkstruktur, eine psychosoziologische Interpretation* (Munich: Wilhelm Fink, 1977), p. 105.

pelgänger, to be sure, rides a horse identical to Lerch's own, but this horse demonstrates its kinship with the gray through the fact that both horses refuse to cross running water. The gray horse refuses to carry the enemy officer across a small brook and thus exposes him to Lerch's attack. The *Doppelgänger's* horse crosses the old stone bridge, which, however, as Hofmannsthal states twice, spans only a dry ditch. Both the *Faustbuch* and Robert Burns' poem "Tam O'Shanter" present the superstition that the devil's horses are unable to cross running water. It is subtly implied that the diabolical aspects of both the gray horse and the *Doppelgänger's* horse may, in a sense, be construed as punishment for the sins of the squadron. The Austrian troops have laid waste to the environs of Milan and have failed to respect in their skirmishes such sacred places as churches and cemeteries, using them for sanctuary or scenes of battle. The setting sun spreads "a monstrous red" over the landscape, reflecting its light in puddles resembling "pools of blood." The soldiers have laughingly wiped the blood smears from their sabers on the soft leaves of a fig tree. In *Elektra* such a fig tree appears as an emblem of the murder of Agamemnon; on the roof of the royal house weighs

> ein riesiger, schwerer, gekrümmter Feigenbaum, dessen Stamm man nicht sieht, dessen Masse unheimlich geformt im Abendlicht wie ein halbaufgerichtetes Tier auf dem flachen Dach auflagert. (P, 2:69)

The fig tree in "Reitergeschichte" seems to have a similar function as living testimony of the soldiers' bloody deeds. Benno von Wiese interprets the death of Anton Lerch, embodiment of the anarchic animalistic elements in the squadron, as necessary to purge the troops of their collective guilt.[24]

Baron Rofrano stands as the judge of these crimes. Wiese views him as representing, in contrast to Lerch, whatever is noble and beautiful, as recognizing that the fine gray horse can not be left to his coarse-natured sergeant.[25] In fact, the gray horse demonstrates that he belongs in the commander's sphere as his nostrils nearly touch the forehead of Rofrano's horse.

---

24 "Hugo von Hofmannsthal, 'Reitergeschichte,' " p. 298.
25 Ibid, p. 300.

Lerch lacks total control over his horse, as was proven by his repeated recourse to force in the village. He opposes his desire to possess Vuic and his plans for a more comfortable future to the horse's instincts. Rofrano, on the other hand, might be aptly characterized by one of Hofmannsthal's favorite adages, "The whole man must move at once" (A, p. 151). He commands "ohne seine Stimme zu erheben" and raises his arm "mit einer nachlässigen, beinahe gezierten Bewegung" to shoot Lerch (E, p. 61; SW, 28:48). His bearing corresponds to the grace and poise of the gray horse. The harmony within himself makes possible control over others; he dominates through singleness of purpose.[26]

Rofrano has been regarded as the representative of an over-refined nobility struggling against the upsurge of crass but viable lower social classes.[27] Although Hofmannsthal recognizes the precariousness of the aristocrat's social position and depicts the dangers of alienation from everyday life frequently in his early works, the portrayal of Anton Lerch indicates that the reader is not intended to sympathize or identify with his crude instinctive nature either. The conflict is not merely a clash between two opposing *social* classes; rather considering the extent to which this particular story was

26 Rolf Tarot offers a contrasting interpretation of Rofrano's behavior. He writes that the Commander's insight into his precarious circumstances springs from a momentary ability to grasp the situation and not from conscious reflection. "Seine instinktive, nicht rationale Verhaltensweise bedingt seine 'nachlässige, beinahe gezierte Bewegung' " (*Hugo von Hofmannsthal; Daseinsformen und dichterische Struktur*, p. 352). In contrast to that assessment of Rofrano's style of command, Carl V. Hansen calls him "capable and resolute." See his analysis: "The Death of First Sergeant Anton Lerch in Hofmannsthal's *Reitergeschichte*: A Military Analysis," *Modern Austrian Literature* 13 (1980), 17-26.
27 See, for example, Alewyn, *Über Hugo von Hofmannsthal,* p. 86; von Wiese, "Hugo von Hofmannsthal, 'Reitergeschichte'," p. 300. Durr, "Der Tod des Wachtmeisters Anton Lerch,..." pp. 37-40. Theodore Fiedler goes one step further, drawing an analogy between Lerch's capture of the gray horse and the rebellion in Austria's Italian provinces, both events which threaten Baron Rofrano's aristocratic existence: "Hofmannsthals 'Reitergeschichte' und ihre Leser: zur Politik der Ironie," *Germanisch-romanische Monatsschrift* n.s. 26 (1976), 140-63.

shaped by Hofmannsthal's experiences in military service, we perceive here a conflict between the realm of intellect, of language, of refinement, and that of unenlightened bestiality. Indeed it is possible, as one critic has done, to interpret the theme of the story as a discussion of form versus chaos: "Das Grundproblem der *Reitergeschichte* ist der Zerfall von Form und Welt und die Frage, wie die Form zu bewahren sei."[28] The "schöne Schwadron," a unit into which Lerch is totally integrated until he dismounts at Vuic's door, represents military form and order. The village demonstrates that war has caused social order to degenerate so deeply into chaos that the trappings of social form, dress and speech, are scarcely apparent; even the ugly dogs are misshapen, formless. In the *Doppelgänger,* Lerch recognizes the shell of military order, his horse and uniform, but in the skirmish following this apparition he is no longer capable of rejoining the unit; the squadron itself is deformed by the soldiers' careless euphoria and the horses they have introduced into their ranks. Finally Rofrano's command and the shot with which he enforces it serve to restore form. Furthermore, it is of the utmost significance that Rofrano restores form by means of *language.*

It is possible, therefore, to draw parallels between "Reitergeschichte" and such poems as "Ein Traum von großer Magie" and "Manche freilich," poems turning upon the confrontation of a creative spirit with chaos. Rofrano, like the *Magier,* acts through command. Like his sergeant, he must enforce his authority with a brutal deed, yet his calm self-assurance when delivering the command characterizes him as one controlling language in its magic powers.

The opposition to Rofrano heightens Lerch's bestial aspect: "ein bestialischer Zorn" rises within him, and in his gaze flickers "etwas Gedrücktes, Hündisches."[29] Recalling our assertion that the animal's

28 Marianne Burkhard, "Hofmannsthals *Reitergeschichte;* ein Gegenstück zum Chandosbrief," *Amsterdamer Beiträge zur neueren Germanistik,* vol. 4:52.
29 The animal attribute of course calls to mind the pack of village dogs. Here, however, in combination with "etwas Gedrücktes" it suggests a lack of freedom, the dog subordinate to and dependent upon others for his very existence, a position analogous to that of Lerch in the army. The state of dependence and subordination is often, as is the case with Lerch, connected to a lack of money. The title figure in "Der Brief des letzten Contarin" realizes as a youth that his parents live on the charity of wealthy acquaintances and

gaze substitutes for human expression of character through speech, the phrase "stumme Insubordination" further intensifies the sergeant's inarticulate bestial nature. Language seems limited to Rofrano and denied to Lerch. Furthermore, it seems appropriate to Milan, yet utterly absent in the village, filled with a deathly silence like the city of the "Märchen." If speech draws men together, as Anton in *Der Turm* maintains, it also creates social order. The village, in contrast, is chaos, the inarticulate realm of the irrational. The ditch seems perhaps to separate the village's territory from that of the victorious squadron, but its effectiveness as a boundary is undermined by the twice repeated notation that it is a dry ditch spanned by the old stone bridge. Chaos may at any time burst into the realm of reason and order. The dry ditch is merely the semblance of a boundary, as were the four open glass doors at the beginning of "Ein Traum von großer Magie."

Earlier in this chapter we described Lerch as something of an exception among Hofmannsthal's protagonists. Now that his portrait has become clearer, several details have gained new significance. The motion with which he bowed Vuic's head revealed that his erotic desires are only a secondary indirect manifestation of his aggressive tendencies. Sexual desire and violence are inseparable forces of his character. The two struggling rats, their position suggestive of the sex act, visually unite these dual aspects of aggression. The same significance must be attached to the killing of the enemy officer into whose mouth Lerch thrusts his saber. The hesitation before Lerch recognizes his *Doppelgänger* may be interpreted as a moment of estrangement from himself ensuing from the temporary dominance of these violent aggressive traits. Completely absorbed in his search for sudden riches, which would enable him to impress Vuic and thus

> comes to envy the honest independence of others who live in open poverty. He describes himself with the gaze of a beggar, "der Blick hoffnungslosen starren Neides, durchflackert von hündischem überschätzendem Verlangen" (E, p. 91). And in 1920 Hofmannsthal writes to Carl J. Burckhardt that the financial need caused by World War I has deprived him of freedom of movement: "Seit 6 Jahren liege ich hier wie ein Hund an der Kette." (*Briefwechsel* p. 39). The dog, then, as a symbol of social or financial oppression adds a further element of contrast between Lerch's existence and that of Baron Rofrano.

gratify his desires, he fails to recognize the *Doppelgänger* who confronts him only with the appearance of the military ego: horse and uniform. The inability to reconcile these poles, the desire for physical gratification and his military role, prevents Lerch from ascending toward Rofrano's selfcontained harmony, and ultimately seals his doom.

The contrast between the animal sphere and that of creative fantasy developed in our discussion of the "Märchen" and "Ein Traum von großer Magie" can be further pursued here, if the concepts are somewhat broadened. Instead of the interest in art objects characteristic of the fantasy sphere of the "Märchen," we might place Lerch's dreams of a comfortable civilian existence. Physical comfort, idleness and wealth substitute for aestheticism and the delights of the mind. To the animal sphere belong the locales of chaos, the disease-infested village, the woods full of enemy troops. Vuic reigns in the fantasy world; her possession would ensure Lerch fulfillment of his erotic desires, good food, comfortable lodging and leisure. The gray horse presents itself to Lerch as the means of realizing his daydreams. The animal brings him not only wealth, but a heightened esteem of his own person, for it would give his self image as cavalryman a new polish. Baron Rofrano, incorporating the self-assured, dignified soldier ideal, a nobleman and an officer, deprives him not only of his prize horse, but simultaneously of the possibility for personal aggrandizement.

His brown horse links the sergeant to reality, to his familiar position within the squadron's ranks, to the old self image. Lerch, like the merchant's son, dies in the clash of fantasy with reality; when he is shot, he falls between the two horses, between the present reality of his mediocre situation and the hopes of a more prosperous future. He, too, pays for his illusions with his life. His illusions, however, consist of an unrealized desire, whereas the illusion of the merchant's son is a long standing habit of flight from reality.

CHAPTER V

DIE FRAU IM FENSTER

Hofmannsthal composed his lyrical drama *Die Frau im Fenster* as well as *Das kleine Welttheater* during an exceptionally productive summer in Varese in 1897. The story of Madonna Dianora is interwoven with animal imagery which prefigures that of *Andreas* and the fragment, "Knabengeschichte." The symbols display a depth and interdependence consistent with the standards for poetic symbolism Hofmannsthal proposed in his "Gespräch über Gedichte."

Turning our attention first to Dianora's situation, we find that her imprisonment in an arranged marriage to Messer Braccio is visually represented by her position on the stage, looking down from the balcony of her husband's massive Lombardic palace. In her long opening monologue, she projects onto the forest or park landscape below her vision of an unconstrained idyllic existence with her lover, Messer Palla degli Albizzi. The spatial contrast between above and below, between palace and nature, provides the content of much of her speech and of the little dramatic action of the play.

Dianora's attempt to reach the natural world below her takes the form of a gesture recurring throughout the play: she throws her long hair over the balcony railing. Later she lowers the rope ladder by which her lover may ascend, and finally throws her torso over the railing in desperate recognition that her husband has condemned her. Her hair, so long and thick that it has not dried even after much walking in the sun, symbolizes the boundless intensity of her passion; her sister Medea, an unhappy child, had thin hair.[1] While Braccio

---

[1] Hofmannsthal knowingly alludes to historical truth in naming Dianora's sister "Medea." Later Dianora gives her father's name as "Bartholomäus Colleoni" (D, 1:75). In his essay, "Die Rede Gabriele d'Annunzios," Hofmannsthal mentions the chapel in Bergamo where "der berühmte Söldnerkapitän Bartholomäus Colleoni, seine junge Tochter Medea und ihr zahmer Sperling begraben liegen" (P, 1:336); see also SW, 3:545, 551.

interrogates her, Dianora asks for a servant to arrange her hair; the wish to put her hair in order indicates a willingness to conform once again to social norms.

Hair as a symbol of female sexuality appears elsewhere in Hofmannsthal's work; in *Die Hochzeit der Sobeide,* Sobeide offers to share Ganem's bed with her rival:

> Wir wollen unser Haar auflösen: welche
> das längre Haar hat, soll den Jungen haben
> für heut − und morgen wieder umgekehrt!
> (D, 1:143)

Vuic's hair comb, visited by a fly, and the greasy knot of curls belonging to the woman in the village of "Reitergeschichte" suggest that a parallel may be drawn between the unclean state of their hair and their loose sexual behavior. Elektra describes her lost beauty with reference to hair: "mein Haar/war solches Haar, vor dem die Männer zittern" (D, 2:63).

Hair as a symbol of sexual passion or virility is, in fact, a little noticed commonplace of literary imagery. The Biblical story of Samson and Delilah comes readily to mind. Goethe's *Faust* also contains an allusion to the seductive powers of woman's hair; in the Walpurgisnacht scene Mephistopheles shows Faust Adam's first wife, Lilith, and warns: "Nimm dich in acht vor ihren schönen Haaren."[2] Gerhart Pickerodt connects Dianora's flinging her hair over the balcony to reach Palla with the fairy tale "Rapunzel" in which an imprisoned damsel lets down her braided hair so that her lover may climb into her tower prison.[3] Indeed Dianora herself compares her hair to the rope ladder she holds ready for Palla. Hugo Wyss, drawing on Bachofen's *Das Mutterrecht,* interprets hair as "Ausdruck hetärischer Zeugung, urverwandt mit den Fäden der Gewebe."[4] The web figures as an erotic symbol, the "Ineinanderweben von männlicher und weiblicher Geschlechtskraft" and "Symbol der ewig zeugenden Natur."[5]

---

2 *Goethes Werke* 3:129.
3 *Hofmannsthals Dramen, Kritik ihres historischen Gehalts,* Studien zur allgemeinen und vergleichenden Literaturwissenschaft, vol. 3 (Stuttgart, J.B. Metzler, 1968), p. 58.
4 *Die Frau in der Dichtung Hofmannsthals,* p. 73.
5 Ibid., p. 18.

Dianora's hair reaches not the ground, as she wishes, but only the nostrils of a bas-relief lion ornamenting the stark facade of the palace. The marble lion's head contrasts with the description of Messer Palla, whose springing gait is "sichrer als der Tritt des jungen Löwen" (D, 1:73; SW, 3:108). The lion, imagined as part of nature, Palla's realm, embodies restrained vitality, but as an architectural ornament captures in stone only the relentless harshness with which Braccio guards all he possesses. The dilated extended nostrils of the cow in "Reitergeschichte" indicated her thirst for life. The lion ornament, however, displays only "kalte Marmornüstern" as if the urge to live had ossified in Braccio's forbidding palace. The fact that Dianora's hair does not reach the ground where Palla walks with his sure lion's gait, but only the lion's head halfway below her balcony (the spatial frame of her captivity in Braccio's world), is also significant. Dianora fails to reach her lover, attaining only her husband's hollow image, itself subordinated to the severe lines of the palace and the strict convention the building represents.

The opposition between Braccio's and Palla's worlds, between the palace and the park, above and below, is overcome only by Dianora's imagination. Her fantasy wishes away the hours until nightfall, and liberates her from captivity in Braccio's realm to wander freely through the park she regards as Palla's sphere. Animals occupy a considerable place in her imaginings, though they are rarely perceived as objective phenomena, but rather subordinated to her wishes or fantasies. We shall examine the animal images as they occur in her monologue before considering the dog and horse symbols salient in the memories awakened by Braccio's interrogation.

Dianora first describes how she has whiled away the time searching "im Laubengang nach Nestern/ mit jungen Meisen" (D, 1:58; SW, 3:96). In her observation of birds, Dianora concerns herself, perhaps for the first time in her young life, with natural events. Her interest in bird life, like that of the grandmother in *Der weiße Fächer,* is evidence of a strong attachment of life. The old woman preserves her love of life in spite of the many hardships she has endured; Dianora, on the other hand, is first awakened by Palla's love to an awareness of other living creatures.

Dianora's interest in birds is further strengthened by the need to confirm her own observations of the passage of time, for she follows in the sky the flight of wild geese (D, 1:58; SW, 3:96). The phrase "das Rudern wilder Gänse" recurs verbatim in *Das kleine Welttheater* (GLD, p. 303; SW, 3:138), probably a result of the contemporaneous composition of the two plays. The flight of wild geese suggests either fall or early spring when the flocks migrate; neither season coincides with the early summer indicated by the nests of young titmice (Meisen).[6] It seems unlikely that Dianora is speaking of an earlier observation, for her interest in wildlife seems to be of recent date, like her affair with Messer Palla. Perhaps the time discrepancy was merely an oversight occasioned by Hofmannsthal's awareness that the flights of migratory birds serve as a poignant image of passing time.

Love seems to have so transformed Dianora that she welcomes even those creatures once repugnant to her. As a spider, which she would earlier have flung off, crawls over her hand, she marvels at the effects of Palla's love: "Wie sehr bin ich verwandelt, wie verzaubert!" (D, 1:60; SW, 3:98). In the poem "Der Jüngling und die Spinne" the youth realizes the cruelty of life while watching a spider seize its prey. He addresses the spider as "Du häßliche Gewalt, du Tier, du Tod!" and feels powerless to hinder this "widrige Gestalt" (GLD, p. 38; SW, 1:71). Hofmannsthal does not, however, associate the spider exclusively with disgust and death. Because it spins its web scarcely noticed, the spider stands for those aspects of life seldom perceived by humans. In the fourth act of *Der Turm* (1925 version) Sigismund refuses to leave his prison, explaining:

> Schön wirds hier; die Sonne geht auf aus dem Finsteren, die Spinnen in der Mauer freuen sich, wie wenn der Frühling kommt über Nacht und der Hecht mit seinem Schwanz das harte Eis zerschlägt. (D, 4:148)

Hofmannsthal gives the following description of an uninterrupted silence in which spiders are the only life:

> 6 Dianora dates her affair with Palla from the feast day of Mary Magdalene (D, 1:79), or July 22. Later she tells her husband that the changes wrought by Palla's love have lasted twelve weeks; thus the action of the play must take place in mid-October, the season of the autumn migration of wild geese.

> Alle Uhren hört man so genau schlagen, die Laternen malen ihre gleichmäßigen, streifigen Schatten an die Wände, hinter den alten Bildern kommen manchmal winzige Spinnen hervor, und es freut einen fast, daß sie da sind... (B, 2:171-72)

Dianora realizes, as she wonders at her changed attitude toward the spider, that through loving Palla she has opened her heart to all living creatures.

There is, however, another side to the spider's presence. Hugo Wyss, drawing on Bachofen's studies, as we have just seen, interprets hair as an erotic symbol because of its similarity to the web. The spider's web might also be taken as a symbol of the interweaving of masculine and feminine sexual power.[7] There existed, furthermore, a German superstition that a spider in one's house foretold the arrival of a suitor, perhaps because a bride needed to spin and weave industriously to prepare her trousseau.[8] One thinks immediately of the fairy tale "Rumpelstilzchen," in which a miller's daughter who succeeds in spinning flax into gold is rewarded with marriage to a prince, or of Penelope's ruse, weaving a tapestry by day and promising to choose among her suitors when her work should be completed, while ravelling out each night the day's work and waiting for Odysseus' return. The spider, which Dianora treats benignly only since her affair with Palla, seems therefore, like her hair, another indication of her strong passion. The spider's connection with her love affair is further strengthened by her comparing the rope ladder she lets down for Palla to a fine spider's web (D, 1:62; SW, 3:99).

A third complex of meanings has been suggested by Werner Vortriede, who distinguishes three characteristics of the spider which have determined its role in mythology: it spins a web, it places itself in the center of the web, and it spins thread out of its own body. The second of these three characteristics seems to pertain to Dianora:

> Die Spinne, drohend im Mittelpunkt ihres Netzes, stellt die Introversion, den Narziß-Trieb, die völlige Absorption eines Menschen durch seinen eigenen Mittelpunkt dar.[9]

7 *Wyss, Die Frau in der Dichtung Hofmannsthals*, p. 18.
8 *Handwörterbuch des deutschen Aberglaubens*, vol. 8, col. 275.
9 "Hofmannsthal, Gottfried Keller und die Weisheit der Spinne," in *Texte und Kontexte: Studien zur deutschen und vergleichenden Literaturwissen-*

Dianora stands at the center of the play, and her monologue shows her complete absorption in her love for Palla, who has become the center of her existence. Thus the spider, in addition to its association with her love affair, may secondarily point to her narcissistic concentration on her own feelings.

Dianora's ecstasy *(Trunkenheit)* suffuses all her impressions of nature with a benign faith in the brotherhood of all living creatures. She imagines any sort of existence in nature, that is in Palla's realm, as pleasurable:

> Fiel' ich ins Wasser, mir wär wohl darin:
> mit weichen, kühlen Armen fing's mich auf,
> und zwischen schönen Lauben glitt ich hin
> mit halbem Licht und dunkelblauem Boden
> und spielte mit den wunderlichen Tieren,
> goldflossig und mit dumpfen guten Augen.
> (D, 1:60-61; SW, 3:98)

Before attempting to interpret the "wunderliche Tiere" of this passage, it will be useful to examine briefly their habitat, the water.

Hofmannsthal's use of water in his imagery seems to fall into two opposing categories. First, and most simply, it serves as a "symbol of life, of undifferentiated vitality."[10] As such, it is very much Palla's element. In interpreting the "Märchen" we mentioned dolphins as one symbol of exuberant joie de vivre; their natural habitat is the rushing water which connotes vitality. It is therefore significant that Palla is described leading a bacchantic chain of revelers to a waterfall where dolphins form part of the ornamental statuary:

> Delphinen sprang er auf die platte Stirn
> an den im Rausch zurückgeworfnen Armen
> der Faune hielt er sich, stieg den Tritonen
> auf ihre nassen Schultern, immer höher,
> der wildeste und schönste Gott von allen!
> (D, 1:72; SW, 3:107)

---

schaft. Festschrift für Norbert Fuerst zum 65. Geburtstag, ed. Manfred Durzak et al. (Bonn: Francke, 1973), p. 301.

10 Michael Porter, "Elements of Hofmannsthal's Lyric Style; 'Erlebnis' and 'Vor Tag,'" *Modern Austrian Literature* 7 (1974), 88.

Palla's excessive vitality seems, in fact, to animate the very statuary, so that the fauns appear to be throwing back their arms in frenzy as he leaps among them.

Often rushing water is directly connected with sexual passion, as in an unfinished short story Hofmannsthal wrote during the summer of 1896:

> Und in diesem Augenblick wußte ich, daß ich in Anna verliebt war. ... Und wie aus einem Brunnen, der lange verstopft war, die Garben von Wasser unaufhaltsam hervorschießen, so zwang es mich unaufhaltsam, ihren Namen vor mich hinzusagen... (SW, 29:68)

Water is, of course, a traditional symbol of sexual passion; one thinks easily of such examples as Mynheer Peeperkorn's visit to the waterfall shortly before his death in *Der Zauberberg,* or of the waterfall near the castle of the von Ketten family in Musil's "Die Portugiesin."

Water as a symbol of sexuality plays an important, though less obvious, role in *Die Frau im Fenster* as well. Dianora observes the village girls going to the well to draw water and comments on the last girl's beautiful hair. The girl, she imagines, may be vain of her hair, but remains ignorant of its attraction for men. The passage connects water and hair as images of sexuality; they have been connected earlier in the play when Dianora recalls rinsing "einen schweren Schwall von klarem Wasser/ Im Bade durch mein Haar..." (D, 1:58; SW, 3:96). Hair has also been linked to the rope ladder; as Dianora holds the ladder ready for Palla's coming, she shakes her hair over the balcony wishing it were long enough so he might touch it as he reaches for the ladder. Later she connects the rope ladder with the water image; she lets the ladder down over the balcony again and says:

> Nun tu ich so als wär es höchste Zeit,
> und lasse dich hinab in meinem Brunnen,
> mir einen schönen Eimer aufzuziehn!
> (D, 1:62; SW, 3:99)

The pail she hopes to draw up is, of course, Messer Palla. Thus the water image, joined at several points with hair and the woven ladder, forms part of the whole complex of subtle imagery surrounding Dianora's relationship to Palla.

The second broad category of Hofmannsthal's water imagery encompasses water as a symbol of death. Dianora's fantasy beginning with the words, "Fiel ich ins Wasser, mir wär wohl darin" implies her death, though her musings are too passive to be construed as suicidal; she does not envisage jumping into the water, but only falling, due to unspecified causes. The same vision of water as a passive sinking into death forms a central image of the poem, "Erlebnis:"

> Und still versank ich in dem webenden,
> Durchsichtgen Meere und verließ das Leben.
> (GLD, p. 8; SW, 1:31) [11]

It is at first puzzling to find that water may represent both vitality or life itself and its complete opposite, namely, death. The paradox is already inherent in water itself; Hofmannsthal's reader is presumably aware that both science and religion visualize life originating in the ocean; at the same time he realizes that man can not survive unaided below the surface of the water. A few passages in *Die Frau im Fenster* suggest further explanations for the apparently contradictory meanings of Hofmannsthal's water image.

First, the very frenzy of romantic passion drowns out the infatuated lover's perception of the exterior world. After Dianora describes Palla's Dionysian leap into the waterfall as "der wildeste und schönste Gott von allen," she continues:

> Und unter seinen Füßen flog das Wasser
> hervor und schäumte durch die Luft herab
> und sprühte über mich, und ich stand da,
> und mir verschlang der Lärm des wilden Wassers
> die ganze Welt. (D, 1:72; SW, 3:107)

---

[11] Michael Porter writes that the ocean in "Erlebnis" is the emblem of the harmonious world which is evoked in the first part of the poem. ("Elements of Hofmannsthal's Lyric Style," p. 89.) He maintains that the poet can enter this world of harmony, of correspondences, only after death. Because he views this world of harmony as representing a higher, mystical form of life, he sees no contradiction between this meaning of the water image and its function as a symbol of vitality and life.

The intensity of feeling makes her oblivious to external reality; thus her passion — symbolized by the shower of water — detaches her from life.

Second, love involves to some extent a loss of self, that is, the lover is changed through the intense experience of another person. Dianora, for example, has lost some of her youthful pride and learned from Palla the pleasure of humility and service. Hofmannsthal expresses this aspect of love through the water image as well; Dianora has periods when she can bear nothing except

>...mich
>zu beugen auf ein wildes schnelles Wasser,
>das meinen schwachen Schatten mit sich reißt
>(D, 1:58; SW, 3:96).

The destruction of her shadow, emblem of herself, corresponds to the changes wrought in her by Palla's love; just as her shadow is obliberated by the swift current, she becomes absorbed in his love and ceases to exist as a separate entity.

Third, water is connected with narcissism, which, carried to extremes, leads to spiritual death, Dianora remarks:

>Wie abgespiegelt in den stillsten Teich
>liegt alles da, gefangen in sich selber.
>Der Efeu rankt sich in den Dämmer hin
>und hält die Mauer tausendfach umklommen,
>hoch ragt ein Lebensbaum, zu seinen Füßen
>steht still ein Wasser, spiegelt, was es sieht,
>und aus dem Fenster über diesen Rand
>von kühlen, festen Steinen beug ich mich
>und strecke meine Arme nach dem Boden.
>Mir ist, als wär ich doppelt, könnte selber
>mir zusehn, wissend, daß ichs selber bin —
>Pause
>Ich glaube, so sind die Gedanken, die
>ein Mensch in seiner Todesstunde denkt.
>(D, 1:69-70; SW, 3:105-106)

The water mirrors its surroundings as Dianora's own imagination mirrors her living self; she does not exactly study her reflection in the water, but after observing that the pool functions as a mirror, she notices that her mind similarly presents an image of herself which is separate from reality. The experience of a doubling of one's self occurs, again through the water image, in "Erlebnis," where the speaker, having left life behind as he sank into the ocean, suffers nostalgia for his past self and visualizes himself as a child sailing past his home.

In "Erlebnis," in Dianora's "Gedanken, die/ein Mensch in seiner Todesstunde denkt" and in her fantasy of falling into the water, the water can be defined as representing not precisely death, but more accurately, the inner world of the speaker. It is Dianora's complete absorption in her mental emotional world, whose center is her affair with Palla, which separates her from life; her detachment from reality is most obvious in the *Aneinandervorbeireden* of her conversation with her nurse. Rushing water represents physical attraction or desire, the contemplation of which may distract the infatuated individual from everyday reality. At the same time, still water represents one possible result of an infatuation which remains unfulfilled, namely, a preoccupation with the inner world of the imagination. This preoccupation with the inner world of fantasy is by no means unique to lovers, for it threatens anyone, artist or poet, for example, who concentrates exclusively on the images presented by his imagination. Hofmannsthal evokes this underwater world of fantasy when he writes that he finds in Amiel's diaries the "Dämmern einer weichen, träumerischen Molluskenseele" (P, 1:23).

Because this underwater world is nothing but fantasy or imagination, it has no reality of its own, specifically, it contains no real plants or animals. The "wunderbare Blumen" in "Erlebnis" are not intended to resemble any real flowers; by the same token the plants surrounding Dianora remain nameless, she slides between "schönen Lauben." The half-light is as indistinct as that of "Erlebnis," where it is neither night nor day. And finally, the "wunderliche Tiere" Dianora imagines (to return at last to our starting point) are not even identified as fish, for they exist only in her fantasy without bearing on any exterior reality.

Elsewhere in Hofmannsthal's work, to be sure, fish are linked to a symbolic meaning. On the simplest level, they are merely precious objects; the reader is perhaps reminded of a colorful fish swimming in ornamental basins in formal parks. Hofmannsthal praises a collection of stories by comparing them to "ganz kleine Teiche, über die man sich beugt, um Goldfische und bunte Steine zu sehen" (P, 1:274). The stranger in *Das kleine Welttheater,* who appears to be an artisan or goldsmith, combines imagination and precious objects in his handiwork. His interest in fish reveals both his fascination with the world of the imagination or dreams, and his affinity for jewelry and other precious objects:

> Dies hängt mir noch von Kindesträumen an:
> Ich muß von Brücken in die Tiefe spähen,
> Und wo die Fische gleiten übern Grund,
> Mein ich, Geschmeide hingestreut zu sehen, ...
> (GLD, p. 305; SW, 3:139)

Fish may also stand for innocence, for creatures whose murder is particularly outrageous. Thus the central figure of the poem "Der Schiffskoch, ein Gefangener, singt" complains:

> Schöne purpurflossige Fische,
> Die sie mir lebendig brachten,
> Schauen aus gebrochenen Augen,
> Sanfte Tiere muß ich schlachten.
> (GLD, p. 28; SW, 1:102)

The fish representing the unborn children in *"Die Frau ohne Schatten"* are also innocent, and may furthermore be connected to Indian superstition that fish, because of their own fecundity, stand for wealth and children.[12]

On another level, fish embody the deep secrets of the universe hidden from man; such is the function of the "alles-wissende Muschel" in *Die ägyptische Helena.* In Hofmannsthal's notes for *Der Schwierige* another woman asks Helene Altenwyl: Wie kannst du wissen, worin die Freude der Fische besteht?"[13] The narrator of the

12 *Handwörterbuch des deutschen Aberglaubens,* vol. 2, cols. 1529-30. It would, however, be erroneous to assume that fish regularly stand for fertility, as does Hans Steffen: "Der Fisch ist das Sinnbild der Fruchtbarkeit, H. verwendet es oft." See his essay, "Wahre Sprachliebe ist nicht möglich ohne Sprachverleugnung," *Germanisch-Romanische Monatsschrift* 24 (1974), 441, and note 39.
13 Quoted by Roger C. Norton in: "Hofmannsthal's 'Magische Werkstätte,' Unpublished Notebooks from the Harvard Collection," *Germanic Review* 36 (1961), 62.

prologue to *Die Frau im Fenster* describes, as evidence of his grasp of all the secrets of the universe, his intuitive knowledge of the ways of fish:

> Ich wußte, welchen feuchten Pfad die Aale
> Hinglitten,
> .... Alle Schwärme
> Der schattenhaft hingleitenden Forellen
> Fühlt ich hinan die klaren Bäche steigen ...
> (GLD, p. 131; SW, 3:124)

By nature of their limbless bodies and lack of voice, fish remain isolated and uncommunicative, as in the following passage from "Gedicht der Muscheln":

> Wir sind allein im Dunkeln, ihr habt oben Lippen, gerollte Blätter, verschlungene Hände mit rosigem Blut und bläulichen Adern, wir sind allein und können uns nicht berühren (A, p. 128).

Fish seem to exist apart from time as humans measure it, perhaps because the average person remains unaware of the cycles of their biological existence. Dianora, for example, confirms the passage of time by observing the migration of birds, yet who is able to confirm the passage of time by observing fish? Hofmannsthal recounts dreaming that he belongs to two different ages and must fly from one to the other over the ocean above which nets are spread in the air:

> — da bin ich schon gegen das Netz geprallt, stürze tief hinunter, finde mich unten zusammen mit Meerestieren, Krabben, Langusten, die gleich mir gefangen sind. Die Fischer greifen nach uns. (A, p. 170)

The fish exist separate from any age. Kari Bühl tells Cresence of his belief:

> ... daß alles schon längst irgendwo fertig dasteht und nur auf einmal erst sichtbar wird. Weißt du, wie im Hohenbühler Teich, wenn man im Herbst das Wasser abgelassen hat, auf einmal die Karpfen und die Schweife von den steinernen Tritonen da waren, die man früher kaum gesehen hat? (L, 3:211)

In "Das Dorf im Gebirge" Hofmannsthal again connects the question of the passage of time with the fish image as he describes rooms

> ... in denen eine alternde Frau mit beängstigtem und staunendem Denken nicht darüber hinauskommt, daß dies traumhafte Jetzt und Hier für sie das

> Unentrinnbare, das Wirkliche bedeutet. Aus diesen Fenstern fällt immerfort das Kerzenlicht ... taucht auch hinunter und wirft in das feuchte Dunkel einen leuchtenden Schacht, in dem die schwarzgrauen Barsche stumpfsinnig stehen und die ruhelosen kleinen Weißfische unaufhörlich beben wie Zitternadeln. (P, 1:279; SW, 28:34)

The woman wrestles with the problem of grasping that her existence is limited by time and space. The light from her window links her sphere, temporal and spatial reality, to the world of the fish, yet the light scarcely diminishes the darkness surrounding them, for the human measurement of time and space is without relevance to their underwater sphere.

The sphere of fish, set apart from man's perception of time, and from his terrestrial environment, in these respects corresponds to the world of the imagination, where neither temporal nor spatial boundaries hold. Thus Sigismund tells Julian:

> Ich liege hier und dennoch zugleich fliege ich dahin, ... und im Fluß, unter dem silbernen Schimmer stehen die Fische und freuen sich an der lauen fließenden Tiefe und ich spiele in ihrer Mitte ... (D, 4:136)

Reality, bounded by space and time, is also defined through language. The world of fish, often representing irreality, presents a further contrast in that it is devoid of language; Hofmannsthal repeatedly characterizes fish as "stumm" (P, 2:20; P, 3:481; P, 1:315). Chandos compares himself mentally to the orator Crassus, who became so enamored of a pet fish that he wept at its death. Although his comments about Crassus defy precise interpretation, Chandos appears to suspect that Crassus fell prey to the some sort of wordless mystical bliss which he has experienced. It is significant that Chandos' reflections on Crassus are not in verbal form,

> ... aber Denken in einem Material, das unmittelbarer, flüssiger, glühender ist als Worte. Es sind gleichfalls Wirbel, aber solche, die nicht wie die Wirbel der Sprache ins Bodenlose zu führen scheinen, sondern irgendwie in mich selber und in den tiefsten Schoß des Friedens. (P, 2:19)

Dianora's fantasy of playing with the curious harmless fish in their watery realm, then, signifies her desire to escape reality, and, particularly, to plunge into a world without time, the time which oppresses her as she awaits Palla's coming.

Dianora continues to fantasize, imagining herself next among the forest animals who, like the fish, do her no harm:

> Ja, müßt ich meine Tage eingesperrt
> in einem halbverfallenen Gemäuer
> im dicken Wald verbringen, wär mir doch
> die Seele nicht beengt, es kämen da
> des Waldes Tiere, viele kleine Vögel,
> und kleine Wiesel rührten mit der Schnauze
> und mit den Wimpern ihrer klugen Augen
> die Zehen meiner nackten Füße an,
> indessen ich im Moos die Beeren äße!
> (D, 1:61; SW, 3:98)

Hofmannsthal finds the weasel a stealthy, agile, easily frightened creature (D, 3:112; P, 1:322; E, p. 251). It is able to ferret out hidden objects, treasure, prey or carrion; the king in *Der Kaiser und die Hexe* commands that the witch's body be carefully buried:

> Aber so, daß auch kein Wiesel
> Davon weiß und je es aufspürt; ...
> (GLD, p. 279; SW, 3:196)

The weasel has the power of locating not a human corpse, but a dragon filled with hidden treasure in one episode of the *Gesta Romanorum*.[14] Its quick furtive behavior apparently gave rise to the popular belief that the weasel possessed knowledge hidden from man. Dianora may be expressing such a belief in the weasel's powers of divination or secret knowledge when describing its eyes as "clever." Medieval superstition held that the weasel conceived through the ear and gave birth through the mouth.[15] The animal therefore lent itself to association with women who were seduced by a lover's persuasion; its proximity to Dianora may thus reflect her situation.

---

14 See the story of Guy of Warwick, entitled "Of Mental Constancy," Tale CLXXII in *Gesta Romanorum,* pp. 327-28.

15 For an explanation of this superstition see T. H. White, ed. and trans., *The Bestiary, A Book of Beasts* (New York: Putnam, Capricorn, 1960), p. 92, note 3. Aristotle refutes the belief that the weasel brings forth her young through the mouth, *Generation of Animals*, trans., A. L. Peck, Loeb Classical Library (Cambridge, Mass.: Harvard University Press, 1963), pp. 315, 317.

Der Kaiser und die Hexe presents an image strikingly similar to the weasel image of *Die Frau im Fenster:* the witch is described as having feet "schimmernder und weicher/Als der Hermelin" (GLD, p. 260; SW, 3:182). The ermine is a near relative of the weasel, which has been earlier associated with the witch in the king's command to bury her body carefully. The ermine is compared to the feet of the witch, and the weasel noses about Dianora's bare feet. The witch's powerful attraction for the emperor consists only of her physical charm; it has been implied through the hair symbolism that Dianora exerts the same kind of sexual magnetism. Finally, the bare feet are a sign of a sexual relationship; in the poem "Vor Tag" the youth who returns from an illicit sexual encounter is also barefoot: "Nun/ Schleicht einer ohne Schuh von einem Frauenbett" (GLD, p. 10; SW, 1:106). By the same token it is significant that Romana appears in Andreas' first dream at the Finazzer estate in half peasant, half city costume and barefoot. The association of bare feet with ermine (in the case of the witch) and weasel (Dianora) indicates these animals must be interpreted as signifying sexual relationships outside marriage.

It is useful to compare Dianora's romanticized view of animals with their rather more threatening aspect in the works studied earlier. The narrator in "Ein Traum von großer Magie" slept exposed by his open pavilion to the intrusion of horses and dogs. Dianora, in a roughly analogous situation, the "halbverfallene Gemäuer," is not cognizant of any threat. The animals encountered in the village of "Reitergeschichte" and the horses in the "Märchen" also posed a threat to man. These, however, were domesticated animals found in an urban environment rather than wild creatures in a natural state.

The opposing views of animals derive from contrasting views of life itself. Dianora reflects: "Wie abgespiegelt in dem stillsten Teich/ Liegt alles da, gefangen in sich selber" (D, 1:69-70; SW, 3:105). Both animal and plant life appear to her self-contained, sufficient in themselves, while she remains isolated in her balcony above them and can only repeat the futile gesture of stretching her arms toward the ground. The life here described as "gefangen in sich selber" must not be confused with "die im Leben gefangenen Wesen." The gross physical appetites of the dogs in "Reitergeschichte" have no place in this idyllic setting. What Dianora addresses as life has nothing in common with the decay of the abandoned village nor with the hopeless squalor of the city in the "Märchen." That corporeal earthbound life forms the subject of the sermons of the Spanish priest, who preaches:

> Die Sonne muß glühen, der Stein muß auf der stummen Erde liegen, aus jeder lebendigen Kreatur geht ihre Stimme heraus, sie kann nichts dafür, sie kann nichts dawider, sie muß. (D, 1:69; SW, 3:105)

His view of earth as mute, as the realm of the dumb creature enslaved by the necessities of his physical existence corresponds to the "Unentrinnbarkeit des Lebens" in the "Märchen," and to the presentation of earth in "Ein Traum von großer Magie" as the chaotic sphere of dogs and horses above which the Magier thrones in omnipotent triumph.

The contrast between above and below in the poem is reversed in *Die Frau im Fenster.* Dianora occupies a superior position analogous to that of the *Magier,* yet suffers from her isolation and remoteness from life. She longs instead for the pulsating surging life below her.

Forest animals continue to shape Dianora's reverie; listening to sounds rising from the wood and garden below she exclaims:

> Was raschelt dort? Der Igel ists, der Igel
> vom ersten Abend! Bist du wieder da,
> trittst aus dem Dunkel, gehst auf deine Jagd?
> (D, 1:61; SW, 3:98) [16]

The hedgehog, a nocturnal carnivore feeding on mice and small animals, is sympathetic to Dianora because its furtive hunt is restricted to the darkness. In folklore it is associated with witches; gypsies supposedly enjoy its meat, and it is much sought after for home remedies. It seems to arouse man's curiosity as to how it copulates; one

---

[16] Annemarie Chelius-Gobbels comments: "Dianoras Beziehung zu den Dingen ... ist nur ein Vorwand, um ihren Zustand auszudrücken. Sie vermag nur das zu verstehen, was sie in irgendeine Beziehung zu ihrem 'Du' bringen kann. So betrachtet sie den Igel, wie er auf die Jagd geht, nur um an ihren eigenen 'Jäger' denken zu können. Alle ihre Betrachtungen haben intentionalen Charakter." *(Formen mittelbarer Darstellung im dramatischen Werk Hugo von Hofmannsthals,* Deutsche Studien, vol. 6 [Meisenheim am Glan: Anton Hain, 1968] p. 68).

source quotes Aristotle in affirming that the female hedgehog must lie on her back facing her mate to avoid his bristles.[17] The assumption of the human position during copulation may be what intrigues Dianora about the hedgehog.

Little attention has been given to Hofmannsthal's use of hunting imagery to describe a love relationship.[18] Because the metaphor is one of the most common images in his work, it is worth examining in some detail.

The hunt as a symbol of a love relationship may be traced as far back as Ovid, whose *Art of Love* appeared at about the time of Christ. Ovid briefly compares the search for a mistress to a hunt, or to the spreading of nets to catch birds.[19] This hunt, identified with Venus, combined easily with the figure of Cupid holding bow and arrow, ready to wound his prey. Later in the same work Ovid recommends hunting as one of the remedies for unrequited love; this diversion absorbs the lover's energies, leaving him no time to brood over his passion. Diana, goddess of virginity, became associated with hunting as a diversion from love, and was regarded as an enemy or rival of Venus. Ovid remarks: "Ofttimes has Venus, vanquished by Phoebus' sister [Diana], beaten a base retreat."[20]

The literary tradition of the hunt of Venus may have influenced Hofmannsthal. Medieval French and English authors enjoyed punning on the word "venerie," meaning the craft of hunting, but suggesting at the same time "the act of Venus."[21] The hunt of Venus functioned as a metaphor for the pursuit of sexual satisfaction and became associated with certain animals. Venus, fearful of losing her lover Adonis, an avid hunter, counseled him to hunt only those ani-

---

17 *Handwörterbuch des deutschen Aberglaubens,* vol. 4, col. 668-670. Aristotle writes that hedgehogs "do not mount on the back as other quadrupeds do, but on account of their spines stand upright for intercourse." See his *Generation of Animals,* p. 23.
18 For a complete discussion of this theme, see my article: "The Hunting Motif in Hofmannsthal's Works," *Modern Language Notes,* 95 (1980), 685-93.
19 Ovid, *The Art of Love and Other Poems,* trans. J.H. Mozley (Cambridge, Mass.: Harvard University Press, 1947), p. 30, lines 253 ff.
20 Ibid., p. 191.
21 D. W. Robertson, *A Preface to Chaucer: Studies in Medieval Perspectives* (Princeton, New Jersey: Princeton University Press, 1963), p. 253.

mals which could do him no harm. In Shakespeare's poem "Venus and Adonis" the goddess counsels her lover:

> But if thou needs wilt hunt, be ruled by me;
> Uncouple at the timorous flying hare,
> Or at the fox which lives by subtlety,
> Or at the roe which no encounter dare:
>   Pursue these fearful creatures o'er the downs
>   And on thy well-breath'd horse keep with thy hounds.
>
> (lines 673-78)

The naming of the roe as object of the hunt of Venus may illuminate the presentation of woman as a hunted deer found in such English ballads as "Three Ravens." Hofmannsthal used the same image in "Die Frau ohne Schatten" where the empress appears to her future husband in the form of a gazelle and is nearly wounded by his falcon.

More commonly, small fur-bearing animals were depicted as the object of this hunt of Venus. Illuminated medieval manuscripts frequently show a lady holding or accompanied by a small furry creature, often a rabbit, but at other times a squirrel or dog, while her lover entreats her favor. These animals came to represent physical intimacy; the lover's conquest of his lady's virtue was fittingly portrayed in hunting scenes. If she granted him the pleasure of her body, the artist might show her handing her lover a rabbit, dog, or other small, furry creature.[22] This literary tradition or its corollary, the artistic tradition, corresponds to Hofmannsthal's association of Dianora with weasel, hedgehog, and whippet, a hunting dog.

We can not be sure, of course, that Hofmannsthal was conscious of employing the Renaissance commonplace of the hunt of Venus. Bearing in mind his fondness for the Renaissance setting in his early plays, including *Die Frau im Fenster,* and his familiarity with the poetry of Ronsard, it would seem possible that he was aware of these antecedents. Furthermore, the hunting image had long been a commonplace of folklore and music. Expressions such as "Schürzenjäger" and ballads such as "Ein Jäger aus Kurpfalz" attest to the widespread association of the hunt with the erotic encounter.[23] There are, how-

---

22 Ibid., pp. 113, 193.
23 See, for example, the collection of Jägerlieder (particularly numbers 1434,

ever, two essential differences between the hunt in folklore and its use in Hofmannsthal's work. The ballads relate a random encounter between a hunter and a woman; in Renaissance symbolism, on the other hand, it applies to an ongoing courtship, and in Hofmannsthal's work, to a relationship of some duration, such as that of Palla and Dianora, which has lasted twelve weeks and is prematurely cut short by Dianora's death. Second, the ballads are to be sung by men; they relate events from the point of view of a male boasting of his conquest. Hofmannsthal, in contrast, presents Dianora's own recognition of her role as prey.

In his work, the hunt of Venus is no longer a refined game of lovers' intrigue, but a manifestation of brutality and sadism. It may seem appropriate that he describes as hunter and prey relationships between men and women who are not happily mated. Dianora, for example, protests to her husband, "Du kannst mich ein Vaterunser und den Englischen Gruß sprechen lassen und mich dann töten, aber nicht so stehen lassen wie ein angebundenes Tier!" (D, 1:475; SW, 3: 110). Yet it is surprising that Hofmannsthal uses the same hunt metaphor to describe happy love relationships. We have already seen that both Palla and Messer Braccio are depicted as lions. Dianora associates Palla with the lion's erotic Dionysian vitality, while the comparision of Braccio to a lion is founded upon the vigilance and strength of the king of beasts. Nonetheless, the shared metaphor reminds us that both are predators; Dianora is trapped between two hunters, longing for the arrival of her "Jäger" Palla but surprised by her husband.[24] The vulnerability of a woman caught between two hunters applies likewise to the Marschallin in *Rosenkavalier,* prey to

---

"Liebesjagd;" 1436, "Jäger und Jungfrau;" 1438-40, "Der verschlafene Jäger;" 1444, "Jägers Fund;" 1454, "Ein Jäger aus Kurpfalz;" and 1456, "Der Glücksjäger") in: Ludwig Erk, *Deutscher Liederhort,* ed. Franz Böhme, (Leipzig: Breitkopf und Härtel, 1894), III, 295-317.

24 Lore Muerdel-Dormer discusses Dianora's position between two hunters in *Hugo von Hofmannsthal; das Problem der Ehe und seine Bedeutung in den frühen Dramen* (Bonn: Bouvier, 1975), pp. 55-56. A summary of various meanings of the hunt image is given by Eva-Maria Lenz, *Hugo von Hofmannsthals mythologische Oper "Die Ägyptische Helena"* (Tübingen: Max Niemeyer, 1972), pp. 89-91.

both her husband and Octavian; the latter relationship, within its limits a happy one, is nonetheless portrayed through the hunting image: Octavian marvels at his fortune in his affair with the Marschallin:

> Der Feldmarschall sitzt im crowatischen Wald und
>   jagt auf Bären und Luchsen,
> und ich sitz hier, ich junges Blut, und jag auf was?
> (L, 1:267)

Baron Ochs pursues the maid Mariandel (Octavian) and when the Marschallin protests that he is about to marry, he replies:

> Macht das einen lahmen Esel aus mir?
> Bin ich da nicht wie ein guter Hund auf einer guten Fährte?
> Und doppelt scharf auf jedes Wild nach links, nach rechts!
> (L, 1:283)

Man as well as woman may be reduced to the animal state in such hunting imagery: Ochs compares himself to a hunting dog; Braccio grasps the rope ladder to form a noose for Dianora "mit der Sicherheit eines wilden Tieres auf der Jagd" (D, 1:81; SW, 3:114). Nor is man any longer content with merely capturing his prey, he seeks to wound or even kill. Hofmannsthal makes extensive use of stabbing as a symbol of the sex act in *Die ägyptische Helena*. The link between love and violence recalls the description of Lerch thrusting his saber into the mouth of the enemy officer; battle and sexual passion are revealed as dual means of sating his aggressive tendencies. Dealing with such brutal urges becomes problematical, especially during adolescence, as we shall observe when treating "Knabengeschichte" and *Andreas*.

Dianora's monologue is interrupted by the entrance of her old nurse, coming to tend her flowers. She and Dianora discuss a Spanish priest whom the nurse greatly admires. Dianora, seeking to form a mental image of this strange monk, asks if he resembles any person of her acquaintance, and the nurse replies that his voice is a bit like that of Messer Palla. Later Dianora muses:

> ...Nur seine Stimme
> hat dieser fremde Mönch, da laufen ihm
> die Leute zu und hängen sich an ihn,

> wie Bienen an die dunklen Blütendolden, ...
> (D, 1:71; SW, 3:106)

Bees serve in Hofmannsthal's work as an image of wealth and fertility; they appear in spring scenes of plentiful vegetation and mild weather when all nature smiles on mankind. The poet in "Gerechtigkeit" sits in a garden:

> In der dünnen durchsichtigen Luft schwebten Bienen
> zwischen den rosenroten über und über blühenden
> Pfirsichbäumen hin und her. (P, 1:119)

A garden scene in "Leda und der Schwan" is filled with "Bisamäpfel, gelbe Pflaumen, Quitten, Granaten voll Bienen, wohlriechende Blätter, duftendes Holz, Cinnamon, unberechenbarer Reichtum" (D, 2: 501).

In addition to embellishing scenes of plentitude and ripeness, bees frequently signify the sort of drunkenness, in the sense of ecstasy, which Dianora repeatedly connects with Palla. The gardener in *Das kleine Welttheater* expresses content at having exchanged his crown

> Für diese Beete, dieses reife Lasten
> Der Früchte, halbverborgen an Spalieren,
> Und schwere Rosen, drin die goldig braunen
> Vom Duft betäubten Bienen sich verlieren.
> (GLD, p. 301; SW, 3:136)

Gianino in *Tod des Tizian* describes the night

> Wo sich die offenen Granaten wiegen,
> Da sah ich deutlich viele Bienen fliegen
> Und viele saugen, auf das Rot gesunken,
> Von nächtgem Duft und reifem Safte trunken.
> (GLD, p. 188; SW, 3:44)

Dianora envisages people clustering like bees around flowers about the Spanish priest whose voice resembles Palla's; Palla and the priest merge into a figure who is the source of the heady pleasure intoxicating their listeners. This image contributes to the characterization of Palla as a charismatic leader capable of exciting his followers to a high pitch of frenzy, as in the description of his leading them to the waterfall.[25]

Dianora's soliloquy containing the references to birds, spider, fish, weasel, hedgehog and bees is, of course, entirely subjective. At no point does she demonstrate any awareness of animal existence as a struggle for survival. Even the hedgehog's nocturnal hunt suggests nothing of hunger, terror, or death. In her purely subjective interest in wild animals, she may be compared to the merchant's son; just as he saw life through art or history, or was aware of animals only through their stylized representation in art, so all Dianora's perceptions of her surroundings are conditioned by a constant preoccupation with her own situation. The birds are a measure of the passage of time, the hedgehog furnishes a link to her wait for her own "hunter," and the life of fish and forest creatures presents an escapist romanticized vision of Palla's realm.

Her fascination with wildlife does not extend to those domesticated animals which form part of her husband's realm. She notes an old man calling in his dog to protect him at the approach of night (D, 1:59; SW, 3:96) and later remarks that the sheep in the fold must be pressing closer together in dread of the oncoming darkness (D, 1:61; SW, 3:99). Sheep and dog, like man whose creatures they are, regard the night with apprehension. Dianora identifies not with these domestic animals, but rather with the forest's nocturnal prowlers, for her clandestine affair, like their hunts, requires the shield of darkness. Moreover, dog and sheep are uninteresting to her because of their association with Braccio. The nurse relates how he, displeased with an emissary from Como, whistled to his hunting dogs, and later on his hunt encountered the emissary and threw him into the river. The nurse heard the story from a shepherd who had to drive his flock into a nearby field to keep them from being trampled by the hunters.

With the unexpected appearance of her husband, Dianora's idyllic vision of wildlife vanishes. She is abruptly swept out of her sub-

---

[25] The bees in the "Lebenslied," "Der Schwarm von wilden Bienen/Nimmt seine Seele mit" (GLD, p. 12), are best interpreted by Exner's statement that they bear away the soul, according to classical mythology *(Hofmannsthals "Lebenslied,"* p. 106). Their presence in the poem contributes to the aura of unrestrained ecstasy surrounding the main figure.

jective fantasy of life with Palla in a tranquil state of nature unthreatened by any struggle for survival. In the presence of Messer Braccio, only those domesticated animals which serve him continue to figure in her memories.

Dianora's confession to her husband includes one incident of paramount importance for our understanding of Hofmannsthal's descriptions of tortured animals, a theme appearing in *Das kleine Welttheater, Jupiter und Semele,* "Knabengeschichte," *Andreas* and *Der Turm.* Dianora describes a wedding banquet at which Palla set near her holding out a bowl of peaches. Suddenly she was overcome with the strength of her passion for him, she relates, and was moved to kiss his hands in humility before the assembled guests. She withstood the impulse, which Braccio's brother, seated near her, nonetheless remarked. She continues:

> ... da kam ein Hund,
> ein großes dunkles Windspiel hergegangen
> und rieb den feinen Kopf an meiner Hand,
> der linken, die hinunterhing: ...
> (D, 1:79; SW, 3:113)

H. Stefan Schultz has established that these lines and the continuation of Dianora's description depict the scene portrayed in a painting by the pre-Raphaelite artist, John Millais, titled "Lorenzo and Isabella."[26] The painting, whose Renaissance atmosphere corresponds to that of *Die Frau im Fenster,* appears to employ the artistic tradition of the hunt of Venus. The whippet, a hunting dog,

---

26 See his article, "Some notes on Hofmannsthal's *Die Frau im Fenster,*" *Modern Austrian Literature* 7 (1974), 49-52. It is significant that Hofmannsthal has altered one detail of the painting in addition to those which Schultz mentions. In the painting, the dog rests his head in the woman's lap; Dianora describes the whippet rubbing its head against her left hand; the hand closer to the heart is always associated with the emotions. Hofmannsthal altered this detail to add to the hand symbolism prevalent in the play; Dianora is fascinated by Palla's hands and wishes her fate lay "in diesen königlichen guten Händen" (D, 1:71; SW, 3:106). She is repelled by the ugly wound on her husband's right hand, the hand of justice and power. When, in their final confrontation, she throws her torso over the balcony, he hastily bandages his right hand and then, using both hands, makes a noose of the rope ladder to draw her body up.

may stand for the woman's lover or "hunter;" the affection she lavishes on the dog suggests her willingness to accept the intentions of its master. Although Hofmannsthal did not invent this scene, the use of the dog symbol within it is entirely consonant with the meaning of that image in his own work. The whippet's function as a sign of female sexuality parallels the use of the white bitch in "Reitergeschichte" to indicate Vuic's erotic attraction for Lerch.

The dog's description evokes its noble refined character, and contrasts sharply with Dianora's characterization of Braccio's "dummer Bruder." Whippets were prized as hunting dogs, renowned for their speed, and often bred by the nobility; hence the whippet functions realistically (as well as symbolically) because it is appropriate to Dianora's milieu, in the same way the degenerate curs of the "Reitergeschichte" were appropriate to the surroundings of Anton Lerch. Indeed Hofmannsthal seems to have esteemed whippets as one of the nobler species of dog: a graceful, long-legged whippet accompanies the angel in "Gerechtigkeit" (P, 1:119), and in the *Josephslegende* slaves present Potiphar and his wife with priceless gifts, among them "zwei weiße Windhunde an goldenen Ketten" (D, 3:127).

The next lines of Dianora's narration contain an important clue to the motivation behind the mistreatment of animals. She explains to Braccio:

> ... da stieß
> dein dummer Bruder mit gestrecktem Fuß
> in Wut mit aller Kraft nach diesem Hund,
> nur weil er nicht mit einem harten Dolch
> nach mir und meinem Liebsten stoßen konnte.
> (D, 1:78-80; SW, 3:113).

In these lines Hofmannsthal gives full expression to what is only intimated elsewhere in his works: cruelty toward animals springs from a repressed desire for revenge. The hatred and aggression which social convention compels Braccio's brother to repress is directed toward a weaker opponent, in this case, the dog. At the same time, his attack on the animal reinforces its function as an image of Dianora's unfaithfulness; the kick is perhaps an unpremeditated striking out in anger; yet wounds the animal which has some inexpressible connection with her sexual magnetism. We shall have occasion, in discussing further instances of cruelty toward animals, to reaffirm the insight Hofmannsthal expresses so lucidly here; the animal is often the victim, though not necessarily the source, of an impulse toward violence; he may be merely the scapegoat for some more feared and powerful opponent.

A second symbolic event takes place on that same day of the wedding banquet. Dianora's nurse relates how Braccio was unexpectedly bitten by his roan horse:[27]

> Wie der gnädige Herr in den Stand getreten ist, hat der Rotschimmel die Ohren zurückgelegt, geknirscht, und auf einmal nach der Hand geschnappt. ... Dann hat ihn der Herr mit der Faust hinter die Ohren geschlagen, daß das große starke Pferd getaumelt hat wie ein junger Hund. (D, 1:66; SW, 3:102)

Braccio's punishment demonstrates his complete mastery of the situation; instead of allowing fury to sweep him away and beating the horse, he retains sufficient self-control to spare the animal bodily injury. The horse's poll, as he knows, is especially sensitive, and therefore his blow is intensely painful to the animal. His calculated brutality in this case prefigures his cold-bloodedness in executing his unfaithful wife.

In interpreting "Reitergeschichte" we suggest a connection between the horse and the erotic encounter; the uneven gait of Lerch's brown horse coincided with his awareness of Vuic and of the shabbily clad village woman. A similar link seems to bind Dianora and the roan horse, for the bite it inflicts on its master becomes a symbol of her infidelity.[28] Both Dianora and the horse supposedly serve Braccio loyally, yet both betray him on the same day without warning. Just as Dianora's secret deception causes him no open scandal, so the bite

---

27 It is not without significance that the horse is of a reddish color, red hair being continuously associated with deceit and treachery.

28 The modern reader is reminded of the connection between love for a woman and a wound in Kafka's "Ein Landarzt," where the young patient's wound is described as "Rosa," the name of the doctor's maid. Although Hofmannsthal does not appear to have been acquainted with Kafka's story, he would certainly have been familiar with the *Rahmenerzählung* of *A Thousand and One Nights,* where King Shahzeman is suffering physically because of his wife's infidelity; the "internal wound" he complains of applies realistically to his physical decline, but symbolically to the psychological loss caused by his wife's unfaithfulness.

on his right hand (the hand of reason and power) heals on the back, leaving only a small dark spot on the palm which stubbornly refuses to heal. As Braccio listens to his wife's confession, he repeatedly raises his hand and studies the wound. Finally, the bite leads indirectly to her death, for it is while fetching more salve for his hand that Braccio discovers his wife waiting for her lover.

We may trace a further connection between the woman and the horse. While interpreting "Ein Traum von großer Magie" we concluded that mastery over the horse stands symbolically for mastery of the self and of one's own existence. Accordingly it is significant that Dianora's cousins set her "auf ein schönes Pferd" (D, 1:77; SW, 3:111) and led her to her bridegroom; she did not come to him of her own volition. She tells Braccio that Palla often held the bridle of her saddle horse as he rode beside her; she admits to his domination as she submitted earlier to the stronger will of her relatives. Apparently his love imbued her with such self-assurance that her demeanor changed noticeably. "Ging ich nicht anders?" she asks. "Saß ich nicht zu Pferd/ wie eine Selige?" (D, 1:80; SW, 3:113). Had her love been fulfilled, perhaps Dianora would have gained enough self esteem to assert her own will, or at least control her own horse.

Continuing this analogy between control over a horse and control over one's own destiny, it follows that a man who succeeds in mastering horses will also successfully dominate women. On the other hand, a man who lacks the forceful commanding gesture (Gebärde) must control both horse and woman by brute strength. Lerch, possessing neither faculty, must bow Vuic's head in order to extort her submission; Braccio must kill his wife in order to possess her entirely.

In the *Rosenkavalier* Hofmannsthal compares the domination of a woman directly to that of a horse. Baron Ochs von Lerchenau first gives Octavian permission to flirt with Sophie, explaining that she must be tamed like a skittish horse:

> Betrachts als förderlich, je mehr sie degourdiert wird.
> Ist wie bei einem jungen ungerittenen Pferd.
> Kommt alles dem Angetrauten letzterdings zugute,
> wofern er sich sein ehelich Privilegium
> zunutz zu machen weiß. (L, 1:328)

Sophie protests against this crude treatment:

> Was sind das für Manieren? Ist das leicht ein Roßtäuscher und kommt ihm vor, er hätt mich eingekauft? (L, 1:320)

Curiously enough, D.H. Lawrence uses much the same image, taming a horse compared to taming a woman, in *Women in Love.* Gerald explains that a horse has two wills: "With one will, it wants to put itself in the human power completely — and with the other, it wants to be free, wild." Ursula asks how a horse can want to submit to human will, and Gerald replies:

> It's the last, perhaps highest, love impulse: to resign your will to the higher being. ... And woman is the same as horses: two wills act in opposition inside her. With one will, she wants to subject herself utterly. With the other she wants to bolt, and pitch her rider to perdition.[29]

Until now we have examined the animal symbols in *Die Frau im Fenster* merely in order of their occurrence. Reviewing them at this time, we may classify them as belonging to the sphere of one of the three main characters in the play, or as forming a link between two of them.

Palla is most directly associated with the lion, embodiment of strength and vigor, with the dolphins found among the fauns in the waterfall, and signifying exuberance, and with the bees, symbolizing the fullness of life. The animal images surrounding him indicate his direct descendance from the *Magier* of "Ein Traum von großer Magie." The *Magier* springs over cliffs like a lion; Palla walks with the sureness of the lion's gait. The *Magier's* leaping over cliffs may be compared to Palla's effortless springing through the waterfall. His association with bees, a symbol of plenitude and even intoxication, reinforces his characterization as "einen Trunkenen", a phrase reminiscent of the *Magier's* "großer Trunkenheit." Palla's world encompasses the harmonious co-existence of man and beast in an unproblematical natural state, yet this world is purely visionary, evoked in the play through Dianora's fantasies. Indeed Palla never appears on the stage, his presence, like that of the Magier, remains only "ein Traum."

---

29 *Woman in Love* (New York: Viking Press, 1965), p. 132.

Braccio's world, by contrast, corresponds to that of the "Hunde und geschirrte Pferde" disturbing the sleeper at the beginning of the poem. Wild animals hold no interest for him, yet the domesticated animal he professes to dominate, namely the *Rotschimmel,* breaks away from his command, as do the "geschirrte Pferde" of the poem. His sphere, framed by the balcony of the austere Lombardic palace, although situated above and remote from the animal-filled park below, corresponds to the "ebne Erde" of the poem, for his is the sphere of earthbound physicality. Both Braccio's sphere and that of the poem's opening lines are aptly evoked in the sermon of the Spanish priest as recalled by Dianora's nurse:

> Die Sonne muß glühen, der Stein muß auf der stummen Erde liegen, aus jeder lebendigen Kreatur geht ihre Stimme heraus, sie kann nichts dafür, sie kann nichts dawider, sie muß. (D, 1:69; SW, 3:105)

Thus Hofmannsthal inverts in the play the spatial contrasts of the poem. The earth, in the poem the realm of dogs and horses, becomes in the play the realm of Dianora's fantasies. Terrestrial reality in the play occupies Braccio's fortress-like residence, situated above in the heights haunted, in the poem, by the omnipotent *Magier.* Dianora, literally and figuratively suspended between the two extremes, longs to transcend the intervening space, though only her imagination enables her to do so. The woven rope ladder and her hair, both images of her sexuality, provide only a tenuous and insufficient link between the two worlds.

Taking a broad view of the play, we conclude that Hofmannsthal is working here once again with the fundamental polarities dominant in those of his works previously discussed. The substance of this play, like that of the "Märchen" and "Reitergeschichte" as well as "Ein Traum von großer Magie," might be summed up as the clash between the sphere of the imagination and that of terrestrial reality. The latter sphere encompasses horses and dogs in each of the works here under discussion. It seems that these domestic animals, because of their very closeness to man, defy any attempt to transform them through the creative imagination.

As well as continuing the fundamental opposition between fantasy and reality, the play presents some new facets of animal imagery. The hunting metaphor used to portray the love relationship appears to have been influenced by ancient literary tradition. The revelation that cruelty towards animals conceals a desire for violent aggression against an opponent who, because of superior strength or social position can not be attacked, will guide us in our examination of "Knabengeschichte." Finally, the equation of domination of a horse with domination of a woman, as well as with mastery of one's own destiny, leads us directly to the consideration of *not* riding as a symbolic act in *Das kleine Welttheater.*

CHAPTER VI

DAS KLEINE WELTTHEATER

Among the "Glücklichen" who present themselves in this series of lyrical monologues, the young lord warrants our attention because of the relationship to his horse and because of his dream of hunting forest animals.

It is significant that the youth walks onstage leading his horse by the bridle. Although he tells of riding out at dawn and dismounting at noon, he does not enter the play as a rider. We discussed Anton Lerch's riding and dismounting, concluding that his horse's hesitant gait in the village represented Lerch's instinctive reaction to the repugnant or menacing sights he encountered. This interpretation was complicated, however, by our recognition that the horse embodies Lerch's military self, the order and discipline of the squadron, as well as his instincts. At best we can reconcile the apparent conflict between the horse as instinct and the horse as military role by emphasizing that Lerch's allegiance to the military is based not on loyalty or patriotism, but on a desire for material comfort and for satisfaction of his brutal urges. If we turn now to the young lord, we may assume that the fact that he does not ride his horse indicates a renunciation of any attempt to control his instincts. This interpretation is substantiated by his account. He removes the horse's bit to permit it to graze; that is, he gives up the instrument by which he dominates the horse. Soon he perceives wild birds close by and throws the bit, killing three of them. Removing his horse's bit, or unleashing his instincts, then, leads directly to the death of the birds and to his subsequent feelings of guilt.

The broadly phrased equation of the horse with instinct or physical urges, and of the rider with controlling reason or intellect holds true not only for Hofmannsthal, but seems almost a commonplace of figurative language. D.W. Robertson, whose *Preface to Chaucer* analyzes many animal images ornamenting medieval manuscripts, quotes St. Gregory in this regard:

> Indeed the horse is the body of any holy soul, which it knows how to restrain from illicit action with the bridle of continence and to release in the exercise of good works with the spur of charity.[1]

A fourteenth century commentator on scripture whom Robertson quotes in the same context states: "Thus *moraliter* our flesh is the horse and the reason [,] spirit is the rider."[2] And five centuries later Sigmund Freud, substituting his concept "ego" for the Christian soul and "id" for the medieval flesh, restates the same relationship in the same symbolic terms:

> Man könnte das Verhältnis des Ichs zum Es mit dem des Reiters zu seinem Pferd vergleichen. Das Pferd gibt die Energie für die Lokomotion her, der Reiter hat das Vorrecht, das Ziel zu bestimmen, die Bewegung des starken Tieres zu leiten.[3]

In the same vein, Mary E. Gilbert writes of the young lord in *Das kleine Welttheater:*

> Does not the consonance between the young man and his horse intimate that he is still living within his unconsciousness before consciousness takes the reins?[4]

We are now in a position to understand more fully the intrusion of the riderless horses in "Ein Traum von großer Magie." They may signify a loss of conscious control over the physical urges in that twilight of consciousness preceding sleep. We may reflect further on the consistency of Hofmannsthal's use of the riding image in "Reitergeschichte," *Die Frau im Fenster,* and in the case of the young lord. Later the *Andreas* novel and *Der Turm* will rework the image once again.

To return to *Das kleine Welttheater,* we may conclude that the young lord's easy companionship with his horse implies a lack of conscious control over his subconscious urges. He relates:

> Zu Mittag saß ich ab im dämmernden Gebüsch,
> Von Brombeer und von wilden Rosen ganz umzäunt,

---

1 *A Preface to Chaucer,* p. 254.
2 Ibid. See also illustrations, figures 7, 8, 61 and 63.
3 *Gesammelte Werke* 15:83.
4 "The Image of the Horse in Hofmannsthal's Poetic Works," p. 61.

> Und neben meinem Pferde schlief ich ein.
> (GLD, p. 303; SW, 3:138)

Recalling the threatening intrusion of the horses in "Ein Traum von großer Magie" one might fear for the youth's safety, yet it is characteristic of the untroubled atmosphere of the play that his complete trust in the animal is not betrayed. In the poem, the *Magier* appearing in the dream banished the intruding horses and dogs. Here, by contrast, reality affords the harmony and contentment otherwise characteristic of dreams, while the dream is the stage of chaos and danger.

The youth continues and describes dreaming of a wild hunt:

> ... Ich jagte, war der Traum:
> Zu Fuß und mit drei großen Hunden trieb ich Wild,
> Gekleidet wie auf alten Bildern und bewaffnet
> Mit einer Armbrust, und vor mir der dichte Wald
> War angefüllt mit Leben, überschwemmt mit Wild,
> Das lautlos vor mir floh. (GLD, p. 303; SW, 3:138)

Hofmannsthal's critics have interpreted this hunt in diverse ways. An early scholar writes of the young lord:

> er spürt das Herannahende mit großer Bereitschaft, doch vermag er es nicht anders zu bezeichnen als mit dem geträumten Gleichnis vom gejagten Wild ... [5]

Werner Metzeler regards the hunt as "eine Jagd nach dem Leben schlechthin."[6] Benno von Wiese considers it a "wilde Jagd nach dem Weltgeheimnis."[7] Erwin Kobel interprets the hunt as signifying that the hunter is oriented toward the future:

> Die Gestalt des Jägers zeigt den Menschen, der das Leben vor sich zu haben meint und es daher einholen, erjagen, erobern muß...[8]

---

5 Max Ittenbach, "Hugo von Hofmannsthals *Kleines Welttheater*," *Germanisch-Romanische Monatsschrift* 20 (1932), 196.
6 *Ursprung und Krise von Hofmannsthals Mystik*, p. 90.
7 "Das Kleine Welttheater," in: *Das deutsche Drama*, ed. Benno von Wiese, vol. 2 (Düsseldorf: August Bagel, 1962), p. 236.
8 *Hugo von Hofmannsthal*, p. 72.

Such statements reveal little about the hunt's function in the play. It will prove more fruitful to consider other hunt imagery in Hofmannsthal's work and to analyze the account of the hunting dream at some length.

In treating *Die Frau im Fenster* we considered the medieval image of the hunt of Venus, whose true object was the favor of a mistress. The hunt of Diana was mentioned briefly as a diversion to distract the lover's attention from an unhappy passion. The hunt of Diana, as well as that of Venus, figures in Hofmannsthal's work. The emperor in *Der Kaiser und die Hexe* attempts to forget the sorceress through pursuing a wild boar:

> Wohl, ich jage! ja, ich jage!
> Dort der Eber, aufgewühlt
> Schaukelt noch das Unterholz,
> Hier der Speer! und hier der Jäger!
> (GLD, p. 256, SW, 3:179) [9]

But suddenly the emptiness of his existence overcomes him and he despairs: "Nein, ich bin das Wild, mich jagt es..."[10]

The emperor's fear that he is now the prey suggests that the hunt places the hunter in constant danger. Basilius' nephew and heir to the throne is killed while hunting when his horse stumbles into a wolf's den (D, 4:35-36). Menelas in *Die ägyptische Helena* returns from a hunt to find Helena missing.[11] The merchant's son in the "Märchen" imagines meeting his death as "ein auf der Jagd verirrter König." The young lord's physical safety is not endangered by his hunt, but the dream reveals the threat posed by his subconscious desires. Just as

---

9 The boar, because of the danger its strength posed to the hunter, was not among those animals Venus counseled Adonis to hunt. He was, in fact, later killed by a wild boar. Therefore the boar indicates that the hunter is not concerned with preserving his life for love, but rather with diverting his mind from his mistress.

10 The emperor's despair contradicts Pickerodt's comment on the passage: "Die Jagd vermittelt dem Jäger die Bestätigung seiner selbst als eines Handelnden, seiner Macht über die Natur" *(Hofmannsthals Dramen,* p. 76).

11 At this point Hofmannsthal departs from Goethe's recounting of the legend, where Helena explains how Paris abducted her while she was worshipping in Cythera's temple *(Faust II,* Act. 3, "Vor dem Palaste des Menelas," lines 8511-12).

the animals in the village of the "Reitergeschichte" embodied certain drives within Lerch, so the hunting dream displays the youth's inner urges which threaten his peace of mind. The peril of the hunt stems in this case not from exterior danger, but from conflicts within the young man himself.

The young lord's dream bears some resemblance to the hunt of Diana, although its similarity is not as clearly defined as was the case in *Der Kaiser und die Hexe*. The youth shuns the "Netze und Fußangeln" which he associates with having a destiny or social role and responsibilities. The net or snare figured in Ovid's *Art of Love* as an image for the attempt to capture a lover.[12] The bird snare served the middle ages as an image for "the sweetness of this life" which might prevent the spirit from ascending toward heaven.[13] The young lord's solitude and the hunt of which he dreams may be viewed then as flight from romantic entanglements and from the ensuing social burden of adulthood and family responsibility.

The youth places himself within the framework of past tradition: he is "gekleidet wie auf alten Bildern" and armed with a crossbow. His love of costume demonstrates the youthful pleasure in role playing and in self-contemplation, traits he shares with the page in *Der Tod des Tizian* and with the narrator of "Age of Innocence." Coupled with his anxiousness to avoid "Geschick" or personal destiny, this fondness for assuming an artificial role reveals that the youth lacks a firm grasp of his own identity. The statement that he is accompanied by three large dogs suggests a stylized representation of the hunt, as if he were imitating some medieval tapestry. In fact, Hofmannsthal's inspiration derived from Gustave Flaubert's treatment of the medieval legend of Saint Julian the hospitaler.[14] An examination of Flaubert's story will further our understanding of Hofmannsthal's re-working of it.

---

12 See p. 30, line 270.
13 Robertson, *A Preface to Chaucer*, p. 95.
14 Hofmannsthal's debt to Flaubert's *Légende de St. Julien l'Hospitalier* has been noted by Michel Vanhelleputte, "Hofmannsthaliana (1968-1970)," *Etudes Germaniques* 27 (1972), 258; and by Gerhart Baumann, *Vereinigungen* (Munich: Wilhelm Fink, 1972), p. 49.

Julien, the only son of noble parents, seeks pleasure in killing animals at an early age. Observing a pigeon in the garden, he touches a loose stone in the wall. "Il tourna son bras, et la pierre abattit l'oiseau qui tomba d'un bloc dans le fossé."[15] Flaubert's choice of the stone as subject of the second clause stresses Julien's passivity: the instrument leads directly to the deed. Julien strangles the pigeon "et les convulsions de l'oiseau faisaient battre son coeur, l'emplissaient d'une volupté sauvage et tumultueuse."[16] The "volupté sauvage" suggests the "Wollust" Hofmannsthal connects with the animal killings or fantasies of Euseb (E, p. 251; SW, 29:167) and Andreas (E, p. 146; SW, 30:64).

Julien receives an education in venery, but abandons himself to the pleasure of unrestrained killing. He does not willfully prolong the suffering of a dying animal, nor does he identify with its plight, as do Euseb and Andreas. Rather he derives pleasure from exercising an unlimited power over animal life. Finally a stag warns him that he will kill his parents. Julien asks himself, "Si je le voulais pourtant?" but rejects the idea as unseemly: "et il avait peur que le Diable ne lui en inspirât envie."[17] To avoid the fulfillment of the prophecy, he leaves his parents' home, as does Oedipus. Years later his wife suggests hunting as a pastime. He goes into the forest, but his arrows fall short of their mark, the animals flee silently before him.

Upon his return home, Julien discovers his aged parents in his wife's bed and kills them under the mistaken impression that his wife is betraying him with another man. He soon recognizes his mistake and, broken by guilt, becomes a beggar. One day he bends over a well and sees an emaciated face whose wretchedness causes him to weep. Without recognizing his own reflection, he confusedly recalls the face resembling that mirrored in the water, the face of his father. He cries out, then gives up all thoughts of suicide and becomes a ferryman, serving travelers without pay.

Comparing Flaubert's story with the young lord's monologue, we find several parallels. The forest animals flee silently before Julien, the young lord describes their flight as "lautlos," later as "stille atem-

---

15 Gustave Flaubert, *Trois Contes* (Paris: Garnier Frères, 1969), p. 87.
16 Ibid.
17 Ibid., p. 99.

lose Flucht." Hofmannsthal evokes not only the silence of dream, but the whole inarticulate eerie stillness characterizing the chaos of city and village in the "Märchen" and "Reitergeschichte."

In keeping with the undisturbed atmosphere of the play, the hunting scene is described without carnage or bloody slaughter. The various forest creatures are not visually presented to the reader, rather, their presence is evoked through synecdoche: one hears only:

> ... das Streifen
> Der Felle an den Bäumen und das flinke Laufen
> Von Tausenden von Klauen und von leichten Hufen
> Auf Moos und Wurzeln, ... (GLD, p. 303; SW, 3:138)

Hofmannsthal weaves Julien's vision of his dead father's face into the young lord's dream; the youth relates:

> ... Ich war vom Übermaß
> Der Freude über diese Jagd erfüllt und doch
> Im Innersten beklommen, und ich mußte plötzlich
> An meinen Vater denken, und mir war, als säh ich
> Sein weißes Haar in einem Brunnen unter mir.
> (GLD, p. 304; SW, 3:138)

What exactly does this evocation of the father signify? Does Flaubert's *Légende* offer any clues?

The well may evoke the sight of the steep-walled ravine into which the youth has driven the forest animals. The dying animals, we may assume, appeared below him as does his father now. The father's white hair suggests old age and accompanying frailty; his disquieting position in the well stresses his vulnerability. It seems an easy step from the young lord's forcing the forest animals into the steep-walled ravine to exposing his father to a similar danger.

In Julien's case, unrestrained slaughter of wild animals leads directly to the prophecy that he will kill his parents. He is overcome while hunting by a sensation of irreality likened to that of a dream:

> Il était en chasse dans un pays quelconque, depuis un temps indéterminé, par le fait seul de sa propre existence, tout s'accomplissait avec la facilité que l'on éprouve dans les rêves.[18]

---

18 *Trois Contes*, p. 95.

He comes upon a herd of deer huddled together in a valley for warmth and begins to shoot them with his crossbow. The scene of Julien's massacre in the valley may have suggested to Hofmannsthal the ravine whose steep sides prevent the forest animals' escape. Julien sees a stag accompanied by a doe and fawn, which he shoots. The stag, a father figure, wounded by Julien's last arrow, approaches and warns him that he will one day kill his parents, an act presented as the culmination of his excessively destructive tendencies.

The juxtaposition of animal killing with patricide in Hofmannsthal's source tinges the young lord's account with the suspicion that he may subconsciously desire his father's death. The father, in his traditional role, provides his son with the concept of identity and social role, educating him to a responsible position in society. The logical conclusion of the father's influence is to impose upon his son the responsibility or "Geschick" which the young lord shuns as "Netze und Fußangeln." Here as in the "Märchen" the father binds his son to a social role he refuses to assume. We have already suggested that similar grounds for friction between father and son existed in Hofmannsthal's own life as he renounced his father's business-oriented career for poetry. In the "Märchen" the merchant's son reacted to society's demands with a longing for his childhood, his bed, and for his mother as a safe refuge. It is important to note that in both the "Märchen" and *Das kleine Welttheater* dread of or hostility towards the father does not necessarily hinge on Oedipal — that is, sexual — passion, but may simply arise from the father's attempt to impose identity, responsibility, and a socially acceptable role on his son.

At the moment when the young lord envisages his father in the well his horse springs up and disturbs his sleep. It would be false, however, to maintain that the horse functions as a kind of censor, destroying the youth's contemplation of substituting his father for the wild animals as the object of his next hunt. Instead the horse forcibly draws the young lord from the dream world to that of reality, where he does, in fact, bring guilt upon himself by killing three wild birds. The horse breaks up the dream world, which remains innocent by virtue of its very irreality, and leads his master into the actual peril of the hunt which now takes place.

The young lord relates the dream's echo in reality; he awakes still under the dream's shadowy influence and walks beside his horse. When he startles birds in the underbrush, he searches for a stone in the deep moss, but, finding nothing, casts instead the horse's bit, killing three birds. The dream has already prepared us for the choice of birds as his prey; in the youth's account of the dream, only the birds were described concretely enough to make their presence felt, rather than merely evoked through synecdoche as were the other animals:

> ... In getrennten,
> Doch durcheinander hingemengten Schwärmen rauschten
> Birkhähne schweren Flugs, das Rudern wilder Gänse,
> Und zwischen Ketten der verschreckten Haselhühner schwangen
> Die Reiher sich hindurch, und neben ihnen, ängstlich
> Den Mord vergessend, hasteten die Falken hin.
> (GLD, p. 303; SW, 3:138)

The birds flee in unison before their pursuer; fear of him causes them to break common behavior patterns to save themselves.

The success of the young lord's throw has been interpreted as evidence of a mystical oneness, "seine augenblickliche Identität von Ich und Welt,"[19] or as creating "den Eindruck der glückhaften Leichtigkeit des ganzen Daseins."[20] That the successful throw does not constitute such an epiphany may be seen from the comparison with a similar incident in the poem "Vor Tag:"

> ... Nun im stummen Wald
> Hebt der Landstreicher ungewaschen sich
> Aus weichem Bett vorjährigen Laubes auf
> Und wirft mit frecher Hand den nächsten Stein
> Nach einer Taube, die schlaftrunken fliegt,
> Und graust sich selber wie der Stein so dumpf
> Und schwer zur Erde fällt. (GLD, p. 9; SW, 1:106)

The stillness of the wood recalls the silence of the young lord's dream. Like him, the vagrant throws his stone without reflecting on his intentions. The success of the throw is indifferent to him, we are

---

19 Tarot, *Daseinsformen und dichterische Struktur*, p. 251.
20 Mauser, *Bild und Gebärde in der Sprache Hofmannsthals*, p. 31.

not even told whether he hits the mark. In describing the vagrant, however, Hofmannsthal inserts the judgement "mit frecher Hand," a condemnation absent in *Das kleine Welttheater*. The vagrant senses his guilt upon hearing the stone hit the ground; the young lord feels it necessary to wash his eyes. The youth's unmotivated throw occurs under the influence of the hunting dream; it is the transference into reality of dreamed guilt, "Sinnbild unausweichlicher Verschuldung."[21]

Feeling the need for purification, the young lord seeks "den Brunnen" and hastily washes his eyes. It is characteristic of his unsuspecting innocence that he washes not the hand, which committed the deed, but only the eyes, the organ of recognition. He thereby negates his part in the birds' death; it suffices to purge his memory of his perception of the killing. The use of the definite article, "den Brunnen" emphasizes the influence of the dream; the youth seeks not any well, but that one which appeared in his dream. The identity of the well in the dream with the real well forges a link between the dream and reality.

In the dream the youth saw his father's white hair in the well beneath him. Now he raises his head from the well and feels himself "um ein Stück/ Gealtert in dem Augenblick." He now recognizes that he must one day grow old, like his father, he has become subject to time, "der Zeit untertan."[22] Furthermore, the identification with his father casts new light on his father's function in the dream. When the father's face becomes visible in the well, he seems to present himself as judge, condemning his son's indiscriminate slaughter. His appearance does put an end to the massacre; the horse starts up suddenly and awakens his master. In Julien's case as well the father embodies his conscience. Julien sees his own reflection, yet without recognizing his own face he visualizes that of his father. Thus his father's image is produced from his own, his conscience warns from within himself and moves him to cease contemplating suicide. The young lord's fleeting sensation that he grows older and comes to occupy his father's place ("als würd ich innerlich/ Durch einen Abgrund

---

21 Benno von Wiese, *"Das kleine Welttheater,"* p. 236.
22 Metzler, *Ursprung und Krise von Hofmannsthals Mystik*, p. 90.

hingerissen") suggests that now he is at one with his conscience, with his father's perspective on the killings.

While trying to comprehend such omens, the young lord speaks of his earlier belief "daß in meinem tiefsten Seelengrund/Das Böse läg und dies Vorboten wären" (GLD, p. 305; SW, 3:139). Earlier he feared the future and the manifestation of such destructive tendencies as those revealed in the dream. Now he senses relief, for his dream has presented the imagined confrontation with his "Geschick" and he has escaped unencumbered by the snares and fetters of an individual fate. He attributes his feeling of relief and joy to a greeting ("Gruß") which must be identical to the "stummer Gruß" of a "sonderbarer Bettler" mentioned at the very beginning of his monologue. Then he recognized the royal bearing of the "beggar" and furthermore intuitively sensed that this ruler had silently abandoned his crown. This figure, a former king who rejected his realm and duty in favor of a simple existence as gardner, appeared on the stage immediately before the young lord. When he first comments on his meeting with the beggar, the young lord is puzzled by the gardner-king's renunciation of power, and can only remark that this inexplicable behavior, like human destiny, reminds him of snares and fetters, encumbering duty from which man can extricate himself only with considerable difficulty and sacrifice. It is only after his dream, after the vision of his father, and after his recognition of his own maturation that the young lord finds pleasure in recalling this encounter, for now he understands the gardner-king as an example. The hunting dream, the killing of the birds, and the only half understood confrontation with the urges and conflicts within him have awakened the young lord to the snare of responsibility for his own actions. Henceforth he resolves like the gardner-king to extricate himself from duty, guilt and encumbrances of human relationships, to remain different from his brothers, secure in his own solitude. Now he feels that all paths have been mysteriously prepared for him, "Von Händen in der Morgenfrühe hingebaut" (GLD, p. 305; SW, 3:139). The dawn, the hour at which he has arisen to ride out alone, signifies innocence, an untarnished purity to which he expects to return:

> Und überall erwarte ich den Pfad zu sehen,
> Der anfangs von ihr weg zu vieler Prüfung führt

> Und wunderbar verschlungen doch zu ihr zurück.
> (GLD, p. 305; SW, 3:139)

The dream vision of his potential guilt, purged from his memory through the simple gesture of washing his eyes, has relieved him of the necessity for real experimentation, with its infinite possibilities of wrongdoing. He now contemplates a future leading back toward his past, a circular passage beginning and ending in the unblemished innocence of childhood and inexperience.

CHAPTER VII

JUPITER UND SEMELE

Although the two-page outline of this drama, composed in 1901, offers only a glimpse of what Hofmannsthal intended to make of the play, it interests us as a forestudy for certain passages in *Andreas* and *Der Turm*.

Hofmannsthal's notes sketch a group of scenes whose content may be summarized as follows:

A girl begs her lover, a poet, to embrace her "im höchsten Glanz seiner Schönheit."

The lovers meet near a crumbling city wall.

In a bedroom scene, the girl repeats her plea. A dog poisoned by her brother appears at the lovers' bedside.

The poet justifies his refusal to appear to her in his full glory.

Before attempting to interpret these scenes, it will be helpful to characterize the two main figures.

The girl is passionate to the point of self-sacrifice:

> Ihr dämonischer, tragischer Zug: bis zum Äußersten gehen zu wollen. So hat sie ihre Familie verlassen. Ihr Bruder ist Offizier. (D, 2:504)

The title's reference to the legend of Jupiter and Semele indicates that the girl is a far humbler creature than her mighty lover. In leaving her family she has severed connections with her own milieu and placed her fate in her lover's hands. Combined with the note that her brother is an officer, the facts of her situation reflect that of Gretchen in *Faust*.

While considering the poet, Hofmannsthal deliberates:

> Ob nicht als seine Geliebte die Muse einzuführen wäre, eine Gestalt ähnlich der geheimnisvollen Königin in "Idyll of the White Lotus." (D, 2:504)[1]

---

[1] Hofmannsthal read Mabel Collins' novel, *The Idyll of the White Lotus*, as early as December, 1892, and valued it highly as an "ethische Allegorie,"

133

This allegorical novel by Mabel Collins relates the adventures of a youth brought as apprentice into a mysterious temple. A dark queen surrounded by night and serpents and served by a priest named Agmahd appears to have been Hofmannsthal's model for the *Bergkönigin* in *Das Bergwerk zu Falun*. Her opponent, the queen of the White Lotus, arrayed in gleaming white, embodies purity and virtue, and leads the youth out of the temple into the garden or among the populace. The Semele figure of Hofmannsthal's play shows little resemblance to the queen of the White Lotus. Unlike a muse, she does not lead him to loftier spiritual heights, rather, as the dog in her proximity implies, she links him to the corporeal sphere of physical desire.

It is significant that Hofmannsthal associates the poet with Jupiter; divine creativity and supremacy are equated with artistic creativity. The artist using his imagination to create a microcosm assumed the role of the Christian god in "Ein Traum von großer Magie"; here the classical deity becomes identified with the creative artist, in this case a poet, in much the same manner.

The poet's material is defined in a series of contrasts:

> Des Dichters eigentliches Gebiet: das Verhältnis von Geist zu Körper, von Idee zum Ausdruck, Mensch zum Tier. (D, 2:504)

The relationship of soul to body, of man to beast, are matters of philosophy or theology, the relationship of idea to expression a matter of aesthetics. The three contrasts are, however, interwoven in Hofmannsthal's own work. As we shall observe when examining *Der Turm,* Sigismund's conversation with his foster mother gropes for the distinction between body and spirit. Because Sigismund is unable to accept the peasant woman's explanation that man is distinguished from animals by his immortal soul, he fails to grasp the relationship of body and soul in his own being. Thus the "Verhältnis von Geist zu Körper" is linked to that of "Mensch zum Tier." And Hofmannsthal expresses these abstractions, the relationships of body to soul and of man to beast, through animal imagery, thereby including the relationship "von Idee zum Ausdruck."

> according to Rudolf Hirsch, "Hofmannsthal und Frankreich. Zwei Beiträge," *Etudes Germaniques* 29 (1974): 150, note 8.

Hofmannsthal seems to have intended the poet in *Jupiter und Semele* to concern himself with the distinction separating man from beast:

> ... (es müssen Tiere vorkommen, zu denen er ein sehr starkes Verhältnis hat; conf. "The Island of Dr. Moreau") (D, 2:504)

H. G. Wells' short science fiction novel describes the experimental attempts of Dr. Moreau to shape various jungle animals into human form by means of surgery. At the center of the book lies the question, to what extent can animals, through social organization or through mastery of speech, approximate human existence? Hofmannsthal treats the same question in a different form in *Der Turm*, focusing on speech as a possible criterion for separating man from the animals.

The events of the drama are briefly outlined. The girl meets the poet near a crumbling city wall, whose presence suggests that in the play, as in "Amgiad und Assad," "Das Märchen," and "Reitergeschichte" the city may have been depicted as squalid and treacherous. The flickering fire where the lovers meet points to the poet's identification with Jupiter, god of lightning. If we compare this unsteady flame to the fire in the bedroom scene of "Das Erlebnis des Marschalls von Bassompierre," a fire representing the all-consuming passion of Bassompierre and the shopwoman, we must conclude that the love shared by the poet and his mistress is as weak and uncertain as the flickering blaze.[2]

It appears that the lovers' next meeting was to be presented as a bedroom scene marked by the bizarre intrusion of a poisoned dog:

> Hund, den ihr Bruder vergiftet haben muß – von einem anderen hätte er sich nicht Nahrung reichen lassen – richtet sich nachts mit brechendem Blick vor dem Bett der Liebenden auf. (D, 2:504)

The conjectural use of "muß" admits a doubt as to whether the girl's brother actually poisoned his own dog. The comment that the dog

---

[2] See Mary E. Gilbert's remarks on fire as a symbol of passion in: "Some Observations on Hofmannsthal's Two 'Novellen,' 'Reitergeschichte' and 'Das Erlebnis des Marschalls von Bassompierre,' " *German Life and Letters,* n.s., 11 (1958), 104.

would have accepted food from no one else confirms the suspicion of the brother's guilt. The nocturnal appearance of a poisoned dog must be considered again in the *Andreas* novel.

The question how a person could bear to torture or kill an animal having full trust in him particularly fascinated Hofmannsthal. In a paragraph of "Der Dichter und diese Zeit" which was subsequently deleted he recalls the fascination exerted on his imagination by the Danish story of a lion tamer who poisoned his own lions.[3] He found in the story "einen dumpfen Schmerz und das mitleidige halb grausende Ausmalen einer Situation, in der etwas Quälendes und etwas Erlösendes sich mischten."[4] The heightened sensation accompanying such deeds arises from the tension between love of the animal and the desire to make it suffer. The same tension characterizes the hunt imagery of *Die Frau im Fenster*.

The tension between love and a desire to make the loved one suffer prevails not only in the case of the girl's brother poisoning his own dog, but in the relationship between the poet and the girl, who explicitly compares herself to the dog: "Ich liege unter dir wie die stumme Kreatur." A passage from an older version of *Die Hochzeit der Sobeide* compares the eyes of a frightened woman to those of a tortured cat. A thief captures Sobeide before she reaches Ganem's house, and, lifting her veil, he remarks:

> ... Ich hab einmal
> ist schon lang her, der Mutter größte Katze
> ins offne Feuer geworfen und sie drin
> so lang als nötig mit der Ofengabel
> gehalten. Solche Augen hat mir die
> gemacht, dieselben Augen. (D, 1:437)

Here, as in *Jupiter und Semele*, the woman is compared to an animal suffering man's cruel abuse. Sobeide's eyes resemble those of the burning cat; in *Jupiter und Semele* the dog's eyes are emphasized: he appears "mit brechendem Blick" at the lovers' bedside, later repeated as "mit brechenden Augen." In discussing "Reitergeschichte" it was

---

3 David H. Miles has identified the unnamed story as "Fratelli Bedini" by Hermann Bang. *Hofmannsthal's Novel Andreas*, p. 171, note 71a.
4 In *Die neue Rundschau* (1907), p. 268.

determined that the animal's gaze fulfills the function of human speech as an expression of character; therefore the dog's dying eyes further stress his muteness.

The dog's appearance at the lovers' bedside is reminiscent of the beginning of "Ein Traum von großer Magie," where the narrator's sleep is disturbed by the intrusion of horses and dogs. In the play, however, the bed is primarily the scene of the lovers' meeting and only secondarily the place of sleep. The dog's proximity to the bed under these circumstances corresponds to what Hofmannsthal seems to regard as the woman's intensified physicality during the sex act.[5] In *Das Mutterrecht,* Johann Jakob Bachofen elucidates this link between woman and dog which becomes evident during intercourse:

> Der Hund ist der hetärischen, jeder Befruchtung sich freuenden Erde Bild. Regelloser, stets sichtbarer Begattung hingegeben, stellt er das Prinzip tierischer Zeugung am klarsten und in seiner rohsten Form dar.[6]

The association woman-dog-earth rests on the concept of earth as mother of all life, that is, as feminine, and of the dog as embodiment of the fleshly or material, of which earth is comprised.

The fact that the dog appears at the lovers' bedside at the point of death suggests several possible interpretations. His suffering deprives him of any non-physical qualities; he has no significance as an emblem of fidelity or loyalty, but exists merely as a suffering body.[7] By extension then, the woman who identifies herself with him exists at that moment only as body. Secondly, sexual intercourse was long believed to shorten life, and therefore naturally associated with

---

5 Wyss comments without elaboration: "Im Augenblick der Zeugung ist sie [die Frau] mehr Kreatur als sonst." *Die Frau in der Dichtung Hofmannsthals,* p. 110.
6 *Gesammelte Werke,* vol. 2: *Das Mutterrecht,* 1st half (Basel: Benno Schwabe, 1948), p. 106.
7 In Thomas Mann's *Zauberberg,* Settembrini declares: "Ein Mensch, der als Kranker lebt, ist *nur* Körper, das ist Widermenschliche und Erniedrigende, er ist in den meisten Fällen nichts Besseres als ein Kadaver." *Gesammelte Werke,* 2d ed., 13 vols. (Frankfurt: S. Fischer, 1974), 3:142. By the same token, the suffering dog exists only as beast, as body, devoid of spiritual attributes.

death.[8] The woman who engages in it may feel that she is dying, like the poisoned dog. Third, her utter self-abnegation in love represents a spiritual death; she gives herself up entirely to her lover and ceases to exist except through him. In begging him to embrace her in his full glory, she is bringing about her own fiery annihilation.

Hofmannsthal adds one element to this chain of associations he found in Bachofen: muteness. As early as the "Terzinen" the dog appeared "unheimlich stumm und fremd" (GLD, p. 17; SW, 1:45). On a subtler level, the dog's sphere, the earth, was characterized by the absence of speech in "Ein Traum von großer Magie" and *Die Frau im Fenster,* where the Spanish priest declares that all things obey divine will: "Der Stein muß auf der stummen Erde liegen" (D, 1:69; SW, 3:105). Muteness, appropriate to the dog and earth, may be applied to all that is material or purely physical, in Hofmannsthal's eyes, including woman, who compares herself to the "stumme Kreatur."

If we focus on the opposite pole, the mastery of language, an instrument of the mind, we perceive that Hofmannsthal in *Jupiter und Semele* exemplifies "das Verhältnis von Geist zu Körper ... von Mensch zum Tier" in the poet's relationship to his mistress. Perhaps the series of contrasts is most clearly represented in the following schema:

poet	girl
Jupiter-heaven	Semele-earth
god	animal
creative-spirit	material-flesh
language	muteness

To the dog's muteness the poet opposes a "Wortgewalt" which will reduce the girl to a "Kotlache." Implicitly his verbal power is equated with Jupiter's command of destructive lightning. Explicitly, his verbal power is equated with sexual potency. His mistress complains: "Du strömst in ein anderes Medium, als ich bin, Zeugungskraft aus" (D, 2:505). This comparison of poetic creativity to sexual potency is also found in Goethe's poem, "Selige Sehnsucht:"

---

8 See John Donne's poem, "The Canonization:" "We [the lovers] are tapers too, and at our owne cost die."

> In der Liebesnächte Kühlung,
> Die dich zeugte, wo du zeugtest,
> Überfällt dich fremde Fühlung,
> Wenn die stille Kerze leuchtet.
>
> Nicht mehr bleibest du umfangen
> In der Finsternis Beschattung
> Und dich reißet neu Verlangen
> Auf zu höherer Begattung.[9]

The circumlocution "höhere Begattung" for poetic endeavors corresponds to the girl's complaint that her lover expends his "Zeugungskraft" in some other medium. In Goethe's poem, the moth which must be consumed by the flame in order to be transformed prefigures the fate of the Semele figure; Semele was destroyed by Jupiter's lightning, but gave birth to Bacchus, or Dionysus, who came to be strongly associated with procreative and creative powers.

If we continue examining the parallels between Hofmannsthal's figures and Jupiter and Semele, we perceive the justification for his choice of that classical legend as a basis for his "Phantastische Dichterkomödie." Bacchus, the offspring of their union, came, through Nietzsche, to be connected with the source of tragedy, which supposedly arose out of the dithyrambs honoring him. Since Bacchus was also revered as a god of vegetation and fertility, poetic and sexual creativity merged in his person.

The equation of poetic and sexual creativity which Hofmannsthal incorporates in his sketch presupposes woman's exclusion from artistic creation; she shelters and nourishes, but the male must supply the creative impulse. This concept of woman's limitations may have been influenced by *Das Mutterrecht,* whose essential principles may be summarized as follows:

> ... Auf dem geistigen Gebiet herrscht der Mann, auf dem der Materie in ihrem ganzen Umfang die Frau. ... Ist alles Stoffliche der Erde zugewiesen, so ist sie hinwieder auf dieses beschränkt. Ist umgekehrt der Mann von dem Stofflichen ausgeschlossen, so fällt ihm hinwieder das Geistige ungeteilt anheim. Plato nennt die Einwirkung des Mannes auf den Stoff unkörperlich. Anderwärts wird sie ... mit der Kraft des Stahles verglichen, der den im Feuerstein schlafenden Funken wachruft. ... Dem Weibe, als stofflicher

9 *Goethes Werke,* 2:18-19.

Grundlage des menschlichen Seins, tritt der Mann als unkörperliche Potenz entgegen. Ist jenes die Materie, so ist er der Künstler. Vertritt jenes die Stelle der Erde, so erinnert er an den Schöpfer, der wie der Töpfer den Topf, so der Erde als eine von außen her einwirkende, unsichtbare Gewalt gegenübertritt.[10]

Bachofen's concept of woman's role may have bearing on Hofmannsthal's portrayal of such women as Vuic and Dianora. Vuic is associated with the white dog, Dianora expresses her longing for the earth and the existence of the forest animals. Perhaps even the decision of the empress in "Die Frau ohne Schatten" to sacrifice her magic powers (among them that of flight) to an earthbound existence may be considered an avowal of her suitable place in life. And certainly Bachofen's imagery echoes in the beginning of Hofmannsthal's "Idylle." The heroine's father was a potter, creating from the raw material of earth forms whose representations of "Liebeslust" fascinated her. Her husband, a blacksmith, urges her to revere his craft:

> Das aus des mütterlichen Grundes Eingeweiden stammt
> Und, sich die hundertarmig Ungebändigte,
> Die Flamme, unterwerfend, klug und kraftvoll wirkt.
> (GLD, p. 59; SW, 3:56)

The poet in *Jupiter und Semele* recognizes his mistress's bond to earth when he warns that his fire will leave no trace of her save a "Kotlache," the residue of her physical being must contain traces of earth.

Our investigation of *Jupiter und Semele,* limited to the sparse details in the sketch, must remain incomplete. We cannot satisfactorily account for the brother's role, nor have we treated the poet's concept of language, nor have we exhausted the possible interpretations of the poisoned dog. The dramatic sketch does serve, however, to prepare our investigation of *Andreas* and *Der Turm,* where its unresolved problems will be dealt with at greater length.

---

10   *Das Mutterrecht,* 1:401-2.

CHAPTER VIII

"KNABENGESCHICHTE"
("DÄMMERUNG UND NÄCHTLICHES GEWITTER")

From 1906 through 1913 Hofmannsthal planned a short story which was never finished. The events in the completed portion of the story, written in 1911, were intended to take place during a single night; thus the fragment was tentatively entitled "Dämmerung und nächtliches Gewitter."[1] Here Euseb, the protagonist, observes the death agonies of a sparrow-hawk which he and other boys have crucified. Then, driven into the village by a thunderstorm, he waits opposite the window of the butcher's daughter, hoping to see her undressing for the night. While he is waiting, a servant steps in front of the house quarreling with his former mistress, a pregnant servant girl. As she walks away in despair, Euseb pursues her, fantasizing that he is hunting a "behextes Tier." At this point the fragment breaks off. Notes show that Hofmannsthal intended to expand the plot to encompass the birth of the servant-girl's child and of a legitimate child born in the same night as well as other material centered about Euseb, his relationship to his father, his awakening sexuality and his adolescent struggle for identity. As the events to be narrated expanded beyond the timeframe of a single night, Hofmannsthal came to refer to his notes simply as "Knabengeschichte."

Regardless of the fragmentary nature of the text, a study of its content is indispensable to an understanding of *Andreas,* for it contains three themes to be taken up again in the novel.[2] Euseb's search

---

1 Under this title Herbert Steiner has published the completed portion of the story and some notes (*Erzählungen,* 248-53). Because *Sämtliche Werke* 29 (pp. 167-88) gives all notes in chronological order, that text will be cited here with a supplementary reference to the Steiner edition if the quoted portion also appears there.

2 For a discussion of the story's relevance to *Andreas* and other works focussing on the father-son relationship, see my article, "Hugo von Hofmannsthal's *Knabengeschichten," Modern Austrian Literature* 17 (1984), 33-47.

for identity is part of a larger complex encompassing the pregnant servant girl and revolving about the issues of paternity, legitimacy, and the relations between father and son, a theme encountered as early as the "Märchen" and as late as *Der Turm*. The second theme, that of animal sacrifice, here forms an analogy to the passion of Christ. Because the significance of Euseb's crucifixion of the sparrow-hawk is more explicitly stated than the meaning of Andreas' half-repressed memories of animal torture, the story fragment may supply insights relevant to the novel. Third, Euseb is at the stage of puberty where he relates to woman as both mother and lover. The lack of a satisfactory relationship to either mother or father hinders the normal development of romantic love, as we shall see again in *Andreas* and *Der Turm*.

Within the story fragment and accompanying notes we can distinguish three complexes of animal imagery corresponding approximately to these three themes. First, a series of relatively minor animal images characterizes Euseb's village milieu and draws attention to his tendency toward self denigration through identifying himself with lowly or repulsive animals. Second, Euseb's search for his father (one facet of his identity crisis) is entwined with the Christian imagery linked to the crucifixion of the bird. Third, Euseb's awakening sexual urges are depicted through imagery of butchery and the hunt. Although these spheres of imagery overlap and intermesh, we shall attempt to discuss them individually in this order.

"Knabengeschichte" opens with the death agonies of the crucified sparrow-hawk whose mate circles about crying piteously. Next appear a bat and a bearded goat-sucker preying on an insect. The goat-sucker, a European nocturnal bird related to the American whip-poor-will, is believed in Tyrol to possess the evil eye. Its cry is said to foretell death and it may show itself only at night.[3] Later Euseb stands near a slaughtered calf hanging head downward. These animal images illustrate the brutality of the struggle for existence in which animals are both predator and prey. Indeed humans are reduced to an animal plane: from the notes we learn that Euseb sleeps

---

3 *Handwörterbuch des deutschen Aberglaubens*, vol. 9, 1/2 Lieferung, col. 934.

on a horse blanket. He feels himself the victim of his father's rejection and becomes predator in killing the sparrow hawk and hunting the servant girl. The harsh ugliness of his surroundings may be compared to the decaying village in "Reitergeschichte," where the fighting rats, the dogs quarreling over a bone, and the cow being led to the slaughter served to illustrate Lerch's condition. In the same way the external landscape of "Knabengeschichte," illuminated by flashes of lightning and buffeted by gusts of wind, reflects the turmoil within Euseb.

The threatening animal realm of "Reitergeschichte" and the caserne in the "Märchen" were characterized by a lack of spoken communication. Similarly Euseb's world is ominously silent. Euseb does not speak to the boys who have joined him in torturing the bird, nor does he take leave of them; he is simply driven into the village by the approaching storm. He does not exchange words with the butcher's daughter, nor with the servant girl. The only words directly quoted in the completed portion of the story are the servant Joseph's rebukes to the pregnant girl. The scarcity of spoken language reinforces the reader's impression of Euseb's isolation and alienation from the human community. He is rooted in an animal world dominated by the biological processes of propagation, birth and death:

> Das gräßliche des Ideen-losen — alles lebt dahin, paart sich, frißt, brüllt, stinkt, übervorteilt, unterdrückt, höhnt, belauert, beargwohnt einander — greift an einander herum... (SW, 29:181)

Because language is the vehicle of thought, its absence typifies this unenlightened realm of chaos inhabited by both Euseb and Anton Lerch.

One specific animal image common to both "Reitergeschichte" and "Knabengeschichte" is the dead calf. While Euseb spies on the butcher's daughter, he stands opposite a calf slaughtered that very afternoon; the animal's mouth still seems to exhale a warm breath. Lerch's progress is blocked by a cow who balks at the hide of a freshly slaughtered calf as she is being led to the slaughter. She inhales "mit geblähten Nüstern den rötlichen Sonnendunst des Abends in sich" (SW, 29:44; E, 57). Both the cow's inhaling the evening air and the calf's warm breath (in "Knabengeschichte") symbolize here (as in "Vor Tag" and in "Prolog" to *Die Frau im Fenster*) the animal's drive to live.

The source of the scene in which Euseb waits beside the calf hanging head downward outside the butcher shop was the eighteenth century Bildungsroman *Anton Reiser*. The still warm corpse, a reminder of the brevity of all physical life, forms a counterpoint to Euseb's awakening interest in sex as he hopes to watch the butcher's daughter undress for the night. Anton Reiser, contemplating a slaughtered calf hanging near the shop of the butcher with whom he boards, considers the merging of his identity with that of the dead animal:

> Er stand oft stundenlang und sahe (sic) so ein Kalb mit Kopf, Augen, Ohren, Mund und Nase an und lehnte sich, wie er es oft bei *fremden Menschen* machte, so dicht wie möglich an dasselbe an, oft mit dem törichten Wahn, ob es ihm vielleicht nicht möglich wurde, sich nach und nach in das Wesen eines solchen Tieres hineinzudenken — es lag ihm alles daran, den Unterschied zwischen sich und dem Tiere zu wissen —[4]

Like Anton Reiser, Euseb identifies with various animals and becomes preoccupied with discerning the difference between their identity and his own. In his fantasies, he is frightened and degraded by the sensation of identity with repulsive animals:

> Traum: eine plötzliche unaussprechliche Gleichheit der häßlichen und gräßlichen Tiere mit den Menschen (diesen Traum hofft er wegzuwälzen; in ihm sind die Tiere vergrößert, besonders die Würmer und Asseln) (SW, 29:185)

Euseb sees wood lice (Asseln) in the cemetery wall; Lerch saw them in the crumbling walls of the village. They are associated also with Ariadne and Sigismund, suggesting that the human observing them has been reduced to a lowly state.

Although Euseb shares the Magier's propensity to lose self-awareness in identification with other creatures, the animals chosen indicate that he has no part in the Magier's mystical union with the cosmos. While the Magier is compared to a mighty lion, Euseb becomes "klein wie die Wiesel, wie die Kröten, wie alles was da an der zitternden Erde raschelte und lauerte" (SW, 29:177; E, p. 251). The toad is

---

4 Karl Philipp Moritz, *Anton Reiser* (Berlin: Aufbau Verlag, 1973), p. 245.

regarded with suspicion as a creature of witches or the devil, also as "Symbol des Geizes und des Neides."[5] In fact, Euseb envies the wealthy city dwellers who command numerous servants, an envy he shares with Anton Lerch. The weasel's significance has been partially analyzed in discussing *Die Frau im Fenster*; its further connotations pertain to the pregnant servant girl Euseb pursues through the woods. The weasel has a reputation for "widernatürliche Lüsternheit," in Carinthia a pregnant woman is said to have been bitten, or elsewhere, breathed upon by a weasel. Because weasels and toads are seen disappearing into burrows in the earth, they are suspected of embodying the souls of unborn, aborted or unbaptized children.[6] Thus when Euseb identifies with weasel and toad, he places himself in the position of the servant girl's illegitimately conceived and unborn child, whose situation is like his own. "Er ist ein uneheliches Kind und kennt seinen Vater nicht" is one of Hofmannsthal's earliest notes, showing that this question was intended as the core of the story (SW, 29:167).

Euseb's father appears to him "als Räuber, Landstreicher, der ein Pferd losmachen will" (SW, 29:168; E, p. 153). In the poem "Vor Tag" a vagrant ("Landstreicher") awakes in a silent forest and throws a stone at a dove. He behaves like an animal, sleeping unwashed in a bed of leaves, and he throws the stone without reflecting on any motives for his action. Toward the end of the poem a barefoot man creeps from a woman's bed through a window into his own room. The last line of the poem, "Nun geht die Stalltür. Und nun ist auch Tag" introduces the stable and by association the horse into the series of glimpses of brutality, suffering, crime and adultery. The scenes in the poem picture a world like that of Euseb's father. He intends to turn a horse loose, or, in Hofmannsthal's symbolic language, to give his libidinous desires free rein: we recall the young lord removing his horse's bit and throwing it at the birds to satisfy his destructive urges. Since we earlier equated directing a horse's gait and path with determining one's fate, we may conclude that Euseb's father reveals in releasing the horse the lack of any conscious control

---

5   Ibid., vol. 5, cols. 608-9.
6   Ibid., vol. 9, cols. 581-83.

over his own existence or that of his son. The father's influence on his son's concept of identity is thus in this case entirely negative.

Euseb's inability to delineate his relationship to his father leaves him without any firm concept of self. Hofmannsthal's portrayal of this state is quite convincing. The reader learns nothing about Euseb's appearance or his speech. We never see the youth from an external point of view; the character exists only as an undefined creature capable of losing self-awareness in identification with vermin, toad, weasel or sparrow-hawk.

Other youths in Hofmannsthal's works, among them Andreas, Sigismund, and Wladimir in the story "Lucidor" demonstrate a similar tendency to identify with animals, a predeliction arising from their uncertain concepts of self. On the one hand these adolescents, in putting themselves in the place of animals, distance themselves from reality; they fail to relate to the external world through a defined self-image. On the other hand, paradoxically, the youth searches for the fine line bounding the self through torturing the animal with which he identifies, or through torturing himself, which he perceives as nearly the same process. This game may stem from the "Gier nach Eindrücken" attributed to Euseb; at the same time, however, the youth attempts, in becoming conscious of suffering, to determine to what point his own self extends and where that of another creature begins. Of Euseb Hofmannsthal writes:

> Er war der Schreckliche, der im Dunkel lauert und am Kreuzweg hervorspringt, und zugleich fühlte er alle Schauer, die von ihm ausgingen; an seinem eigenen Rücken herunterrieseln. (SW, 29:177; E., p. 251)

Euseb shares the inclination to produce sensation purely for its own sake with the child in "Age of Innocence" who also plays the double role of torturer and sacrifice:

> Er spielte und sah zu, fühlte die Schauer des Mordes und das Grauen des Opfers, weidete sich an seinen eigenen Qualen, brachte sich selbst Botschaft um sich selbst, weinte aus Rührung über seine eigene Stimme, verriet sich selbst Geheimnisse seines Innern und erweiterte die Scala seiner Empfindungen; sein eigenes reiches Reich. (SW, 39:18; P, 1:13)

Since Euseb has not yet ascertained the distinction between self and external world, he is incapable of distinguishing sadism from masochism; he derives similar sensations from tormenting the sparrow-hawk, himself, or the servant girl.[7]

Yet Euseb's crucifixion of the sparrow-hawk is more than an experiment with the production of sensation and emotion, more than an investigation of his own identity. He intends the crucifixion as an act of vengeance against the father who has created and then abandoned him:

> Er suchte den Vater — auch in Hammerschlägen auf die Nägel, die den Leib des Sperbers am Holz kreuzigten, suchte er den Vater — und fand sich. (SW, 29:178; E, p. 253)

We shall turn our attention first to the sparrow-hawk, then to the significance of animal sacrifice and its bearing on Euseb's relationship to his father.

Although the sparrow-hawk is named in Hofmannsthal's other works, its presence seems devoid of any symbolic significance. He mentions the bird's piercing cry in "Knabengeschichte," in an essay again its "seltsames Rufen" (P, 1:240), and in the "Märchen von der verschleierten Frau" its "heftiges Schreien" (SW, 29:144; E, p. 82). The bird is elsewhere characterized as swift (P, 1:31) and a fierce predator; Prince Eugene of Savoy has eyes like those of the sparrow-hawk (P, 3:294) and Sigismund warns the courtiers: "Ich will mit euch hausen wie der Sperber im Hühnerhof" (D, 4:125-26). Sometimes the bird is equated with the eagle; Josef Kainz's eye is praised as "Aug des Sperbers, der auch vor der Sonne/ Den Blick nicht niederschlägt" (GLD, p. 52; SW, 1:109). The eagle, but not the sparrow-hawk, is supposedly capable of gazing directly at the sun. A miner in

---

[7] Wolf Wucherpfennig analyzes evidence of Hofmannsthal's ambivalent relationship to his father in both "Age of Innocence" and "Knabengeschichte." He finds that the child (Hofmannsthal and the protagonist of "Age of Innocence"), confronted with the parental image of a "good" boy while he knows himself to be deeply flawed, reacts with aggression toward himself which he struggles to suppress. "Age of Innocence" details numerous fantasies of self punishment which lead to a splitting of the child's identity into torturer and victim. Euseb, on the other hand, attempts to assume the father's role as torturer and externalizes his aggression, directing it against the sparrow-hawk and the servant girl. See "Das junge Wien und seine Väter," pp. 166-67.

"Das Märchen von der verschleierten Frau" identifies with a circling sparrow-hawk as does Andreas with the eagle circling above the Finazzer valley.

Hofmannsthal's essay "Die Wege und die Begegnungen" begins with the return of a pair of young swallows to their home; the birds represent the mystery and power of sexual attraction, the instinct for mating and raising young. The crucified sparrow-hawk and his mate hovering frightened nearby also embody this erotic drive:

> der Sperber ... hört sein Weib in den wüthenden Lüften, ist selber schon halb im jenseits, meint er sei ein viel größerer Vogel, zu größerem Horst, zu größerer Wollust geboren. (SW, 29:173)

The pair of sparrow-hawks experience the same strong sexual tie as do the human couples in the story; their instinctive bond is as firm as the human moral bond of fidelity in love.

In Hofmannsthal's notes for "Knabengeschichte" the bird's special significance for Euseb becomes clear. Euseb equates the bird he wishes to torture with his father because of its habit of throwing its young out of the nest: "er sieht das von einer unfaßbaren Gewalt aus dem Mutterleib herausgeworfene (Association der aus dem Spernest geworfenen Jungen) – das töricht ins Sein herausgelaufene – nun angewiesen, sich des Daseins zu erwehren" (SW, 29:177). Euseb's unknown father has cast him carelessly into existence and left him exposed, devoid of any sheltering family. But from Euseb's point of view rejection of the young appears to begin immediately at birth. His story was to have been complemented by the narration of two births, one a legitimate but stillborn child born to the innkeeper's wife, the second, a child of the same father born illegitimately in the same night to the servant girl. This second birth Euseb feels is like "ein Herausfallen eines nackten aus einer Tür – das wars schon!" (SW, 29:184). Euseb's feeling of loneliness and anonymity would have comprised the main theme of "Knabengeschichte," paralleling the vulnerability of a newborn baby and driving him to retaliate symbolically against his unreachable father by crucifying the bird which casts its young out of the nest.

Whether Euseb was conscious of the significance of his choice of a mature male sparrow-hawk to represent his father, Hofmannsthal does not say, but he leaves no doubt that Euseb equates the two. The boy is horrified by the suffering of the bird he has nailed to a barn door, "Dennoch ergriff er nochmals den Hammer, um seinen Vater zu finden" (SW, 29:173). Perhaps the very explicitness of this equation forced Hofmannsthal to leave the story unfinished. The last sentence quoted was an insert into the manuscript, the other direct references are found in the notes. Works in which Hofmannsthal touched upon the father-son conflict remained fragments like the "Knabengeschichte" and *Andreas* or were later substantially revised, like *Der Turm*.

According to Hofmannsthal, the first human to sacrifice an animal was an individual who

> ... fühlte, daß die Götter ihn haßten: daß sie die Wellen des Gießbaches und das Geröll der Berge in seinen Acker schleuderten; daß sie mit der fürchterlichen Stille des Waldes sein Herz zerquetschen wollten; ... (P, 2:88)

Man's awareness that he is at the mercy of greater hostile powers (Euseb feels his father, the "Verächter seines Lebens" to be such a hostile power) gives the first impulse toward animal sacrifice. Returning for a moment to *Die Frau im Fenster,* we recall that Braccio's brother kicked the whippet from similar motives, striking out at a weaker creature because he felt constrained by the superior powers of social convention.

Before sacrificing any animal, the despairing human, overcome by the sense of his own helplessness, is prepared to take his own life. Suddenly he becomes aware of the presence of a familiar animal:

> ... auf einmal zuckte dem Tier das Messer in die Kehle, und das warme Blut rieselte zugleich an dem Vlies des Tieres und an der Brust, an den Armen des Menschen hinab: und einen Augenblick lang muß er geglaubt haben, es sei sein eigenes Blut; einen Augenblick lang ... muß er die Wollust gesteigerten Daseins für die erste Zuckung des Todes genommen haben: er muß, einen Augenblick lang, in dem Tier gestorben sein, nur so konnte das Tier für ihn sterben. (P, 2:88-89)

The phrase "Wollust gesteigerten Daseins" echoes in the "Übermaß der Freude" the young lord feels on his hunt. The same heightened sensation, or "Wollust" accompanies Andreas' dreamed recollection of a cat he maimed as a boy.

A comparison of the above passage to Freud's theory of the origin of animal sacrifice contributes to our understanding of the bird's crucifixion. Freud assumes that the original state of human society must have consisted of:

> ... ein gewalttätiger eifersüchtiger Vater, der alle Weibchen für sich behält und die heranwachsenden Söhne vertreibt. ... Eines Tages taten sich die ausgetriebenen Brüder zusammen, erschlugen und verzehrten den Vater und machten so der Vaterhorde ein Ende.[8]

According to Freud's theory, the brothers who had murdered their father joined in rites of commemoration to strengthen the bond among them. In these rites, they killed in the father's stead an animal consecrated to him and then devoured it. After the repentant sons elevated the slain father to the status of a god, the animal sacrifice as a commemoration of the original patricide evolved into a reverent offering to the deity. Freud detects in the mourning and repentance accompanying the patricide the origin of the Christian concept of original sin. Christ relieves his brothers of their common inherited guilt by dying as a voluntary sacrifice and atoning for the sin of patricide.

The hostile yet sorrowful attitude toward the father, and parallels to the life of Christ connect "Knabengeschichte" with Freud's explanation of animal sacrifice. It seems justifiable to assume that the bird's crucifixion springs chiefly from Euseb's initiative: "plötzlicher Schreck wie er erkennt, daß die Gemeinschaft der anderen ihm dabei nichts hilft, die anderen hängen nur so daneben herum wie aufgeblasene Därme, die der Wind bewegt, neben dem Kalb" (SW, 29: 169; E, p. 146). Yet Euseb acts not only out of a desire to create sensations such as brutality and sympathy; he carries out the crucifixion as a Christian sacrifice which, in his stead, purges the evil of his own nature:

> Zustand des Knaben Euseb: an das Gute der Welt nicht heran –, zu ihm nicht hinüberkommen zu können – will sich hinüberschwingen, – sich hin-

---

[8] *Gesammelte Werke*, vol. 9: *Totem und Tabu*, p. 171. Appeared 1912 in the periodical *Imago* under the title: "Einige Übereinstimmungen im Seelenleben der Wilden und der Neurotiker."

übertasten — auch der Mord an dem Sperber ist so eine folternde Ungeduld, hinüberzukommen in das Andere. (SW, 29:178; E, p. 253)

The bird's crucifixion discloses Euseb's attempt to attain the "Heiliges" which comes too close to him, and from which his father holds him back.

> Er suchte den Vater — auch in Hammerschlägen auf die Nägel, die den Leib des Sperbers am Holz kreuzigten, suchte er den Vater — und fand sich.
>
> So gekreuzigt war auch er durch den Vater, den Verächter seines Lebens.
>
> Predigt des Katecheten: der Vater habe die Verachtung kundgegeben für das von ihm hinterlassene Geschöpf. (SW, 29:178; E, p. 253)

This passage unequivocally expresses Euseb's hostility toward his father. The youth wishes to torture or crucify him, yet is unable to imagine his father as an inferior being. In his fantasy the youth is always the weaker power and accordingly is compelled to identify himself with the helpless bird. The fragmentary nature of the reference to the catechist does not admit its interpretation, though it is doubtless significant that Andreas, during the first night spent with the Finazzers, thinks of a gaze "den er als Knabe gefürchtet hatte wie keinen zweiten, der Blick seines ersten Katecheten" (E, p. 146; SW, 30:64). This allusion to Christian instruction opens a new perspective: the father who crucifies Euseb must signify God the father as well as the youth's natural parent. The creature whom God has abandoned and despised may be Adam (whose first sin, disobedience, represents rebellion against the father) or may be Christ, who lamented on the cross that his father had forsaken him.

If we now consider the pregnant servant girl, we find our allusion to the story of Christ measurably strengthened. From Euseb's fantasy of taking the shape of weasel and toad, we determined that he identifies with the girl's unborn child. In a letter written in 1907 to Florens Christian Rang, Hofmannsthal mentions a book by Johannes Schlaf entitled *Christus und Sophie*. Schlaf presents the thesis that Christ was an illegitimate child, born not in Bethlehem of the lineage of David and Abraham, but in Nazareth among mixed races. When Joseph learned that his bride, the Lord's handmaiden ("Magd"), was already carrying a child, he accused her of infidelity and wanted to abandon her. The manservant in Hofmannsthal's story is named Joseph, the servant girl is a stranger to the village, and as Joseph accuses her she supports herself on the rim of a well: the entire scene has Biblical overtones. We can draw parallels between the unborn child and Christ, between the child and Euseb, and finally, between Euseb and Christ crucified. Hofmannsthal's notes describe a midwife attending the birth of the innkeeper's illegitimate child. The sign of the midwife's trade shows "die Mutter mit dem vaterlosen Gotteskind" (SW, 29:182). The fatherless child also refers to Euseb who acknowledges God as his father and seeks him as a replacement for his natural father: 'Ich will zu dir dürfen' wen meint er? den himmlischen oder den irdischen Vater?" (SW, 29:183).

The actual details of the scene between Joseph and the pregnant servant girl were modeled on Robert Musil's *Verwirrungen des Zöglings Törless* which appeared in 1906.[9] Early in the book young Törleß, student at a military academy, accompanies a youth named Beineberg to a tavern located in the ground floor of an old bath house outside the town. From a nearby thicket the two observe a scene between Bozena, a country woman and servant now turned waitress and prostitute, and a drunken man. Bozena asks him for money; he refuses her and threatens her with a stone. Bozena, like the servant girl in Hofmannsthal's story, may be asking for money because of an illegitimate pregnancy, although this is not explicitly stated in the story. Beside their common atmosphere of a nocturnal prowl, both scenes are narrated from the point of view of the youths, Törleß and Euseb, who observe them from a distance with a mixture of fascination and fear.

The scene in "Knabengeschichte" forms the core of the problematical man-woman relationship, which, in Hofmannsthal's other

---

9   Hofmannsthal mentions Musil's book and its relevance to his own adolescence in "Ad me ipsum" (A, p. 244). There he makes the following comments about the period around 1895:
    "Das Lebendige, das Wahre in dem aufweisen was schweigt, z.B. Epoche der Freundschaft mit Poldy ('Kaufmannssohn' 'Garten der Erkenntnis;' vgl. hierzu das zwölf Jahre spätere Buch 'Verwirrungen des Zöglings Törleß')" (A, p. 224).
    Twelve years after 1895, the year 1907, may be the date Hofmannsthal read Musil's book.

works, is frequently represented through animal imagery. It will be useful to discuss certain aspects of that relationship at this time as a preface to their recurrence in the *Andreas* novel.

One symptom typical of the adolescent whose sexual urges are awakening is the avoidance of direct confrontation with a woman or of firsthand experience. We recall, for example, the failure of the merchant's son to establish direct contact with his servant girl. Euseb also shuns face to face confrontation, preferring instead to wait in the darkness for the appearance of the butcher's daughter, and to observe from a distance Joseph's argument with the servant girl. This tendency may be equated with the aesthete's habit of experiencing life through art, or preferring fantasy to the realization of his fantasies. It is typical of such a preference for indirect modes of experience that Euseb awaits the butcher's daughter not with the hope of speaking to her, but simply in the desire to glimpse the shadow of her breasts on the drawn curtain as she undresses, an erotic stimulus suggested not by his own urges, but by the gossip of an older boy.

The association of eroticism with butchery was found to be a common feature in "Reitergeschichte," *Die Frau im Fenster* and *Jupiter und Semele*. In "Knabengeschichte" the association of eroticism with violence is also suggested by imagery of butchery and the hunt. The butcher's daughter whom Euseb spies upon belongs to the animal sphere of blood and slaughter; he awaits her standing next to the freshly slaughtered calf. A butcher's daughter also figures among the memories of the narrator of the "Briefe des Zurückgekehrten." And an anecdote in Hofmannsthal's *Buch der Freunde* (to which he refers in the notes for "Knabengeschichte") explicitly connects eroticism and butchery:

> Der Fleischhauer in Kaschau ... der an seinem Hochzeitstag sich so fröhlich, so glücklich fühlt, daß er − bevor er zu seiner Frau hingeht − sich den stärksten Ochsen heranführen läßt und ihn kunstgerecht abschlägt, seinen Gefühlen Lauf zu lassen. (SW, 29:364; A, p. 22)

In Euseb's fantasy the imagery of butchery merges with that of the hunt as he becomes "der Metzger, der ein ihm entlaufenes Tier beschlich, um es zu Tode zu führen, das Tier aber war ein behextes Tier; es war dieses Weib da vor ihm" (SW, 29:177; E. 252). The woman Euseb hunts is the pregnant servant girl. Hofmannsthal has already alluded to her role as prey, for the servant accompanying Joseph is dressed as a hunter. Euseb senses "eine innige Übereinstimmung zwischen den Atemzügen des Windes und seiner wilden geheimen Jagd;" he feels that the lightning flashes "um ihm seine Beute immer zu zeigen, wenn sie im Dunkel entschlüpfen wollte" (SW, 29: 177; E, p. 252). Karl Groos, whose *Spiele der Thiere* belonged to Hofmannsthal, confirms this "enge Verknüpfung der Quälerei und der Rauflust mit sexuellen Regungen" as common to man and beast alike. The desire to fight and kill, he writes, is such a predominant attribute of the male sex, that an intimate connection between the same tendency and the sex drive is unquestionable.[10] Groos, however, offers no explanation for Hofmannsthal's view that the woman chooses voluntarily to assume the role of the hunter's prey; such self-destructive tendencies on the woman's part hardly seem to belong to common human experience. Nor is the alliance of sexual urges with violence entirely obvious. Perhaps the inexperienced youth, in this case, Euseb, envisages the sex act as a wounding of the woman; accordingly Joseph's "messerscharfe Worte" fill the youth with a sort of "grausamer Wollust."

In conclusion, we may point to animal imagery as the focus about which the three spheres of Euseb's development revolve. His state of mind is presented in terms of the animals inhabiting his environs; he imagines himself taking the shape of a weasel and toad. The lack of verbal communication isolates Euseb and condemns him to his father's bestial realm, dominated by the sign of the horse. The sparrow-hawk's crucifixion proved to be a ritual animal sacrifice, in which Euseb's desire to torment his father corresponded to Freud's explanation of animal sacrifice as originating from the commemoration of the first patricide. The youth's identification with a butcher pursuing an animal, the servant-girl, revealed the connection between eroticism and brutality, a connection to be further developed in the *Andreas* novel.

---

10   Karl Groos, *Die Spiele der Thiere*, pp. 130-31.

CHAPTER IX

ANDREAS ODER DIE VEREINIGTEN

In discussing "Ein Traum von großer Magie," "Das Märchen der 672. Nacht" and "Reitergeschichte" we observed Hofmannsthal's use of animal symbolism to give indirect poetic expression to certain of his own experiences: the struggle for mastery of his horse had bearing on the composition of the poem; the financial worries brought on by the expense of caring for his mare in Göding forced him to recognize the inadequacy of wealth as a means of ensuring an aesthetic existence like that of the merchant's son; the struggle to overcome or transcend the ugliness of his surroundings during military service is reflected in the threatening appearance of the degenerate dogs in "Reitergeschichte." Autobiographical reminiscences are once again apparent in the portrayal of Andreas von Ferschengelder, the twenty-two or three year old hero of the novel which Hofmannsthal sketched at between 1907 and 1927.[1] Several critics have noted that the parallels between Hofmannsthal and Andreas surpass the frequent resemblance between an author and his protagonist. Herman Broch maintains that Hofmannsthal's "Ichverschweigung," his reluctance to reveal any more about himself, forced him to give up the story of Andreas through which he had already divulged so much.[2] In the same vein, Karl Gautschi contends that the confessional nature of the material prevented the work's completion.[3] Ursula Renner-Henke concurs, conjecturing that the tension between "gestalteten oder angedeuteten seelischen Tiefenschichten und deren Verschweigung oder

---

1 Particulars of the novel's composition are given by the editor of the critical edition, Manfred Pape, SW, 30:303-311. Because the definitive text is that of the new edition, it will be cited first in this chapter with subsequent reference to *Erzählungen* in the Steiner edition, if the quotation appears there as well.
2 *Hofmannsthal und seine Zeit*, pp. 172-73.
3 "Hofmannsthals Romanfragment 'Andreas'," p. 93.

Mystifizierung" constitutes the novel's chief attraction, while probably causing it to remain a torso.[4]

The strongly autobiographical nature of the work is further confirmed by the striking importance of animal imagery, which appears, as in the early works mentioned above, in connection with those events which bear a direct resemblance to actual crises in the author's life; we have, for example, already noted the similarity between Hofmannsthal's feelings of helplessness when confronted by his horse's infirmities and Andreas' reaction to the brown horse which goes lame.

On the basis of the understanding of animal symbols gained in previous chapters, we shall now attempt a coherent interpretation of their function in the novel, focussing on the Carinthian episode, where the animal symbols are most significant.

In light of the autobiographical nature of the novel, it is enlightening to note that the entire Carinthian flashback constitutes a repressed experience. Just as the animals in "Ein Traum von großer Magie" were forced into a secondary position instead of opening the poem, the journey through Carinthia appears not at the very beginning of the novel, but after the reader's introduction to Andreas in Venice. The episode is prefaced by the remark that Andreas is compelled to think back on it daily, whether he wants to or not (SW, 30: 46; E, p. 122).

On its simplest level, the animal imagery serves Hofmannsthal as a means of characterization, comparing one figure in the novel to some animal, a technique we shall now begin to examine.

The comparison of Gotthelf to various animals characterizes him as belonging wholly to their realm. Andreas finds him "widerlich wie eine Spinne" (SW, 30:51; E, p. 128). The attribute "repulsive" evokes the deadly spider of "Der Jüngling und die Spinne" and the belief that the spider is poisonous and a creature of the devil.[5]

---

4 " '... daß auf einem gesunden Selbstgefühl das ganze Dasein ruht ...'. Opposition gegen die Vaterwelt und Suche nach dem wahren Selbst in Hofmannsthals *Andreas*-Fragment," *Hofmannsthal-Forschungen* 8 (1985): 238.
5 *Handwörterbuch des deutschen Aberglaubens*, vol. 8, cols. 266-67; 274. Compare also the spider as the poisonous creature of the devil in Jeremias Gotthelf's "Die schwarze Spinne."

Furthermore the spider is said to possess an affinity for money, and its appearance often foretells sudden acquisition of wealth, associations reminiscent of Gotthelf's uncanny power for divining where Andreas' money is hidden.

When treating *Die Frau im Fenster* we observed that the spider running across Dianora's hand may signify her affair with Messer Palla. Since Hofmannsthal was familiar with Bachofen's interpretation of weaving as an erotic symbol, it seems likely that he extends this association to the spider as well.[6] Hofmannsthal noted in his copy of Morton Prince's *Dissociations of a Personality* (a psychoanalytical work used as a source for the portrayal of Maria-Mariquita): "Sally [the prototype of Mariquita] ... macht BI [the model for Maria] Tausendfüßler und Spinnen sehen (B I weiß, es sind Halluzinationen, fürchtet sich aber davor.)" (SW, 30:21). This note confirms our supposition, made in connection with Dianora, that Hofmannsthal connects the spider with non-binding sexual relationships. Maria and Mariquita differ radically in their attitudes toward love and physical intimacy; Maria is tormented by any allusion to sex, as she is by the visions of spiders and centipedes which Mariquita, the embodiment of her sexual being, has the power to call forth in her. The note also illuminates a possible link between Mariquita, who causes the apparition of spiders and Gotthelf, who is compared to one precisely at the moment when he arouses Andreas' fantasy with tales of his lascivious adventures. Mariquita and Gotthelf share such traits as strong erotic desire and a disregard for moral authority. (Their lifestyles are, to be sure, quite different; Mariquita's carefree promiscuity can not be equated with Gotthelf's criminality.) We may conclude that Gotthelf and Mariquita, like Dianora, are connected with the spider because of the strong sexual urges all three have in common. The spider-like Gotthelf is therefore particularly repugnant to Andreas, whose only fleeting acquaintance with sex has been unpleasant and frightening.

In a second animal simile, Gotthelf is characterized as greedily licking his "feuchten dicken Lippen wie eine Katze" (SW, 30:48; E, p. 123). The cat's stealthy gait, luminous eyes, and its fur suscep-

---

6 Hugo Wyss, *Die Frau in der Dichtung Hofmannsthals*, p. 18.

tible to static electricity have long made it the object of popular superstition.⁷ Its portrayal in literature bears out the suspicion with which man regards the cat. The cat's wariness and ferocity when cornered have caused many writers to depict it as sinister: the cat which claws Mahlke's Adam's apple in Günter Grass's *Katz und Maus* comes immediately to mind. Gottfried Keller in *Der grüne Heinrich* describes his young protagonist's terror when attacked by a cat in the attic room where he has been playing with wax figures in human form.⁸ Hofmannsthal stresses these combative strengths when describing Elektra as "giftig/ wie eine wilde Katze" (D, 2:9) and as hissing cat-like at the servants who come too near her (D, 2:10).

The cat has long been associated with evil supernatural forces and witches. In Theodore Storm's *Schimmelreiter* the relationship between the old woman, Trina Jans, and the angora cat left by her drowned son suggests something of the attachment a witch and her familiar. In Hofmannsthal's work the cat's association with evil forces is only hinted at in the strength and cunning attributed to the animal. When the merchant's wife in "Der goldene Apfel" discovers that her daughter has lost that treasure, the child stands behind her in the semi-darkness (the realm of evil)⁹ "lauernd wie eine Katze und über die feinen Züge einen eigentümlich lügenhaften Ausdruck gebreitet" (E, p. 44; SW 29:105). Elis in the mine at Falun mistakes Agmahd for Anna and marvels at her furtiveness:

> Wie immer dus erklärst, ob dus dem Vater
> Hast abgeschmeichelt, ob dich heimlich her-
> Gestohlen wie ein kleines Kätzchen, nichts
> Ist so, wie daß du da bist, wundervoll! (GLD, p. 427)

It is this dishonest stealth that Hofmannsthal attributes to Gotthelf in the cat simile. Gotthelf pretends that his desire to serve Andreas stems from the longing for a master-servant relationship based on mutual trust rather than on corporal punishment, which was used

---

7 *Handwörterbuch des deutschen Aberglaubens*, vol. 4, col. 1123.
8 See the tenth chapter of the first volume of *Der grüne Heinrich*, „Das spielende Kind."
9 Miles has stressed the half-light or darkness surrounding Gotthelf as symbolic of his evil power, *Hofmannsthal's Novel Andreas*, pp. 159-60.

to enforce discipline among the royal troops, where he served previously. The greedy cat-like licking of his moist lip, once its connotations are understood, arouses the reader's suspicion that he prefers such a relationship to an authoritarian one merely because it allows free play for his treachery. The old adage that a dog would save his master nine times while a cat would destroy him as willingly attests to the cat's reputation for treachery.[10]

In addition, the cat image suggests Gotthelf's lasciviousness, for Hofmannsthal repeatedly associates the cat with sexual infatuation. In *Der Bürger als Edelmann* Jourdain sings a ditty comparing an imaginary mistress to a cat, at once tame as a kitten and ferocious as a tiger (L, 3:76).[11] Theodor in *Silvia im "Stern"* accuses the Baron of being "verliebt wie ein hagerer Kater" in Silvia (L, 2:27), and the mulatto in *Der weiße Fächer* confesses that she too was once "verliebt wie eine Katze" (GLD, p. 249; SW, 3:122). The heroine of *Die Hochzeit der Sobeide* leaves her new husband to return to her lover. A thief stops her, claiming to serve her lover's father, and explains:

> ...er hat mir aufgetragen,
> sooft sich eine solche Katze durchschleicht,
> zu überprüfen, ob sie für ihn paßt:
> die schlechtern läßt er nämlich dem Herrn Sohn.
> (D, 1:435)

---

10 *Handwörterbuch des deutschen Aberglaubens*, vol. 4, col. 1117.
11 Molière's Jordain sings:
"Je croyais Jeanneton
Plus douce qu'un mouton.
Hélas! hélas! elle est cent fois,
Mille fois plus cruelle
Que n'est le tigre aux bois."
(Oeuvres Complètes 2 [Paris: Librairie Gallimard, 1956]: 518.) Hofmannsthal omits the comparison to a sheep:
"Ich glaubete, mein Schätzchen
Ist zahmer als ein Kätzchen;
Doch ist sie wilder hundertmal,
Ja, wilder ist sie tausendmal
Als Tiger, die im Walde gehn" (L, 3:76).
Here the cat image emphasizes the tension between docility and ferocity in the woman's nature while alluding more clearly to her sexual attraction.

The thief knows, though Sobeide does not, that her lover and his father keep several women in their house: he assumes Sobeide to be of the same loose moral character as these, and in comparing her to a cat, places her on the same level as the other sexual playthings.

Hofmannsthal's association of the cat with sexual infatuation is consistent with both the popular view of this animal and with its function in literary imagery. In *Kater Murr*, E. T. A. Hoffmann makes much of the cat's renowned sexual appetite, even allowing his feline hero, Murr, to become infatuated with his own daughter. Another cat tells Murr: "überall ist schnöder Wankelmut zu Hause und leider vorzüglich bei unserm Geschlecht."[12] This statement of the cat's fickleness and infidelity is borne out by the plot of the story. Thomas Mann alludes to the same popular image of the cat when naming the Slavic seductress of *Der Zauberberg* Clawdia Chauchat. D. H. Lawrence describes the meeting between a stray female and a tomcat in *Woman in Love* and uses the scene to expound his views of human sexual relationships. He considers the female alone promiscuous, "a mere stray, a fluffy sporadic bit of chaos," and finds it the tomcat's function "to bring this female cat into a pure stable equilibrium, a transcendent and abiding *rapport* with the single male."[13]

The cat's agility enables it to climb to considerable heights to reach a lover. Theodor ("der Unbestechliche") makes a sign to Hermine "er werde wie ein Kater geklettert kommen" (L, 4:403). This ability may become indicative of the strength of passion in those compared to cats. Andreas realizes what Mariquita undertook to reach him in the grape arbor:

> Sie hatte, um einen unauslöschlichen Eindruck auf ihn zu machen, auf eine unbegreifliche Weise den Weg gefunden: eine hohe Mauer, unter der vielleicht das Wasser dahinfloß, hatte sie nicht abgehalten: das zu machen, was außer einer Katze jedem Geschöpf versagt schien, ... (SW, 30:92-93; E, p. 185)

---

12 E.T.A. Hoffmann, *Poetische Werke*, vol. 9: *Lebensansichten des Katers Murr* (Berlin: de Gruyter, 1960), p. 199.
13 Lawrence, *Women in Love*, p. 142.

In the comparison of Mariquita to a cat, Hofmannsthal emphasizes first her climbing ability, but secondarily the strength of the desire whose fulfillment is her goal. The shared cat image again implies that Mariquita and Gotthelf have certain traits in common: strong sexual urges and a penchant for deviousness in the clever gratification of their desires.

Although superior to the dog in cunning and stealth, the cat appears to be its counterpart as a symbol of latent or active sexual desire. Hofmannsthal sketches King Kandaules' entrance into his wife's bedchamber:

> Rhodope steht nicht auf, weil auf ihrer Schleppe eine Katze schläft. Sie ist fortwährend angstvoll, sich zu verschulden, und wäre es gegen die Dämonen, die in der leeren Luft fliegen. Sie nennt die Tiere die wortlosen Heiligen.(D, 2:516)

In another note for the same unfinished play Hofmannsthal writes:

> Im Gemach der Königin. Die Königin regungslos, weil ein Hund auf der Schleppe ihres Gewandes eingeschlafen liegt. (D, 2:516)

The substitution of the sleeping dog for the cat suggests their equivalence as images of Rhodope's latent eroticism. It is further proof of their interchangeability that wordlessness, elsewhere an attribute of the dog-symbol, is here also mentioned in close proximity to the cat.

From these examples, we may derive those qualities evoked in the cat image as cleverness and agility but with an emphasis on their negative aspects, cunning and stealth, qualities characteristic of Mariquita as well as Gotthelf. The similarity of cat and dog as symbols of concupiscence representative of both figures will be further discussed when we examine the dog imagery in the novel.

The same attributes of cunning and illicit or excessive sexual desire implied in the cat image are evoked again by the comparison of Gotthelf to a fox; his face reddens "vor wilder frecher Lust wie ein Fuchs in der Rage" (SW, 30:51; E, p. 128). Superstition has it that the fox's red fur signifies falseness, and fables from Aesop to Goethe's *Reineke Fuchs* attest to his cunning. He is associated with witches and is supposed to give off an unpleasant odor.[14] Hofmanns-

---

14 *Handwörterbuch des deutschen Aberglaubens*, vol. 3, cols. 174f.

thal emphasizes particularly the fox's connection with lust or illicit sex. He writes that Baron Ochs von Lerchenau's aria in the souper-scene of the *Rosenkavalier* should be imagined "buffonesk gesungen" "von einem fetten lüsternen Gesicht, halb Fuchs halb Schwein."[15] The fox's cleverness enables him to gratify his desires through trickery; accordingly Gotthelf describes a countess enamored of his former master and adept at securing her pleasure as "verliebt ... wie eine Füchsin" (SW, 30:50; E, p. 127).

It is proof of the dominant role allotted to animal imagery in the novel that not only Gotthelf and Mariquita, who frequently succumb to their animal urges, but Sacramozo as well, representative of the spiritual world, is characterized through the use of animal symbolism. Hofmannsthal describes the knight of the Maltese cross in the following manner:

> Der Kopf war bei weitem zu klein für die Gestalt und die gelbliche, etwas leidende Miene so seltsam verzogen, daß Andreas der ungereimte Gedanke an das vertrocknete Gesicht einer toten Kröte durch den Sinn fuhr. (SW, 30:83; E, p. 172)

The actual source of the image is Philippe Monnier's *Vénise au XVIIIe Siècle*, whose importance for Hofmannsthal's novel has been documented by Richard Alewyn.[16] There Monnier describes the eighteenth century author, Gasparo Gozzi, as follows:

> Os et longueur; si sec qu'en taillant sa carcasse en morceaux, on en ferait des bouchons pour les bouteilles; ressemblant, s'il faut l'en croire, à un crapaud enfilé au soleil sur un baton ....[17]

Even after identifying the source of the toad image, there remains the question of its significance. Chapple explains this rather repellent metaphor by stating that Sacramozo

> ... is a knight of the mind, and the physical world, "the completely non-metaphysical" (Erz 215), is abhorrent to him. Only later in the novel does the full implication of the "dead toad" come to light: by stifling the physi-

---

15 Hugo von Hofmannsthal and Harry Graf Kessler, *Briefwechsel*, ed. Hilde Burger (Frankfurt: Insel, 1968), p. 226.
16 *Über Hugo von Hofmannsthal*, pp. 136-36.
17 (Paris: Perrin, 1970), p. 117.

cal side of his nature, Sacramozo is unable to appeal to that side of Maria symbolized by the sensuality of Mariquita.[18]

Yet rather than stressing the dominance of his spiritual and intellectual powers in Sacramozo's nature, as Chapple maintains, Hofmannsthal seems to underscore in the toad image the base, repulsively physical aspects of the living creature. Elsewhere the toad is likened to the worm as the lowest of living things: Sigismund laments that he considers "Wurm und Kröte meinesgleichen!" (D, 3:383). In keeping with its base earthy nature, the toad is often equated with the most condemnable of human traits, such as dishonesty. When Creon's boyservant tells his master that he has dreamt of Creon as king, the latter grows pale, and the boy asks why. Creon replies: "Vor Ekel über dich/ schmeichelnde Kröte, lügnerische" (D, 2:334; SW, 8:57). Lorenzo in *Der Abenteurer und die Sängerin* asks Vittoria how they can continue their life together:

> ... wenn in deinem Reden, deinem Schweigen
> so wie in einem Nest und einem Abgrund,
> wie Kröten, Lüge neben Lüge wohnt. (D, 1:231)

The toad repels Hofmannsthal not only because of its association with dishonesty, but because it is supposedly capable of secreting poison.[19] The dyer's wife in "Die Frau ohne Schatten" complains of the empress to the nurse, "Stumm hockt sie dort, die Kröte, und schwitzt ihr Gift aus" (E, p. 325; SW, 28:159). Yet at the same time the toad is valuable for its supposed possession of magic forces. The witches whose incantation opens the fourth act of *Macbeth* use a toad for their evil charm:

> Toad, that under cold stone
> Days and nights has thirty-one
> Swelter'd venom sleeping got,
> Boil thou first i' the charmed pot.[20]

In *Bergwerk zu Falun* Elis ascribes to the toad knowledge of the innermost secrets of the earth, its own element:

18 "Themes and Symbols in Hofmannsthal's *Andreas*," p. 18.
19 *Handwörterbuch des deutschen Aberglaubens*, vol. 5, col. 608.
20 *Macbeth* 4.1.6-9.

> ... Seht die Unke,
> Das tagblinde verborgene Geschöpf,
> Ist strahlend gegen unser Finsternis
> Und winkt mir mit bediademtem Haupt:
> Denn ihr ist noch Gemeinschaft mit der Erde!
> (GLD, p. 343)

The words "Mit bediademtem Haupt" allude to the superstition that certain toads bear in their heads a precious stone. This stone, when extracted by man, was said to protect the bearer from disease, misfortune, enchantment, and poison.[21] Shakespeare refers to the same belief in *As You Like It:*

> Sweet are the uses of adversity,
> Which, like the toad, ugly and venomous,
> Wears yet a precious jewel in his head; ...[22]

If we attempt then to define the toad's symbolic qualities, we may conclude that its ugly exterior conceals magical and valuable attributes; its appearance does not coincide with its essence, but rather opposes it. Fairy tales in which a handsome prince has been transformed into a hideous frog or toad (the two are sometimes interchangeable) play upon the same fundamental opposition between appearance and reality.

It is fully in keeping with Sacramozo's role in the novel that his physical being should embody this dichotomy, for it is under his tutelage that Andreas learns to distinguish appearance from reality: "Andreas hat vom Malteser zu lernen: das Erkennen des Wesenhaften" (SW, 30:113; E, p. 216). Until his meeting with Sacramozo, Andreas has been gravely led astray by appearances. He was motivated to buy the brown horse and to accept Gotthelf's services by the false emphasis he placed on appearing in Venice as a gentleman. The undue importance attached to outward show is identified as a Viennese trait: "Im Wien kommt es jedem darauf an, etwas vorzustellen" (SW, 30:113; E, p. 216). The contrast between Sacramozo's toad-like appearance and his noble nature is only one of the many examples of this opposition between appearance and reality pre-

---

21 *Handwörterbuch des deutschen Aberglaubens*, vol. 5, cols. 631-33.
22 *As You Like It* 2.1.12-14.

sented in the novel; the animal images used for characterization serve to depict reality.

In general, the animal images used for characterization of figures in the Venetian episode are rarer and more limited in scope than those of the Carinthian episode. Besides the identification of Sacramozo with a toad, Zustina and her brothers are briefly compared to a squirrel. "Etwas in ihr (Zustina) ließ an ein Eichhörnchen denken, doch war sie eine resolute brave kleine Frau" (SW, 30:79; E, p. 166). Her twin brothers glance at each other "mit flinken Eichhörnchenaugen" (SW, 30:43; E, p. 117). The image communicates their quick furtive movements, and in Zustina's case, her efficient housewifery; as the squirrel is often observed storing nuts against the coming winter, so Zustina seems to take charge of providing for the welfare of her family. Nora in Ibsen's *Doll's House* is also compared to a squirrel; Hofmannsthal describes Eleanora Duse as playing her role, "das Eichkätzchen und die Lerche" (P, 1:69). Nora, like Zustina, is troubled by her financial worries, and forced into deviousness; she combines something of the squirrel's anxiety about providing for the future with the animal's quick, darting movements, which may be construed as furtiveness. Curiously enough, the Finazzer's coat of arms shows a squirrel holding a crown (SW, 30:56; E, p. 135). However, the squirrel appears to seldom in Hofmannsthal's imagery that it is impossible to draw valid conclusions about its significance here.[23]

The application of one animal image to two figures in the novel may imply either a correspondence between them, as in the spider and cat images common to both Mariquita and Gotthelf, or a contrast, as in the association of both Gotthelf and Romana with goats.

During the noonday meal at the Finazzer estate, Gotthelf behaves "frech ... wie der Bock im jungen Kraut" (SW, 30:54; E, p.

---

23 In popular superstition the squirrel, because of its reddish fur and hasty movements, may be regarded as a personification of lightning, and consequently is sometimes hunted and sacrificed to ward off lightning storms. Its meat is sought after for home remedies, and is believed particularly effective in preventing dizziness; as the squirrel is a good climber and unafraid of heights, its meat is thought to give men the same properties (*Handwörterbuch des deutschen Aberglaubens,* vol. 2, col. 655).

132). Ancient peoples regarded the goat as a harbinger of storms and linked him with the fertility brought on by the rain.[24] Hofmannsthal alludes to antiquity's connection of the goat in the mythological figure of satyr or faun with lasciviousness when describing Andreas' identification with "Onkel Leopold, der wie ein Faun im Wald sprang, einer Bauerndirn nach" (SW, 30:71; E, p. 155). Through the god Pan, who had the legs and horns of a goat, the animal became suggestive of chaos and disorder signified by such words as "panic" and "pandemonium" deriving from his name. With the introduction of Christianity, the exaggerated lewdness attributed to the male goat was condemned as an attribute of the devil.

Gerhart Hauptmann chose the conflict between pagan and Christian attitudes toward sexuality as a central theme of *Der Ketzer von Soana* and embodied these contrasts in the goat symbol. On the one hand, the herd of goats sustaining the novella's protagonists contributes to an idyllic vision of a paradisiacal communion with nature. On the other hand, the fight between two rival male goats as described by the heretic of the book's title becomes symbolic of the destruction inherent in the struggle for sexual dominance. Hauptmann concludes with a glorification of the procreative and creative powers symbolized in the goats:

> Jupiter Ammon wurde mit Widdershörnern dargestellt. Pan hat Bocksbeine, Bacchus Stierhörner. Ich meine den Bacchus Tauriformis oder Tauricornis der Römer. Mithra, der Sonnengott, wird als Stier dargestellt. Alle Völker verehren den Stier, den Bock, den Widder und vergießen im Opfer sein heiliges Blut. Dazu sage ich: ja! — Denn die zeugende Macht ist die schaffende Macht, Zeugen und Schaffen ist das gleiche![25]

Romana's identification with the goats is concerned with the opposite pole of the image. Since the goat was domesticated early in human history and provided its keepers with milk, meat and clothing, it was venerated as a symbol of female fecundity and docility. The description of Romana among the herd of goats calls forth bucolic scenes of innocence and peace, like the ancient patriarchal

---

24 Ibid., vol. 9, cols. 898f.
25 In Hauptmann's *Sämtliche Werke,* ed. Hans-Egon Hass, vol. 6: *Erzählungen; Theoretische Prosa* (Berlin: Propyläen Verlag, 1963), p. 92.

life among sheep and goat herds evoked in Hofmannsthal's "Augenblicke in Griechenland." She regards each of the animals as a distinct personality:

> Sie zeigte Andreas die bösartigste und die gutherzigste, die langhaarigste und die am meisten Milch gab, die Geißen kannten auch sie und kamen willig zu ihr. (SW, 30:56; E, p. 135)

Romana's anthropomorphic tendency to regard the goats as individuals and raise them toward the human level stands in sharp contrast to Gotthelf's habit of relegating humans to the animal niveau through such comparisons as that of the Pormberg countess to a vixen.

As Romana shows Andreas the goats, she lies down on the ground and immediately one of them stands over her to let her drink its milk. Later she lies down to try out the length of the bed where Andreas will sleep and draws him down to kiss her: "So fröhlich und arglos lag sie unter ihm, wie sie sich auch unter die Geiß hingestreckt hatte" (SW, 30:59; E, p. 139). She confronts both the animals and Andreas with the same unquestioning trust. Her supine position beneath Andreas hints at the physical intimacy which may later develop between them. It is significant that this prefiguration of a possible later union takes place in a room sanctified by strong familial associations; Romana tells Andreas that her grandmother gave birth in this very bed.

In its alliance with both Gotthelf and Romana the goat is laden wih implications of sexuality. As it corresponds to Gotthelf, the goat embodies the male power, at once destructive, chaotic and procreative. As it relates to Romana, by contrast, the goat represents the fertile nurturing female life force which draws the sexual relationship into familial order. The goat image stands then at the confluence of these extremes, embodying the two contrasting possibilities open to Andreas in the fulfillment of his desire. Similarly in Hofmannsthal's essay "Griechenland" he describes two goats on a cliff:

> Ihr Klettern, ihr Kopfheben, dies alles ist wirklich und zugleich wie vom geistreichsten Zeichner gezeichnet. Zu ihrem Animalischen haben diese Geschöpfe etwas Göttliches hinzu, aus der Luft: ... (P, 4:154-55).

The goats symbolize animal and human sexual desire, yet incorporate at the same time the sacred power of procreation.

Far more complex than the comparison between an animal and a figure in the novel which Hofmannsthal utilizes for the purpose of characterization are the symbolic interrelationships between man and beast: horseback riding, animal torture and hunting. Each of these man-animal relationships is used to elucidate some vital facet of Andreas' developing personality or of his interaction with his surroundings or with other people important in his life. Each constitutes a repeated motif echoed throughout the novel and expanded to include several people and animals: the imagery connected with horses and riding provides insight into both Andreas and Gotthelf; the motif of animal suffering encompasses the Finazzer dog Gotthelf poisons, and the dog and cat Andreas killed as a boy; the hunt metaphor Gotthelf chooses to describe his amorous adventures exercises a telling influence on Andreas' erotic fantasies and on his second dream of Romana. An investigation of these recurring animal images will lead us into a discussion of the most significant events of Andreas' *Bildungsreise*.

David Miles has identified Gotthelf as a major force shaping the plot of the novel, and Gotthelf, through a chain of circumstances, does indeed bring Andreas to Romana.[26] Probing deeper, we perceive that the brown horse plays an equally decisive role in determining the course of events: the sojourn at the Finazzer estate is necessitated by its lameness. As Andreas learns later, the horse was stolen from Finazzer and his return to the estate seems more fate than coincidence. Just as the uncertainty in his horse's stride first drew Lerch's attention to Vuic, so the disabled gait of the brown horse leads to a comparable erotic encounter between Gotthelf and the stable girl, and, less directly, to the meeting of Andreas and Romana.

Without pursuing the association of the horse with sexual relationships (a connection familiar to us through the examination of the "Reitergeschichte" and *Die Frau im Fenster*) to its logical conclusion, Miles nonetheless quite correctly assesses the import of the horse symbol:

26 *Hofmannsthal's Novel Andreas,* p. 128.

> The imagery of the horse and stable ... connects throughout the flashback with the forbidden realms of sex, guilt, and erotic desire—realms most generally associated with Gotthelf.[27]

The horse symbol may be profitably divided into two categories for further study: the act of riding horseback and the realm of the stable.

As has already been noted, the tension between horse and rider often represents that between the rider's desires and his conscience. Thus the youth in "Die Beiden" evinces perfect self-control in the compelling gesture with which he reins in his spirited young horse, a control so shattered by his sudden passion for the girl, that his hands shake when he reaches for the goblet of wine. Lerch's brown horse instinctively shies away from the bleeding rats, the shabbily clad woman and the cow being dragged to her death, but Lerch, whose ambitions dictate that he win a substantial sum of money in the desolate village, overcomes the resistance of his horse and his own desire for escape.

In much the same manner the interplay of horse and rider in the novel reveals the inner conflict between the rider's urges and his will. While bragging of his amorous exploits with a Carinthian innkeeper's wife, Gotthelf

> ... trieb ... sein Pferdchen an und ritt ganz dicht an Andreas, daß der ihn mahnen mußte, er solle achthaben, nicht aufzureiten, sein Fuchs vertrüge das nicht. (SW, 30:50; E, pp. 126-27)

He gives his erotic fantasies, symbolically embodied in the horse, free rein and approaches Andreas as if his physical proximity would extend his influence to encompass the youth. Andreas condemns this behavior, but only momentarily; soon Gotthelf rides beside his master "anstatt dahinter, aber Andreas achtete es nicht" (SW, 30:51; E, p. 128). Andreas succumbs to the suggestive power of his servant and is soon lost in daydreams of an affair with a countess. At the climax of his imaginary adventures he becomes aware that he has reined his horse in sharply (SW, 30:52; E, p. 129). The awakening of his moral censor, the realization that he has permitted his imagina-

---

27 Ibid., p. 163.

tion to carry him too far, is transformed through his movement into action.

Hofmannsthal's use of horseback riding to symbolize the tension between man's desires and his conscience offers a striking parallel to an analogy drawn by Freud and cited earlier in connection with *Das kleine Welttheater:*

> Man könnte das Verhältnis des Ichs zum Es mit dem des Reiters zu seinem Pferd vergleichen. Das Pferd gibt die Energie für die Lokomotion her, der Reiter hat das Vorrecht, das Ziel zu bestimmen, die Bewegung des starken Tieres zu lenken.[28]

Applying Freud's analogy to Gotthelf and Andreas, we note that they both temporarily submit to their libidinous urges, a submission symbolized in the quickened tempo of their ride. However, while Gotthelf deliberately urges his horse on, or implicitly, indulges his desires, Andreas seeks to suppress his carnal fantasies and signifies that he wishes to do so by reining in his horse sharply.

Returning to our contention that the brown horse becomes a significant force behind the plot of the novel, we remark that, because Gotthelf is following Andreas too closely, the brown horse stumbles as a result of Andreas' sudden reining in of his horse. When the brown horse goes lame soon after they set out the next morning, Gotthelf lays the blame on Andreas' thoughtless deed and criticizes his horsemanship. Considering that the brown horse goes lame as an indirect result of Andreas' attempt to suppress his erotic fantasies, and that its injury, necessitating the postponement of the journey, draws Andreas to Romana, the first encounter of the young lovers derives, albeit rather circuitously, from Andreas' lack of conscious control over his sexual urges. This chain of events casts a threatening shadow over Andreas' love for Romana and hints that the inner conflict between his desires and his conscious will menaces its fulfillment.

At the Finazzer estate, the dusky carnal atmosphere surrounding Gotthelf centers in the stable, now the scene of his illicit sexual encounters with the stable girl. Andreas finds the pair brewing a medicament "which can make a sick horse well and a healthy dog ill"

---

28 *Gesammelte Werke,* vol. 15, p. 83.

(SW, 30:58; E, p. 138). Gotthelf's position, more on top of the girl than next to her, is heavily suggestive of the physical intimacy developing between them. He has chosen the partner appropriate to his own animal nature; the horse blanket in which the stable girl is wrapped after the disastrous fire proves her link with the animal realm of the stable. She facetiously dubs Gotthelf "Herr Wachtmeister," perhaps underscoring his association with horses or referring to his past service in the royal troops.

Andreas experiences in the stable his first confrontation with illicit sex and behaves in the unsure hesitant manner appropriate to his innocence. When he and Romana enter the stable to look at the brown horse, Andreas seems repelled by his recognition of the developing physical intimacy between Gotthelf and the stable girl and unsuccessfully attempts to enforce his authority over the servant by repeating the order to carry his baggage to his room. Later that same evening Andreas nearly stumbles over Gotthelf who appears hurriedly in the half light of the stable mouthing praises of the clever stable girl who is supposedly helping him to cure his horse. He launches into an exposition of the free mores current among Carinthian women, implying that Andreas should try Romana's virtue. Enraged at his servant's presumption, Andreas feels a violent desire to strike Gotthelf. But his surge of fury is overcome by a vision of Romana awaiting him in bed, a vision conjured up by Gotthelf's lewd boasts and indicative that Andreas has succumbed for the second time to the suggestive eroticism of his servant.

The function of the stable as scene of an erotic encounter is not unique to Hofmannsthal's novel. The personification of a carnal animal stable atmosphere in the figure of a *Stallmeister* carries connotations of sexual adventure in Goethe's *Wanderjahre,* where the impulsive Felix sends Hersilie the message: "Felix liebt Hersilien. Der Stallmeister kommt bald." Hersilie replies: "Hersiliens Gruß an Felix. Der Stallmeister halte sich gut."[29] The mysterious groom in Kafka's "Landarzt" appears with his horses in the pigsty, an animal shelter more cramped and lowly than the stable, and pursues the doctor's

---

29 *Goethes Werke,* vol. 8, pp. 265-66.

servant, Rosa.[30] Like Kafka, Hofmannsthal frequently associates the kind of surging animal passion germane to the environment of horses with evil and violence. In a letter dated 1891 Hofmannsthal writes:

> ich habe wenigstens einmal mit einem Mexikaner gesprochen, ... der täglich ein wildes Pferd fängt und seine Geliebten alle zweiten Tage ersticht. (B, 1:18)

Gotthelf attempts to murder the stable girl after she has noticed that he is brandmarked as a criminal. the *Stallmeister* of the unfinished story "Der goldene Apfel" commits adultery with the wife of a carpet merchant, who subsequently murders him.

The poem "Vor Tag," composed about the same time as the first half of *Andreas*, juxtaposes these same elements: the stable, violence, and illicit sex. The stall is first mentioned early in the poem:

> ... Nun streckt
> Die junge Kuh im Stall die starken Nüstern
> Nach kühlem Frühduft. (GLD, p. 9; SW, 1:106)

The cow inhaling vigorously appeared in the "Reitergeschichte" and in the "Prolog" to *Die Frau im Fenster* as a symbol of the animal hunger for life; here as in the "Prolog" it bears strong connotations of fertility and sexual potency. The poem concludes with the description of a youth slinking into his room after a sexual experience heavily tinged with guilt; he is frightened by his own reflection in the mirror as if this "stranger" had murdered his former innocent self. Indeed the burden of his wrongdoing is so great that the very air seems heavy with it:

> Und darum sei der Himmel so beklommen
> Und alles in der Luft so sonderbar.
> (GLD, p. 101; SW 1:107)

The final line follows these immediately:

> Nun geht die Stalltür. Und nun ist auch Tag.

---

30 See Michael Lakin's discussion of the horses and their significance in "Hofmannsthal's Reitergeschichte and Kafka's Ein Landarzt," pp. 44-45.

In realistic terms, the line probably signifies only that someone is entering the stable to tend the stock. But the pairing of the two brief sentences implies a temporal or causal relationship: "Now since the door has been opened," or "because the door has been opened, day has come." The stable, where it is presumably dark and still, seems to form part of the nocturnal sphere, that scene of the youth's sexual adventure, of the vagrant's attempt to kill a dove, and of the sick man's wakefulness mentioned earlier in the poem. Dawn penetrates the stable while the door is opened; thus seeming to banish the atmosphere of violence and sin associated with night.

We may summarize the import of these two aspects of the horse symbol: horseback riding and the stable, by concluding that these images are chiefly allied with sexual experiences. While they center around Gotthelf, they also reveal his influence over Andreas, whose behavior as a rider and in the stable is colored by the lascivious tales through which his servant first makes him acquainted with sex.

Focusing our attention now on the horse motif as related to Andreas, we find that it pertains, secondarily to be sure, to the theme of sexuality stressed in connection with Gotthelf. Primarily, however, Andreas' experiences as owner of the brown horse and as a rider are indicative of his capability as master of his own fate. This significance of the horse image is familiar to us through the study of *Die Frau im Fenster,* where Madonna Dianora's lack of control over the horse which carried her to her husband or on pleasure rides with Messer Palla was interpreted as a failure to shape her own destiny in congruence with her conscious will. Through our understanding of riding as a symbolic act, we perceive that Andreas gives up directing his future in much the same manner. He permits Gotthelf to change the route of the journey he had planned to include a trip through Carinthia. His clumsiness at managing his own horse during the narration of Gotthelf's lewd exploits is evidence of his ineptitude: until he can control his subconscious urges effectively, he will remain incapable of channeling all his energies in one direction. The sojourn at the Finazzer estate is determined not by Andreas' decision, but necessitated by the injury to the brown horse which goes lame as a result of his poor horsemanship. Finally Andreas gives up riding altogether; he refuses Finazzer's offer to let him keep the brown horse

173

and leaves the valley in the teamster's wagon. He no longer directs the means of his own conveyance, but places himself in the hands of others. Even the circumstances of his arrival in Venice derive not from his own volition, but from the whim of the gondolier, who leaves his passenger in a quarter unknown to Andreas, but where he subsequently lives. Sacramozo seeks to cure Andreas of this tendency to follow the line of the least resistance; he attempts to transmit to Andreas "die Vereinigung mit sich selbst, völlige Identität, Übereinstimmung von sich-Wollen und sich-Wissen" (SW, 30:104; E, p. 244).

Effective horsemanship is only one of several attributes which Hofmannsthal equates through symbolism with mastery over one's life. True nobility and wealth, discussed in connection with the "Märchen" and with "Reitergeschichte" as additional symbols of control over one's own existence, also play a role in the novel and are inextricably interwined with the horse image. Furthermore, their undeniable relevance to the biography of the novelist suggests that Hofmannsthal was in danger of revealing in his fiction his awareness of his own shortcomings in trying to plot a successful future.

Turning first to the question of nobility, we recall that Hofmannsthal's great grand-father was raised to the nobility in 1835 for his philanthropy and achievements in industry. Andreas' nobility is of a more recent stamp: his grandfather, whose name he bears, rose from humble origins to the position of royal bodyservant and was subsequently ennobled. This sudden rise in fortune has left its imprint on Andreas, whose membership in the Viennese "Bagatelladel" gives him a feeling of inferiority and an unbounded reverence for the true landed gentry. Indeed his dubious social standing exposes Andreas to Gotthelf's sinister influence; the brutish servant impresses him merely by naming his past noble masters.

Andreas' original purchase of the spirited little brown horse turns on precisely this question of his second-rank aristocratic status. Since he is well aware that his father is snobbishly more concerned with the favorable appearance of having sent his son on an expensive journey than with his son's education and pleasure, Andreas undoubtedly hopes to win his father's approval by choosing to enter Italy in the manner befitting a young gentleman — with a servant riding behind him. Gotthelf appears to sense Andreas' vulnerability to arguments aimed at his obsessive desire to present a suitably aristocratic facade. Accordingly, instead of praising desirable qualities in the horse, such as strength or good disposition, Gotthelf argues only on the basis of the horse's attractiveness, claiming that it would surely learn the "Spanish step" within a week, a prancing gait better suited to show than to covering long distances in comfort.

It is symptomatic of Andreas' naiveté that he trustingly buys the horse without examining it first hand. Anyone else would have known that horsetraders are proverbial deceivers, a fact Gotthelf alludes to as he boasts, "daß er jeden Rosstäuscher übers Ohr hauen könne, auch einen ungarischen, das seien die gefingertsten, geschweige denn einen deutschen und wällischen" (SW, 30:47; E, p. 123). The fact that the horsetrader deceives Gotthelf as well as Andreas proves that the servant has no superior knowledge or insight.

It has already been suggested that Hofmannsthal esteems horsemanship as an innate capability of those who are noble by ancestral lineage. Thus the merchant's son confesses to the jeweler that he is not interested in the saddle ornaments offered for sale because, as the son of a merchant, he has no knowledge of horses or riding. Andreas, in social standing not much superior to the merchant's son, is likewise scarcely more knowledgeable about horses, as is proven by his unwise purchase of the brown horse, by his thoughtlessness in reining his own horse in too suddenly, and by his incompetence in helping to care for the lame animal in the Finazzer stable. Finazzer's self-assured behavior contrasts sharply with Andreas' ineptitude. The farmer, who belongs to the older landed gentry, looks quickly between the forelegs of the brown horse when the strangers arrive and immediately recognizes the stolen animal, though he says nothing at the time.

Andreas' insecurity about his social status forms a major part of his search for identity, and weakens his chances for success in the relationships (to Sacramozo, Maria-Mariquita, Nina, Zustina, and Romana) through which he seeks to establish a firm self concept. Hofmannsthal notes that Andreas "Schämt sich auch vor Romana, daß er nicht zu den Herrschaften gehört –" (SW, 30:27). In an essay on "The Nobility and the Cult of the Nobility in the German Novel around 1900" Egon Schwarz analyzes some aspects of this theme which have bearing on Andreas. Although he excludes Austrian literature from consideration, his conclusions should hold true for Hofmannsthal as well as his German contemporaries. Schwarz writes that in this cult of the nobility, "extravagance and ostentatious display are considered noble and valuable," precisely Andreas' line of thought in hiring Gotthelf.[31] He continues: "when genuine military deeds are not possible, substitute actions such as ... hunts can be valuable in proving one's courage and skill," affirming Andreas' interest in Gotthelf's hunting stories.[32] He explains further that the cult of the nobility is reinforced by dictates against intermarriage with a member of another class; thus Romana's attraction for Andreas is strengthened by the knowledge of her family's coat of arms: marriage with her (as outlined in his imaginary letter) would satisfy his parents by reinforcing their own tenuous grip on noble status.

For Hofmannsthal, the concept of nobility is inextricably interwoven with mastery over horses, so much so that he notes for inclusion in the novel an anecdote about Maria Theresia (whom he idealized as the embodiment of Austrian aristocracy):

> Anekdote von Maria Theresia als ganz junger Frau auf einer Reise durch die Lombardei: Die Leichtigkeit, wie ihr das Blut ins Gesicht stieg, wie ihr die Thränen und das Lachen kamen. Die Art zu Pferd zu steigen: sich dabei des Pferdes zu bemächtigen... (wie sie ein Pferd bändigte und einen Schwan kochte). (SW, 30:172-173)

We shall return to this coincidence of nobility and absolute domination of the horse in connection with Sigismund in *Der Turm*.

Andreas' ineptitude as a horseman extends also to the care of horses, and causes him to shun the stable as the scene of repeated defeats. After the noonday meal, he orders Gotthelf to carry his baggage up to his room and then see to the horse. He then intends to go down himself and see the horse, but hesitates because of his reluctance to confront Gotthelf again. Romana leads him off for a tour of the environs, after which they enter the stable together. Andreas attempts to assert his authority again by telling his servant to carry up his baggage, but Gotthelf counters that the brew must

---

31 *German Quarterly* 52 (1979), 178.
32 Ibid.

first be finished. Andreas then tries to assess the condition of the brown horse, but realizes only his own inexperience:

> "Was ist mit dem Pferd," sagte Andreas und that selber Fuss in den Stand hinein, stockte aber ehe er den zweiten Schritt that, weil er wußte, er verstands nicht, und der Braun trübselig dreinschaute. (SW, 30:59; E, p. 138)

The autobiographical reflection here of Hofmannsthal's feeling of "Ratlosigkeit" when confronted with his lame mare in Göding is unmistakeable, even though this passage was written more than a decade and a half afterward. Depression over the horse's melancholy expression saps Andreas' resistance and he leaves the stable with Romana, carrying his own baggage and pretending to have forgotten the repeatedly ignored command to his servant. The inability to enforce his authority over Gotthelf is further evidence that Andreas lacks the tone of command natural to a born nobleman and essential to the mastery of both horse and servant. Undoubtedly his selfassurance in dealing with Gotthelf is further weakened by feeling out of his element in the stable. Therefore it is significant that the scene of his taking leave from Romana occurs in the stable, the setting of his defeat, a fact which jeopardizes his potential success with her even further.

Besides being tied to the question of nobility, the power of command over others, and the erotic encounter, the imagery of the horse and stable connects with wealth, yet another aspect of a fictitious character's dominance over his environment. Lerch and Euseb, subjugated to a higher authority, be it that of the military or of class distinction, long for the easier life of the well-to-do. Richard Exner and Günther Erken have commented on the central role money plays in several of Hofmannsthal's dramas where a marriage is arranged for financial considerations: *Hochzeit der Sobeide, Silvia im "Stern", Danae, Rosenkavalier,* and *Arabella.*[33] H. R. Klieneberger has suggested that the marriages arranged between an impoverished noble partner and a wealthy bourgeois may reflect the situation familiar to

---

33 Günther Erken, *Hofmannsthals dramatischer Stil,* Hermaea, germanistische Forschungen, n.s., vol. 20 (Tübingen: Max Niemeyer Verlag, 1967), pp. 215-16. Richard Exner, "Arabella: verkauft, verlobt, verwandelt?" *Hofmannsthal-Forschungen* 8 (1985): 55-80.

Hofmannsthal through the marriage of his paternal grandparents or the parents of his close friend, Leopold von Andrian.[34] To return to the novel, the lottery for Zustina places the problem of a loss of wealth and a loss of control over one's own future in the foreground of the Venetian episode.

From the first, Andreas' financial affairs, and therewith his control over his life, are closely tied to horses. The financial catastrophe brought on by the purchase of the brown horse and Gotthelf's theft of his own chestnut horse is compounded by the fact that more than half of his travel money was sewn into his saddle. The ensuing loss represents a loss of control over Andreas' surroundings or his future, pointing in the same direction as his giving up riding for passage in conveyances he does not steer. This motif opens the most nearly completed draft of the novel, as Andreas is left by a gondolier in a part of Venice he knows nothing about. His now relatively modest means are a factor in his decision to take lodgings in Count Prampero's house. Upon meeting Nina he indulges in a fantasy of freeing her of obligations to Camposagrado and her other admirers, and winning her favor by renting a neighboring roof garden for her, but realizes that his entire remaining fortune would hardly suffice to keep the courtesan for even a few days.[35] Reality gains power over him because he, unlike the adventurers or aesthetes in Hofmannsthal's works, lacks the financial means to shield himself from its hard grasp.

The causal link between bad luck as a horse owner and a financial loss not only reminds us of Hofmannsthal's experiences in Göding, as noted earlier, but influences the relationship of both author and protagonist to their fathers. Andreas' depression over his loss stems from the conviction that he has severely disappointed his father: "So etwas kann nur Dir passieren," he hears his father say accusingly

---

34 "Hofmannsthal and Leopold Andrian," *Modern Language Review*, 80 (1985), 620. It is interesting to note that in earlier drafts of the novel Andreas was named "Leopold," and that a similarity exists between "Andreas" and "Andrian."

35 This passage has been analyzed in detail by Fritz Martini in "Hugo von Hofmannsthal: Andreas oder die Vereinigten" in his book, *Das Wagnis der Sprache* (Stuttgart: Ernst Klett Verlag, 1954), pp. 225-57.

(SW, 30:68, E, p. 151). In analyzing the "Märchen" we treated Hofmannsthal's almost obsessive worry over money and traced it to the necessity of repeatedly asking his father for funds to meet the cost of caring for his horse.[36] As late as 1903 Hofmannsthal expresses the tension between father and son arising from disagreements in financial matters. Significantly, he dates his money worries from his twentieth year, that period when the expense of caring for his horse forced him to write frequently to his father for money. In order to judge the tone of his letter, it will be necessary to quote at some length:

> ich muß schon sagen, daß Dein gestriger Brief über mein harmloses Vergnügen mit den Antiquitäten mich ziemlich gekränkt hat. ... Besonders geärgert hat mich der Punkt eins, in welchem Du mich zu größerer Sparsamkeit ermahnst. Kennst Du mich wirklich so wenig trotz unserer großen Intimität. Wenn etwas in mir bekämpft werden muß, so ist es eine seit meinem zwanzigsten Lebensjahr fast krankhaft entwickelte, mit dem Temperament eines Dichters so gar nicht zusammenhängende angstvolle Kleinlichkeit und fast unaufhörliche Geldsorge, die mir alle Reisen und was nicht schon alles in meinem Leben zerstört hat, deren tiefster Wurzel das innige Bestreben ist, Euch einmal durch Erwerb einer beträchtlichen Geldsumme Freude zu machen. (B, 2:105-106)

It is surprising to read that Hofmannsthal wishes to please his parents not through poetic creation, surely the field of his highest achievement, but through gaining a substantial sum of money! We are reminded of the merchant's son's pitiable attempts to win the favor of the little girl in the greenhouse and the soldier by giving them money, and of Lerch's conviction that the acquisition of a substantial sum of money will raise his stature in Vuic's eyes. Andreas' calculations regarding his finances both in Carinthia and in Venice show him falling prey, like Hofmannsthal himself, to the niggling worries that similarly destroyed the novelist's pleasure in travel.

Wolf Wucherpfennig determines that in spite of the paucity of information available about Hofmannsthal's relationship to his father, it is nonetheless evident "daß mit dem Gegensatz zwischen beruflich-finanziellen Zwängen und Dichtertum ein tief reichender Konflikt

---

36 See especially the letter dated August 2, 1895 (B, 1:159-60).

zwischen Vater und Sohn verknüpft war."³⁷ Apparently Hofmannsthal's finances became more worrisome around the time of the novel's composition and continued to concern his father. Hofmannsthal had established an account in Munich administered for him by Eberhard von Bodenhausen; his father asked Hofmannsthal the account's balance because of a new tax law going into effect. In a letter to Bodenhausen Hofmannsthal explains his tendency to exaggerate the importance of financial losses such as those he had recently sustained in the stock market; he writes that this tendency is a „hereditärer Umstand; so wie es mir da geht, so ist es ... meinem Vater, meinem Großvater lebenslang gegangen." His parents had suffered heavy stock market losses in 1873, and he feels himself "von diesem Wölkchen einer etwas betrübten Familienerfahrung umschwebt..."³⁸ Thus the novel's treatment of financial worries and Andreas' anxiety about answering to his father are further traces of autobiographical material in the story.

To summarize now the importance of the horse image, we conclude that it reveals Andreas' defeat in several areas critical to his eventual successful maturation. First, his lack of conscious control over his horse corresponds to a lack of control over his sexual urges. Second, his willingness to give up riding altogether indicated the relinquishing of power to direct his own future. Third the insecurity about his social standing gives rise to the false vanity visible in his decision to hire a servant and purchase a horse for him, while at the same time his membership in the "Bagatelladel" excludes him from the innate power of command over horse and servant unique to the genuine nobility. Fourth, the financial setback incurred through the loss of his own horse and saddle deprives him of the means to smooth his own way in Venice. Fifth, this last aspect of the horse image reveals its derivation from Hofmannsthal's own experiences.

These experiences have been reworked in a way which sheds light on Hofmannsthal's creative process. The beginning chapters of this

37 "Das junge Wien und seine Väter...," pp. 162-63.
38 See his letter dated 6.VII.14 quoted by Günther Fetzer, *Das Briefwerk Hugo von Hofmannsthals,* Deutsches Literaturarchiv: Verzeichnisse, Berichte, Informationen, vol. 6 (Marbach: Deutsche Schillergesellschaft, 1980), pp. 73-74.

study attempted to explain the crisis of self doubt brought on by Hofmannsthal's growing awareness of reality as dominated by the "widerstrebende Mächte"; his horse in Göding became a focal point of this experience and thus came to represent those forces which he felt to be resisting his will. His horse resisted his dominance through its unreliable temperament and physical disabilities, to which Hofmannsthal reacted with feelings of helplessness, incompetence, and guilt at the necessity of repeatedly asking his father for money to care for the horse.

The horse's insubordination confronted Hofmannsthal with forces beyond his comprehension, hostile chaotic powers lying beyond the pale of his art. When he later attempts to weave this experience into his novel, he is faced with the problem of working in these "widerstrebende Mächte" in such a way that they do not destroy the ordered design of his fabric. As an artist, he creates a world within a world,[39] ruled by logically comprehensible forces, a miniature cosmos in which these chaotic forces have no place. He resolves the dilemma of subordinating such irrational elements as the defiance of his horse to human intellectual power by altering the facts of the case: the brown horse goes lame, not, like Hofmannsthal's mare in Göding, for imponderable reasons, but because of human deceit. It has been stolen from the Finazzers, has grown rather thin, and possibly has been artifically treated to give it the appearance of health and spirit. On the second morning of Andreas' journey, it appears to be a different animal, the eyes listless, the head seeming much older. But Andreas is not victimized by the unknown evils which plagued Hofmannsthal, he is simply at the mercy of human failings: of Gotthelf's treachery and his own vanity. The horse is no longer a demon, as it seemed to Hofmannsthal when describing his wild ride in Göding, it is simply a sick animal. Its resistance to the human will no longer presents itself as an abnegation of human authority, as seemed the case at the beginning of "Ein Traum von großer Magie," but rather as physical frailty. Reality's resistance

---

39 See his letter to Beer-Hofmann of May 15, 1895 (B, 1:130-31), Hofmannsthal and Beer-Hofmann, *Briefwechsel,* pp. 47-48.

to the domination of the artist's will no longer manifests itself through supernatural forces, instead it is revealed in human failings.

The dog, perhaps the central animal symbol of the novel, is interwoven with Andreas' past, present and future. He dreams of a dog he had as a boy and killed by breaking its back with the heel of his shoe; he watches the death agonies of the Finazzer dog poisoned by Gotthelf, and later has some sort of mystical experience at the dog's grave. In Venice he encounters people who behave like dogs and makes the acquaintance of Maria-Mariquita, owner of a spaniel named Fidèle. It will facilitate our investigation if we begin by examining the more transparent dog symbols, those found in Venice, and progress to the more difficult analysis of the tortured dogs in the Carinthian episode.

The bond between the dog and female sexuality which has been stressed in previous chapters may be seen, from a few illustrations, to obtain for the novel as well. Mariquita is associated with the dog on two occasions:

> Scene, wo die Curtisane sehr aufgeregt darüber, dass Maria ins Kloster gehen will von Leopold [Andreas] verlangt, dass er Marie verführe; — ihr unheimlicher hündischer Blick bei dieser Scene. (SW, 30:10; E, p. 210)

Because Maria and Mariquita are diametrically opposed personalities inhabiting the same body, Mariquita perceives Maria's decision to enter a convent as a threat to the casual sexual encounters which fill her own life. Mariquita, the "cocotte," sees the seduction of the "countess" Maria as a means of depriving her of the spiritual purity which seeks fulfillment in a religious life and thus of ensuring the freedom of movement essential to her own promiscuity. Mariquita's dog-like regard as she pleads with Andreas enhances the reader's awareness of her uninhibitedly sexual nature.

Mariquita and her alter-ego share a distrustful, short-winded haughty spaniel named Fidèle:

> Dunkel ahnt sie [Maria] das Chaotische in sich, das was sie mit Mariquita gemein hat. So haben sie das Hündchen gemeinsam. (SW, 30:9; E, p. 207)

Just as the woman's personality is split into the chaste dutiful widow Maria and the carefree Mariquita, the dog embodies contrasting halves. His name, Fidèle, an obvious sign of his traditional significance as the emblem of loyalty and constancy (in which function he appears in the Finazzer tombstone) corresponds to Maria, whose life has been fatefully determined by her allegiance to these ideals. Her schizophrenia stems from what she regards as a breach of faithfulness to her late husband. While nursing him in a roadside inn, she caught a glimpse of her former lover. According to another draft of the novel, she prayed to Christ for assistance in her extramarital affair. In any case she is unable to reconcile the yearning for her lover with the strict concept of marital fidelity alluded to in the dog's name. At the same time Fidèle represents, by virtue of the dog's association with the mother earth and the uninhibited sex drive, the exact opposite of faithfulness, namely, the promiscuity characteristic of Mariquita. Her total disregard for sexual mores poses a threat to the entire social fabric and therefore evokes the chaos which would ensue from its collapse. These chaotic elements are also present in Maria, but relentlessly suppressed, or as Hofmannsthal expresses it symbolically, the dog is always hidden in her house. Hofmannsthal writes that the dog is visible only on one unspecified occasion, in all likelihood the moment when, in Andreas' presence, Maria stands before her mirror and is unexpectedly transformed into Mariquita. At the moment of her transformation from the austere noblewoman into the intriguing cocotte, she incorporates both contrasting aspects of the dog image, the mythical ideal and the concupiscent creature.

Hofmannsthal may also use the dog symbol to illuminate the opposition between the physical earthly realm and the higher sphere of ideals. Thus, Sacramozo, representative of the spiritual realm, is characterized by his "Antipathie gegen rohes Geschrei, Hundegebell" (SW, 30:105; E, p. 236). The contrast between the two realms is epitomized by the rivalry between two of Nina's admirers. The Duke of Camposagrado, "ein breiter Mensch," whose name signifies "level field" belongs entirely to the animal sphere or earth. When attacked by a dog, he defends himself by lowering himself to the bestial level rather than utilizing his superior human powers to defeat it: "...ein Hund geht ihn an. Er besteht den Hund mit den Zähnen" (SW, 30: 325; E, p. 194). His rival's name, dalle Torre, signifies "from the towers"; his link to the higher sphere is further confirmed by his gift of a songbird to Nina. In a jealous rage Camposagrado bites off the bird's head, again indicating his brutish nature by the violent animal means of destroying the bird.

Having now ascertained that the dog symbol functions in the novel in much the same way as in the other works, we shall approach the interpretation of the poisoned Finazzer dog, concerning ourselves not only with the plight of the animal, but with the insight into Andreas' past offered through his connection of the sight of the suffering dog with his parents and their bedtime conversations.

During the night Andreas leaves his own room intending to seek out Romana in her bed. While standing in the hall, he overhears Finazzer and his wife talking in bed and his heightened perception enables him to distinguish other sounds as well:

> ... er konnte hören, daß die Bäuerin unterm Reden ihr Haar flocht und zugleich wie unten der Hofhund ging und etwas fraß. (SW, 30:60-61; E, p. 141)

It seems probable that Hofmannsthal conceives of hair here, as in *Die Frau im Fenster* as a sexual attribute, as the "Ineinanderweben von männlicher und weiblicher Geschlechtskraft," to use the terminology of Hugo Wyss.[40] The fact that Andreas hears her braid her hair seems to indicate his growing awareness of Finazzer and his wife as sexual beings; what Romana has told him of their common childhood and strong affection for each other is now substantiated by his own observations.

The juxtaposition of the woman preparing for bed with that of the watchdog eating in the courtyard below suggests a subtle link between them. In *Jupiter und Semele* the appearance of the poisoned suffering dog at the lovers' bedside was interpreted as pointing to their sexual activity: since the dog's torment reduces its behavior to that of a dying animal and deprives it of individual personality and capacity for relationships with humans its presence gives the impression that the two lovers, by analogy, similarly exist only as physical creatures. This impression, of course, is compounded by Hofmannsthal's association of the dog with physical urges. The connection be-

---

40 *Die Frau in der Dichtung Hofmannsthals,* p. 18. Wyss refers to weaving, which he equates with hair as a symbol of sexuality.

tween the woman and the dog symbol's connotation of sex has been established with respect to Mariquita, and for Finazzer's wife can be inferred through the reference to her hair and through the simultaneity of Andreas' perceptions of woman and dog.

In the sentence following that quoted above, Andreas' awareness of the physical intimacy between Finazzer and his wife evokes recollections of his earliest suspicions about the private affairs of his own parents:

> Wer füttert jetzt in der Nacht den Hund, dachte es in ihm, und zugleich war ihm gepreßt zumut, als müsse er nochmals zurück in seine Knabenzeit, als er noch das kleine Zimmer neben den Eltern hatte und sie durch den in die Wand eingelassenen Kleiderschrank mußte abends reden hören, er mochte wollen oder nicht. (SW, 30:61; E, p. 141)

The passive mood of such phrases as "dachte es in ihm," "war ihm gepreßt zumut" and the constraint implied in the phrases "als müsse er" und "er mochte wollen oder nicht" suggests that the awakening of these memories is involuntary and even undesirable. Andreas' dream during the same night confirms the suspicion that his first awareness of his parents' activities represents a painful and unwelcome knowledge which Andreas suppressed from the very first. One of the threatening figures who hinders Andreas in the chase after Romana in his dreams is a repulsive boy, "der ihm in dämmernder Abendstunde auf der Hintertreppe erzählt hatte, was er nicht hören wollte" (SW, 30:64; E, p. 146). Quite probably this figure was a second source of the information about sex which Andreas tried so desperately to avert. The boy's appearance between Andreas and Romana in the dream demonstrates that the fear of sex which he represents forms an obstacle to their union.

Other critics have noted these tendencies in Andreas. Hugo Wyss speaks of his "Triebunsicherheit" and "Angst vor dem Weibe."[41] Miles phrases them more succinctly as "a desperate fear of sex."[42] A closer examination of Andreas' dream reveals the possible origin of his anxiety. Andreas hears a cry (in reality that of the stable girl whom Gotthelf has bound before setting her bed on fire) which he

---

41 Ibid., p. 112.
42 *Hofmannsthal's Novel Andreas*, p. 126.

assumes to come from Romana. In his dream he tries to reach her but he must take his way through a clothes closet, struggling through the cast-off clothing of his parents.[43] Because of his childhood memories of listening to his parents in bed through a clothes closet connecting their room with his, we recognize that in his dream where the same closet appears between his room and Romana's, he has momentarily returned to his childhood state. The woman who cries out and whom he attempts to help seems to be at once Romana and his mother. Without reading too much into the dream, we may conclude that he once heard his mother cry out from her bed and assumed that she was somehow being hurt, quite possibly during lovemaking, which Andreas visualizes as a kind of "Morden im Dunkeln." He transfers his misconception of the love act from his intimations about his parents, which he found so horrifying that he resisted any further enlightenment in the matter, to his vision of Romana, whom he fears to wound in the same way that he believes his mother was hurt.

After Andreas listens to the Finazzers conversing quietly in bed, and to the dog eating in the courtyard below, he goes to Romana's room where he finds, contrary to his expectations, that she is not waiting for him, but fast asleep. Afraid of awakening the servant woman who shares the bedroom, he leaves and returns to his own room. There he observes the dog suffering the first effects of the poison:

> der Hund stand mitten im Licht, er hielt den Kopf sonderbar ganz schief, drehte sich in dieser Stellung immerfort um sich selber: es war, als erduldete das Tier ein großes Leiden, vielleicht war er alt und dem Tode nah. (SW, 30:62; E, p. 144)

Andreas' speculation about the animal's age is an understandable attempt to attribute its suffering to some normal cause. The evocation of old age through a description of animal suffering is reminiscent of

---

[43] Miles interprets the closet only as representative of Andreas' "unresolved past" because of the "undiscarded clothes" it contains (Ibid., p. 127). But the clothes do not belong to Andreas, and therefore can hardly signify his own past, but rather to his parents. The discarded clothing may indicate past roles or masks of his parents, who have not achieved a happy marriage and are not as candid and familiar with each other as Romana's parents.

Das kleine Welttheater, where the young lord dreamt of driving countless forest animals into a ravine beneath him and saw his aged father's white hair floating in a well below. Again in a letter to Beer-Hofmann Hofmannsthal connects thoughts of age and infirmity with a dying animal. He imagines watching a dog drown, and consoles his companion by reminding him that the aging dog would only have forced them to reflect on their own mortality:

> Denn kläglich häßlich ist ein altes Tier
> Und grauenvoll in mancher Abendstunde
> Dann später uns, den Jungen, Dir und mir:
> Denn er wär alt und wir noch jung gewesen
> Und wie aus eines offnen Grabes Munde,
> So hätte Gott geschrien aus diesem Wesen...[44]

This passage illuminates Andreas' observation of the poisoned Finazzer dog: the dying animal obliges the observer to recognize that he too exists by means of a physical body susceptible to age, suffering and death. Andreas is moved to sorrow not only by compassion for the dog, but by the recognition that all mortal creatures must succumb to a similar fate:

> Andreas fiel eine dumpfe Traurigkeit an, ihm war unmäßig betrübt zumut über das Leiden der Creatur, wo er doch so glücklich war, als werde er in diesem Anblick an den nahebevorstehenden Tod seines Vaters gemahnt. (SW, 30:62-3; E, p. 144)

Without exception Hofmannsthal's critics have passed over this unusual sentence; not one has attempted to explain why the sight of the suffering dog conjures up reflections about Andreas' father and the anticipation of his death. Even more puzzling than the link between the youth's father and the dying dog is Andreas' pleasure at the thought of his father's death.

Leaving aside for a moment the identification of the dog with the father, let us attempt to discover why Andreas would welcome thoughts of his father's death. It has already been pointed out that Andreas feels that his parents are more concerned with the favorable impression of having sent their son on a journey than they are about

---

44 Hofmannsthal and Beer-Hofmann, *Briefwechsel,* p. 38. Also B, 1:115.

his pleasure in the trip. The conviction that he has failed by losing his travel money is by no means a new sensation. Rather, Andreas is already conscious, while lying in bed after contemplating the suffering dog, that his parents have had too little pleasure in him. He strikes upon a new failproof way of satisfying their expectations of him through marriage:

> Nun habe er ja durch Gottes plötzliche Fügung das Mädchen gefunden, die Lebensgefährtin, die sein Glück verbürge. Von jetzt an gebe es für ihn nur ein Trachten: an der Seite dieser durch die eigene Zufriedenheit auch die Eltern zufriedenstellen. (SW, 30:63; E, p. 145)

In his eagerness to win his parents' approval, Andreas ceases to view Romana as an individual and regards her instead only as a means of reaching his goal. He depersonalizes her in much the same way that his parents utilize him as an object to ensure their social standing and thus their satisfaction. Andreas' readiness to subordinate his own self-fulfillment to the demands of his parents casts new light on his relationship to Romana: although his love for her may be genuine enough, she has also become an expedient, an instrument of his happiness and that of his parents.

In a similar manner Andreas desires children not as human beings in their own right, but as gratification for his parents:

> Wäre er eine Tochter statt eines Sohnes ... so wäre ihnen schon lange das Glück zuteil gewesen, in noch rüstigen Jahren Enkel zu umarmen und Kinder ihrer Kinder heranwachsen zu sehen — durch ihn hatten sie auf dieses Glück allzulange warten müssen das doch einer der reinsten aller Glücksfälle des Lebens sei und gewissermaßen selber ein erneutes Leben. (SW, 30:63; E, p. 144)

Andreas places his hope for satisfying his parents not in himself but in a renewal of their lives through their grandchildren. Andreas' desire to procreate his parents and himself through children does not represent, as in the majority of Hofmannsthal's work, integration into the whole of society, but rather an abdication of his responsibility: his children are to be a replacement for himself, and their existence a recompense for his shortcomings.

This conception of their role is expressed earlier in the novel when Andreas, weary of the responsibility of the unruly Gotthelf, wishes to escape the present situation by substituting his future son for himself, a son who would succeed where he has failed:

> er möchte, das wär alles längst vorüber, möchte älter sein und schon Kinder haben, und das wär sein Sohn, der nach Venedig ritte. Aber ein ganz anderer Kerl als er, ein rechter Mann, nichts als ein Mann und alles rein und freundlich wie an einem Sonntagmorgen, wenn man die Glocken hört. (SW, 30:52; E, p. 129)

We now perceive a two-fold basis for Andreas' pleasure in the contemplation of his father's death: first, he would then be free of the burden of responsibility placed upon him by his father's expectations, and free too of the fear, or even worse the conviction, that he has failed to live up to these expectations. Second, the hope of satisfying his parents through substituting his son, "ein rechter Mann," for his inadequate self forces Andreas to confront marriage as an alliance for engendering progeny, a prospect which calls forth his terror of sex. This fear of an act which Andreas views as indispensable to his future forms an integral part of the dream following Andreas' contemplation of the poisoned Finazzer dog, of his obligation to his parents, and of their fulfillment through marriage to Romana:

> The dream obviously re-enacts, in condensed symbolic form, the unconscious dilemma in Andreas' relationship to Romana, the deepening conflict between a desperate fear of sex and an almost obsessive desire for marriage and children.[45]

It is significant that Andreas' obligation to fill his much dreaded sex role is evoked indirectly through a dog, of all the animal symbols in Hofmannsthal's work the one most inextricably intertwined with sexual relationships.

Having now established why Andreas welcomes the thought of his father's death, we must ascertain exactly how he comes to associate the dog with his father. It has already been suggested that Andreas suspects the dog is old, like his father, and therefore nearing death. To further our discussion, it will be useful to examine the dog

---

45   Miles, *Hofmannsthal's Novel Andreas*, p. 126.

images from Andreas' childhood and from his future in Venice as they shed light on the link between the dog and the father.

As Andreas reflects on the death of the Finazzer dog, he is reminded of a little stray dog which attached itself to him when he was twelve years old. The boy seems to have been flattered by the dog's obsequiousness:

> Die Demuth, mit der es in ihm, von der ersten Begegnung an, seinen Herrn erblickte, war unbegreiflich, die Freude, die Seligkeit, mit der es sich bewegte wenn er es nur ansah. (SW, 30:70; E, p. 154)

One day he sees the dog assume an ingratiating position before a larger dog, and, overcome by disgust at the animal's fickleness, severely maims it with the heel of his shoe. The interplay of master and subservient creature delights Andreas so long as it gratifies his desire for dominance over an inferior being. But when he perceives how readily the dog exchanges his domination for that of the next stronger creature, he feels compelled to assert his own authority by fatally crippling the little dog.

Thomas Mann treats a similar incident in his short story, "Tobias Mindernickel." Tobias, an old man lacking the germ of self esteem necessary to maintain a semblance of worth or dignity, can react favorably only to those creatures delivered powerless into his hands. He buys a puppy Esau, whose youthful enthusiasm and vigor soon threaten his fragile sense of superiority over the animal. Tobias accidentally cuts the dog while slicing bread, but his sorrow at the mishap soon vanishes before his delight at having secured the animal's complete dependence on him, and he cares for it tenderly. When Esau recovers and resumes his boisterous behavior, Tobias deliberately cuts him again, hoping to render him helpless and thus assert his dominance over the wounded animal once more. But Esau is fatally wounded and soon dies. Just as Tobias acquires the puppy for the pleasure of ruling one creature lowlier than he, Andreas, perhaps already conscious of falling short of his father's expectations, relieves his sense of failure in successfully dominating the puppy which attaches itself to him. Like Tobias, he finally kills his pet in the ultimate act of domination.

Probably not until he sees the little puppy fawn on the larger dog does Andreas recognize the parallels between himself and the underdog as creatures subservient to those superior in physical strength or authority. The little dog submits to the larger dog as the boy defers to his father. Andreas can tolerate neither the dog's forgetting of his authority when it humbles itself before the larger dog, nor its reminding him of his own subservient position.

The interplay between a lowly creature and its superior in strength or authority is explicitly compared to that of dog and master in the coffee-house scene in Venice. The nephew of a wealthy Greek appeals to him for financial assistance, but the unforgiving uncle ignores him "as if he were a dog" (SW, 30:82; E, p. 171). Their voices and gestures become bestial; Andreas is repelled by the "Fauchen der einen und Winseln der anderen [Stimme]" and watches their departure with repugnance:

> Der reiche Grieche und sein bettelhafter Neffe standen auf: die plumpe Herzenshärte des einen, die hündische Demut des andern waren abscheulich — in beiden schien die Menschennatur entwürdigt. (SW, 30:83-84; E, p. 173)

The nephew's financial dependence on his uncle suggests a parallel to Andreas' constant worry over his considerable financial obligation to his father for the cost of the journey.

To summarize briefly, we may repeat that Andreas identifies with the dog-like begging nephew or with his own little dog, creatures whose dependence on beings superior in wealth or power calls to mind his own dependence on his father. Quite possibly the association of his father with the larger dog whose favor his puppy seeks to win is later transferred to Finazzer's watchdog. The suffering of the poisoned dog foreshadows not only the liberation from filial duty which his father's death will bring, but his vicarious triumph over the more forceful being who has dominated his existence.

Now that we have treated Andreas' associations of the Finazzer dog with his parents, his childhood anxiety about sex, and his father, we may turn to other aspects of the multi-faceted dog image in the novel.

The behavior of Andreas' puppy as it tries to curry favor with him or that of the larger dog bears covert sexual overtones:

> Meinte es, sein Herr zürne, so warf es sich auf den Rücken, zog die Beinchen angstvoll an sich, gab sich ganz preis, mit einem unbeschreiblichen Blick von unten her (SW, 30:70; E, p. 154)

Karl Groos, whose treatise on animal behavior was found in Hofmannsthal's library, describes the habit of various baboons which try to please their captors or fellow creatures by taking a position which exposes their genitals. He compares this form of ingratiation to the behavior of dogs:

> ...wie auch manche Hunde, wenn sie sich recht freundlich und unterwürfig zeigen wollen, den Körper merkwürdig drehen und winden, gerade als wollten sie dem Herrn ihre Hinterteile zeigen.[46]

The comparision of Andreas' fatally wounded dog to a snake further enhances these sexual overtones in its movements:

> das Hündlein gab einen kurzen Schmerzenslaut und knickte zusammen, aber es wedelte ihm zu. Er drehte sich jäh um und ging weg, das Hündlein kroch ihm nach, das Kreuz war gebrochen, trotzdem schob es sich seinem Herrn nach wie eine Schlange. Er blieb endlich stehen da heftete das Hündlein einen Blick auf ihn und verschied wedelnd. (SW, 30:71; E, p. 155)

Since the cat which appears in Andreas' first dream approaches him "creeping like a snake" it seems worthwhile to examine briefly the import of the snake in Hofmannsthal's work.[47]

The snake is frequently suspected of treachery: both the dyer Barak and his wife in *Frau ohne Schatten* address the old nurse as "snake" (D, 3:194). Its stealth and deadly poison are compared in *Jedermann* to death itself; Buhlschaft says:

> Der Tod ist wie die böse Schlang,
> Die unter Blumen liegt verdeckt,
> Darf niemals werden aufgeweckt. (D, 3:35)

---

46 Karl Groos, *Die Spiele der Thiere*, pp. 246-47; 268.
47 Chapple's comment on the snake-like aspect of the cat and dog describes the serpent as "a traditional emblem of evil; the animal simile enhances the animal symbol," but contributes nothing original to our understanding of the image ("Themes and Symbols in Hofmannsthal's *Andreas*," p. 10). Nor does Miles go beyond the standard interpretation of the snake as "the time-honored symbol of sin, in particular of original sin" (*Hofmannsthal's Novel Andreas*, p. 127).

On the other hand, the writing serpent suggests the lovers' arms; Jedermann replies:

> Wir lassen sie unter Blumen verborgen
> Und wissen nirgends nichts von Schlangen,
> Als zweien, die gar hold umfangen. (D, 3:35)

This image calls to mind Hofmannsthal's definition of myth as the conjunction of opposites in which everything has a dual meaning: "Schlangenkampf-Liebesumarmung" (A, p. 35). The association of the snake with the lovers' embrace forms the basis of a note for the composition of *Das gerettete Venedig*; Hofmannsthal writes that Belvidera and Jaffier have enjoyed an innocent romance and continues:

> Wie Belvidera nach dem Tod ihrer Mutter das bereute und schwor, lieber sollte eine giftige Schlange sie berühren, als seine Lippen. Wie den Tag nach diesem Schwur, ... eine Schlange unter der Steinbank hervorschießt und ihren Zahn in Belvideras herabhängende linke Hand drückt. Wie Jaffier dazukommt, sich über die Hand stürzt und die Wunde aussaugt, Belvidera darin den Wink des Himmels sieht, sie dürfe, ja sie müsse ihm ganz gehören. (A, p. 132; cf. SW, 4:201)

Just as the greyhound which pressed itself caressingly against Madonna Dianora's dangling left hand in *Die Frau im Fenster* symbolized her passion for Messer Palla, the serpent becomes a visible sign of the erotic desire linking Belvidera and Jaffier.

Hofmannsthal's use of the snake comparison to illuminate the sexual connotations of the dog and cat symbols is wholly in keeping with an interpretation of the snake's significance given by Herbert Silberer:

> Als ein mythologisches (auch im Traumleben häufiges) Symbol für die sich introvertierende und in den gefährlichen Bannkreis des Inzestwunsches (oder auch bloß der lebensträgen Tendenz) geratende Libido ist die Schlange anzusehen; ... die phallische Bedeutung der Schlange ist bekannt genug; die Schlange als vergiftendes, als schreckliches Tier bezeichnet aber einen besonderen Phallos, eine mit Angst behaftete Libido...[48]

---

48 *Probleme der Mystik und ihrer Symbolik*, pp. 175-76. It is probably superfluous to note that Freud considers the snake the most important male genital symbol. Cf. his *Gesammelte Werke*, vols. 2/3, p. 362.

In Silberer's emphasis on the introverted and ineffectual qualities of the sex-drive as represented by the snake image we recognize an element particularly appropriate to the signification of Andreas' troubled desires: his fear of the sex act as a kind of murder or wounding of the woman does indeed constitute a libidinous urge inhibited by anxiety. Further, the snake embodies contrasting forces: the love-embrace alluded to in the second passage quoted from *Jedermann* and in the note for *Das gerettete Venedig* is opposed to the power of death in its poison. This dichotomy of attraction and fear was embodied in the snakes accompanying the statues of Indian deities carried by the older servant girl to whom the merchant's son felt momentarily attracted. In the novel, the comparison of both dog and cat to a snake heightens the reader's awareness of the threatening but attractive sexual urges incorporated in both animals.

Although one would expect Andreas' observation of the poisoned Finazzer dog would call forth in his dream of that same night memories of the little dog he killed as a boy, we find instead that a cat which he caused to suffer and die in the same manner appears in place of the dog. We have already discussed in the characterization of Gotthelf the virtual interchangeability of cat and dog as symbols of sexual desire. The substitution of the cat for the dog is further necessitated by Andreas' complete repression of his torturing the dog; the memory is too painful even to be admitted into his subconscious: "Ihm war unsicher, ob er es getan hatte ob nicht; — aber es kommt aus ihm" (SW, 30:71; E, p. 155).

Several details attest to the symbolic unity of cat and dog as dream images. Both animals die only after extended suffering caused by the manner of their deaths: Andreas breaks the puppy's backbone with the heel of his shoe and fractures the spine of the cat with a wagon axle. The cat's snake-like movement and the gaze it fixes on Andreas correspond to the visual impression left by the tortured dog. Andreas' dream of the cat is described as follows:

> So war sie noch nicht gestorben nach so viel Jahren! Er sieht den Gang der Jahre indem er vor sich den Vater grau dann weiß werden sieht und der Mutter Gesicht schlaffer und immer bleicher werden. Kriechend mit gebrochenem Kreuz kommt sie ihm entgegen, und er fürchtet über alles ihre Miene, wenn sie ihn ansieht. Es hilft nichts, er muß über sie weg. Den schweren

linken Fuß hebt er mit unsäglicher Qual über das Tier, dessen Rücken in Windungen unaufhörlich auf und nieder geht, da trifft ihn der Blick des verdrehten Katzenkopfes aus einem zugleich katzenhaften und hündischen Gesicht, erfüllt mit Wollust und Todesqual in gräßlicher Vermischung... (SW, 30:64; E, p. 146)[49]

The sentence beginning "Er sieht den Gang der Jahre..." does not appear in the Steiner edition, but expresses with remarkable clarity Andreas' equation of both parents with the tortured animal. The basis of this equation is not only the weakness brought on by age, (which Andreas sees progressing toward senility with exaggerated speed) but his dream projection of his own complete power over them. The inclusion of his mother in this dream of domination indicates that Andreas' feelings of inadequacy stem from confronting the expectations of both parents, not merely his father. Furthermore, the appearance of his parents together, following upon his overhearing Romana's parents in bed, reveals that his imagination is dwelling on their sexual relationship, (at times unhappy, even a "verkappte Hölle, SW, 30:134) possibly as a model for his own developing intimacy with Romana.

Andreas' unusually heavy left foot symbolizes his guilt in the murder of both animals, for although in the dream he lifts his foot over the cat, in reality he maimed the puppy with the heal of his shoe. Hofmannsthal undoubtedly knew the meaning of the swollen foot from which Oedipus derived his name as evidence that he embodied the male procreative power.[50] Whether the swollen left foot symbolizes Andreas' guilt in torturing animals or his sexual urges, it stands in the way of his union with Romana, for he dreams that it catches repeatedly in cracks in the pavement as he pursues her through the streets and prevents him from catching her.

49 The remark that the head of the animal appears both cat-like and dog-like points to a possible source in Philippe Monnier's book on Venice, where he describes a news item from a Venetian newspaper:
    Il y a peu de jours que dans la maison d'une pauvre femme à S. Margherita une chatte et un chien s'accouplèrent ensemble; la chatte mit au monde cinq petits, dont deux ont une tête de chien, et le reste du corps du chat.
Venise au dix-huitième siècle, p. 42.
50 See Bachofen, *Das Mutterrecht*, vol. 1, pp. 439-40.

We have now established that cat and dog are virtually synonymous as symbols, and that both represent Andreas' parents, both as authority figures and as somewhat faulty models for a sexual relationship. We must now approach the puzzling question of torture; if the dog and cat have displeased Andreas, why does he prolong their death agonies rather than dispatching them quickly?

Hofmannsthal's critics have judiciously skirted this question. Manfred Hoppe points out that Hofmannsthal endowed those fictitious characters closest to his heart (Andreas, Euseb, Sigismund) with a sympathy for suffering creatures and maintains that the source of this sympathy is the "Zwang zur Identifikation" which the author shared with these figures.[51] Likewise, Karl Gautschi accentuates Andreas' "boundless sympathy for the defenseless creature" at the expense of any awareness of the youth's brutality.[52] Werner Metzeler writes that Hofmannsthal's feeling for animals surpassed empathy and speaks of a "mystischer Selbstidentifizierung" with them.[53] Chapple hints at an understanding of the problem when he writes: "Cruelty is often the reflex reaction of a person who feels that life is persecuting him" and argues that cruelty toward animals is part of a search for self.[54]

If we return to the conclusions drawn from our examination of the "Knabengeschichte," we perceive that they are valid for *Andreas,* the most autobiographical of Hofmannsthal's works, as well. The individual who feels himself the pawn of some greater power exercises his own limited capabilities in the only way left open to him: by turning on a weaker creature. Thus Messer Braccio's brother, restrained by social convention from denouncing Dianora and her

---

51 *Literatentum, Magie und Mystik,* p. 13.
52 "Hugo von Hofmannsthals Romanfragment 'Andreas'," pp. 26-27.
53 *Ursprung und Krise von Hofmannsthals Mystik,* p. 57.
54 "Themes and Symbols in Hofmannsthal's *Andreas,* p. 24. However, his conclusion: "Whereas in the earlier works the animals portray the external more often than the internal forces of life, the accent in the later works is more on the inner forces; the animals project human instincts as they did in Victor Hugo's writings, but Hofmannsthal stresses the dark side of Andreas' character with them more than the positive side." is not borne out by our study of the animal imagery in Hofmannsthal's work (Ibid., pp. 25-26).

lover, vents his wrath by kicking the sleek greyhound fondled by the woman he could not attack directly. Euseb temporarily assumed his father's dominant role in crucifying the sparrow-hawk as he felt himself crucified by his father. Andreas, infuriated by the realization that his little dog submits to the larger dog as it does to him or as he defers to his father asserts his superior strength by maiming the puppy. Finally, one of Sigismund's guards correctly interprets the prisoner's exultation in the slaughter of vermin as a reflex reaction to the inexorable authority of Basilius and his henchmen: "Sie kujonieren ihn seit er am Leben ist, so kujoniert er was ihm unter die Hände kommt" (D, 4:12).

In three of the cases of the mistreatment of animals cited above, the oppressor is the father. Thus the imagery of animal torture in the novel revolves around the same father-son conflict (it is remarkable that Hofmannsthal nowhere depicts women torturing animals) that was discovered at the root of the imagery connected to horse ownership. In analyzing that complex, we suggested that Andreas' fear of disappointing his father, and the uneasy relationship to his calculating status-conscious parents seem at least in part reflections of Hofmannsthal's own concerns when he was of the same age as his youthful protagonist.

Guilt and remorse brought on by the suppressed enmity toward the father may lie at the root of the masochistic tendency revealed in Hofmannsthal's descriptions of tortured animals. He seems to have been particularly drawn to the identification of a youth with the animal he is tormenting. Andreas and Euseb regard themselves not only as directors of a weaker creature's fate, but as the agonizing animal itself. Andreas is saddened by the pain of the Finazzer dog, Sigismund loses himself in the contemplation of a slaughtered pig. Hofmannsthal's fascination with the sensation of a person who kills an animal to which he feels some attachment is reflected again in the notes for *Jupiter und Semele,* from which it may be inferred that the brother of the Semele figure poisons his own trusting dog. This interest extends to the work of other authors as well: in the Danish story mentioned in "Der Dichter und diese Zeit" it is the lion tamer whose animals trust him completely who betrays them by feeding them poisoned meat. Similarly Hofmannsthal admires in Hans Carossa's

Rumänisches Tagebuch the portrayal of the death throes of a kitten for whom the author feels a particular affection.[55]

He who tortures a beloved animal indulges not only in the hunger for self-assertion over a weaker being, but engages at the same time in self-torture. Identifying with the crippled or dying animal, he suffers with it. Thus Euseb views the sparrow-hawk's twitching as "furchtbar." Andreas finds the memory of his puppy "martervoll," yet both are held by the desire for a vicarious mortification of the flesh, a sort of penance by substitution, as an integral part of animal sacrifice.

A further attraction of the experiences surrounding animal suffering is the production of sensation for its own sake. The tendency to create and magnify unpleasant or terrifying physical or psychological sensations forms the core of the prose sketch "Age of Innocence" whose young protagonist takes perverse delight in forcing himself to touch repulsive insects, to hang out the window until he nearly faints, and to create frightening reflections in the mirror. He is both the stage director and the audience in these nightly orgies of self-torture, just as the tormentor of animals is at once the source and sharer of their pain.

The purpose of such masochism may be the alleviation of guilt feelings toward the feared and hated father through self-punishment, or it may be a sort of confirmation of one's own existence, the means of drawing a boundary between the individual and the great void surrounding him. Friedrich Hebbel (about whom Hofmannsthal planned a story, "Hebbels Eiland") called such attempts to affirm his own identity through masochistic games "Mittel, die Langeweile zu würzen" and explained their effect as follows:

> Man hält den Odem an, so lange, bis die Augen aus dem Kopf herausspringen wollen und die Brust zu zerreißen droht – dann stößt die Lunge den Mund gewaltsam auf, man atmet wieder und hat darin ordentlichen Genuß. Eben so könnte man sich mit Nadeln die Haut aufritzen oder sich auch wirkliche Wunden mit einem Messer beibringen, man hätte dann doch etwas zu erwarten, die Heilung und das Aufhören der Schmerzen. Jede Gegenwart läßt sich ertragen, nur nicht die vergangenheit- und die zukunftslose, und so

---

55 See Hofmannsthal's letter to Carossa dated October 15, 1924 in Hugo von Hofmannsthal and Hans Carossa, "Briefwechsel 1907-1929," *Die neue Rundschau* 71 (1960), 403.

> ist die meinige beschaffen. Hinter mir nichts und vor mir nichts – ich weiß, wie alles gekommen ist und wie alles kommen wird, und das ist der Tod![56]

For Hofmannsthal and his fictitious characters, many of whom lack a firm concept of the self as a fixed entity continuous through time, such games may affirm through physical suffering the existence of an individual consciousness.

Andreas' relationship to the cat and dog he killed as a boy seems to resolve itself when he throws himself down on the fresh grave of the Finazzer dog:

> Zwischen ihm und dem todten Hund war was, er wußte nur nicht was, so auch zwischen ihm und Gotthelf, der schuld an dem Tod des Thieres war – andrerseits zwischen dem Hofhund und jenem anderen. (SW, 30:72; E, p. 156)

Critics agree that Andreas' throwing himself down on the dog's grave is a gesture of spiritual renewal. Chapple views the act as "a traditional symbol of regeneration as well as death" and maintains that "from this point on Andreas is changed, as if the vicarious experience of death had heightened his sense of the value and meaning of life."[57] In a like vein Miles emphasizes Andreas' identification with the dead animal; he describes Hofmannsthal as "extraordinarily sensitive to the presence of animals" and continues:

> Because of this mythical kinship with human beings, animals, in Hofmannsthal's eyes, could also die a sacrificial death for human beings, functioning in a sense as redeemers.[58]

Both Chapple and Miles stress Andreas' feeling for the dead dog at the expense of his identification with Gotthelf. The power of redemption deriving from Andreas' experience of the dog's death stems less from a recognition of any sort of animal sacrifice (or identification with the dog) than from his identification with his servant who poisons the dog. We have already remarked that Andreas suppresses the consciousness of the murder of his own little dog; in "Das venezianische Erlebnis des Herrn von N." Hofmannsthal writes: "Zweifel,

---

56 Friedrich Hebbel, *Werke*, vol. 4, p. 577.
57 "Themes and Symbols in Hofmannsthal's *Andreas*," pp. 10-11.
58 *Hofmannsthal's Novel Andreas*, pp. 169-70.

ob er jenes Verbrechen an dem Hund wirklich begangen" (SW, 30: 108; E, p. 195). This refusal to acknowledge part of his own past sets Andreas at odds with his childhood:

> In den Erinnerungen der Kinderzeit bleibt etwas peinlich Verwickeltes, das aufzulösen kaum das ganze Leben hinreicht. Mit seiner Kindheit versöhnt sterben. (Tagebuch, "ich möchte mit meiner Kindheit versöhnt sterben"). (SW, 30:115; E, p. 222)

Although Andreas resolutely denies responsibility for his childhood deed, he is able to accept the experience indirectly or subconsciously through taking Gotthelf's guilt as a dog-killer on himself. He imagines himself "ein Verbrecher und der Mörder wie der Gotthelf" (SW, 30: 71; E, p. 155). Gotthelf's misdeed confronts him with an inescapable reminder of his own past, an objectification of his own guilt, which, once presented as external to his own person, embodied now in his servant, can be passively absorbed into his own being.

His acceptance of his past misdeeds does not, however, occur on a conscious level and his cure therefore remains incomplete. Meditating on the ties between himself and Gotthelf, between his puppy and the poisoned dog, Andreas reflects:

> Das lief alles so hin und her, daraus spann sich eine Welt, die hinter der wirklichen war, und nicht so leer und öd wie die. Dann staunte er über sich: wo komme ich her? und ihm war, da läge ein anderer, in den müßte er hinein, habe aber das Wort verloren. (SW, 30:72; E, p. 156)

Andreas becomes cognizant of his past self, that being he came from, as another person whom he seeks to re-enter, with whom he wishes to be entirely re-unified, as the novel's title implies. But although he recognizes the need for a reunification with his past self, his attempt fails, for he has lost "the word." The reader is reminded of the hero of some fairy tale who has forgotten the magic word which would change him into another person. At the same time, the statement indicates that Andreas lacks the final strength of character necessary to give verbal expression to the traumatic experience separating him from his past self, or to draw that experience into his conscious mind and so alleviate the trauma. In his *Studien über Hysterie,* a book familiar to Hofmannsthal,[59] Freud clearly underscores the necessity

---

59 See the letter from May 1904 in which Hofmannsthal asks Hermann Bahr to lend him Freud's book (B, 2:142).

of verbalizing trauma in order to draw it into the patient's consciousness and thus bring about his cure:

> Wir fanden, ... daß die einzelnen hysterischen Symptome sogleich und ohne Wiederkehr verschwanden, ... wenn dann der Kranke den Vorgang in möglichst ausführlicher Weise schilderte und dem Affekte Worte gab.[60]

Andreas' failure to seize upon this moment of paramount consciousness of self to complete the process of reunification with his past must be viewed as a critical one. Upon return from his journey he remains "ohne das Gefühl des Selbst auf welchem wie auf einem Smaragd die Welt ruhen muß" (SW, 30:129; E, p. 247).

Until this point we have been concerned primarily with the animal imagery surrounding Andreas and Gotthelf. Like Gotthelf, Romana is closely allied with the animal world. Her sphere, however, is not that of the stable, but rather of a paradisacal realm where man and beast co-exist in harmonious interdependence. She represents a unity with the natural environment into which Andreas, whose previous experience with animals consists of cruelty and mistreatment, must be assimilated if he is to become at one with his universe. Animal symbols associated with Romana fall into two categories: those surrounding her idyllic existence on her father's farm, goats (whose significance was examined earlier) and birds, and the hunted animal in whose image she appears in Andreas' dreams.

Romana is connected with the ducks and chickens in the farmyard, with the birds which upset the basin of holy water she tends in the cemetery, and with the family's captive eagle. The dead bird which awakens Andreas from his second dream appears as a messenger from her; a swallow flits through the door of the stable where she takes leave of Andreas, and the youth visualizes in the soaring eagle his future with Romana. As we have previously concerned ourselves only with the interest in bird life shared by Dianora and the grandmother in *Der weiße Fächer*, it is now necessary to examine Hofmannsthal's bird imagery more closely before concentrating on Romana.

---

60 *Gesammelte Werke*, vol. 1, p. 252.

Miles briefly states that the bird represents "the realm of the spirit" and then turns to a discussion of spiritual love.[61] Various passages in Hofmannsthal's works make it clear, however, that the bird represents the spirit in the dual, often invisible, aspects of intellect or fantasy and soul or heart. With unusual explicitness Hofmannsthal communicates the origin of thought through the bird symbol:

> Was ein Vogel in der Luft für den Seemann, für den, der die Hundswache hat und allein dalehnt, in den Mantel gewickelt: totenstill das schwere dunkle Meer und darüber nicht Nacht nicht Tag; ... unerträglich ist die wortlose Erwartung, die Stummheit der lichtlosen, der schattenlosen Welt: was hier der Flügelschlag eines wundervollen Meervogels ist, der heransegelt hoch im Osten, königlich die Schwingen schlagend, der erste Abglanz des heraufblitzenden Tages funkelnd auf ihm: das ist für eine frühe dumpfe Welt der Gedanke. (P, 2:93)

It will be useful to retain two contrasts occurring in this passage for the study of bird imagery in the novel. First, the bird appears simultaneously with the morning light; the dawn of a new era, that of rational thought, illuminating a dark world, coincides with, or more exactly seems to be brought forth by the appearance of the bird. Second, the bird stands for thought or reason, which Hofmannsthal invariably connected with language; he effectively suggests the contrast between the deathly stillness of the predawn hours, the wordless expectation, the silence of the lightless world, and, on the other hand, the bird which heralds thought, or, implicitly, language. Darkness contrasts to light as silence to the spoken word.

Elsewhere the bird as an image of thought or language develops into a symbol of poetic creativity: in the fragment *Die Freunde* Hofmannsthal writes:

> Wie eine Schwalbe vor dem Gewitter hinkommt in ungeheurem Schaukelfluge, wo sie sonst nie hinkommt, bis an die Gesichter der Menschen, an die Erdscholle, schon vor der geahnten Gewalt im voraus im großen Fieber in der Luft hin und her geworfen, so streift jetzt seine [Amyclas] Phantasie durch Leben, Traum und Tod hin. (D, 1:427)

The poet in "Vorspiel für ein Puppentheater" listens to the repeated calls of a cuckoo and apostrophizes the bird: "Ja, du sollst hinüberrufen ... in die andere Welt, die ich aufbauen will..." (D, 2:496).

61 *Hofmannsthal's Novel Andreas*, p. 165.

Where the spiritual influence is totally lacking, birds are absent or still, as in the deserted village in "Reitergeschichte": "Das Dorf blieb totenstill; kein Kind, kein Vogel, kein Lufthauch" (SW, 28:43, E, p. 55). The silence creates an opressive threatening ambiance. By contrast, an excess of noise and confusion where birds remain silent determines the atmosphere in one scene of *Der Abenteurer und die Sängerin*. Vittoria wishes to tell Baron Weidenstamm that Cesarino is his son, but finds the tumult around her not conducive to such confidences:

> ... Was dir verborgen,
> dachte ich in einer reineren Begegnung
> an einem stillern Strande dir zu zeigen.
> Nun ists wie eine wilde Hafenstadt
> voll Lärm, in dem die Nachtigallen schweigen. (D, 1:217)

The writer of the "Briefe des Zurückgekehrten" describes the vision of the sixteen-year-old Rama Krishna as occurring when the image of white cranes flying against the blue sky left an indelible imprint on his soul:

> ... nichts als diese zwei Farben gegeneinander, dies ewig Unnennbare, drang in diesem Augenblick in seine Seele und löste, was verbunden, und verband, was gelöst war. (P, 2:307)

Chapple points out that "the circling bird which reflects light and inspiration down to man is one of Hofmannsthal's favorite motifs." As in the instance quoted above, the circling hawk in "Verse zum Gedächtnis des Schauspielers Josef Kainz" is connected with an "illuminating experience."[62] These ciphers of soaring birds as media of higher natural truths function not unlike the osprey pair in *Der Ketzer von Soana*, whose flight Hauptmann describes as follows:

> Aber wer mochte verkennen, daß die wechselnden Kurven ihres Flugs auf die blaue Seide des Himmels eine deutliche, unverkennbare Schrift zeichneten, deren Sinn und Schönheit aufs engste mit Leben und Liebe verbunden war.[63]

---

62 "Themes and Symbols in Hofmannsthal's *Andreas*," pp. 180-81, note 17.
63 *Erzählungen; Theoretische Prosa*, p. 103.

Turning to the domesticated birds in the novel, we find that they connote something of Romana's harmony with the surrounding natural world and evoke an atmosphere of peace and plenty surrounding the Finazzer estate. Upon first entering the courtyard, Gotthelf and Andreas find "niemand als ein schöner großer Hahn auf dem Mist mit viel Hennen" (SW, 30:53; E, p. 130). The word "niemand" seems to equate the rooster with a person who might appear to welcome them, and foreshadows Romana's tendency to regard animals, specifically the goats, as distinct individuals. Nearby the travellers perceive several small ducks swimming in a pond; their presence indicates the security of a limited existence. Jaffier in *Das gerettete Venedig* accuses Belvidera of a desire for just such safety when she wishes to return to her father: "Wie die Ente treibt es dich/ zurück in deinem Pfühl" (D, 2:224; SW, 4:110). Later Hofmannsthal connects these ducks more closely with Romana through the use of color and light symbolism:[64]

> ... der Tümpel mit den aufgeregten Enten wie sprühendes Feuer und Gold, der Epheu drüben an der Mauer der Capelle wie Smaragd, aus dem glitt ein Zaunschlüpfer oder Rothkehlchen hervor überschlug sich mit einem süßen Laut in der webenden Luft, der Hahn und die Henne glänzten wie indische Vögel, das Schönste waren Romanas Lippen, durchsichtig wie pures Blut und ihre eifrigen arglosen Reden kamen dazwischen heraus wie eine Feuerluft in der ihre Seele glänzend hervorschlug... (SW, 30:58; E, p. 137).

The progression of the deepening colors from the fiery gold of the duck pond to the red on the robin's breast to the dark crimson of Romana's lips causes her to appear as the culmination of all natural harmony and beauty. Once again the birds are connected with light illuminating the darkness, which here is that of sunset rather than dawn.

In a similar fashion a bird heralds Romana's arrival in the dusky atmosphere of the stable where Andreas waits to take leave of her:

64 This passage bears out Miles' statement: "In general, the bird represents the realm of the spirit and thus of Romana and the world of light" (*Hofmannsthal's Novel Andreas,* p. 165). Throughout his chapter on the symbolic background of the flashback, Miles emphasizes the contrast between the darkness surrounding Gotthelf and the stable and the light emanating from Romana.

> Andres stand eine unbestimmte Zeit in dem dämmernden Raum und horchte auf das Zwitschern. Da fuhr durch das kleine vergitterte Fenster ein goldener Strahl schräg hindurch bis gegen die Stalltür und blieb so, eine Schwalbe glitt aufleuchtend hindurch, und hinter ihr Romanas Mund, offen, feucht und zuckend vor unterdrücktem Weinen. (SW, 30:74; E, p. 159)

Here, as in the passages cited earlier, the bird's appearance is accompanied by a ray of light. And for the second time the bird is brought into juxtaposition with Romana's lips, most simply the organ of expression of her love for Andreas. Yet the repeated juxtaposition of bird and mouth, which is at the same time the organ of speech, suggests that Hofmannsthal connects the bird not only with the dawn of thought, but with language itself. The equation of the mute dog symbol with the wordless animal phrase of human existence has been repeatedly stressed throughout this study. The bird, opposite counterpart of the dog, may signify language, the instrument of the implementation of human fantasy often symbolized in the bird image. Thus the rivalry of Nina's admirers, Camposagrado and dalle Torre, is fittingly rendered through their link with the dog and bird symbols respectively. Camposagrado, representative of the bestial urges in human nature defends himself against a dog by baring his teeth and later bites off the head of a rare songbird given Nina by her Jewish admirer, dalle Torre.

Both Nina and Zustina keep caged birds as pets.[65] Chapple has suggested that in the Venetian chapters the novelist draws a subtle analogy between the bird's captivity and that of his mistress, who is subjugated and confined by the man who keeps her.[66] Far from being restricted to the latter part of the novel, the image is one of the more common in Hofmannsthal's work. The heroine of *Christinas Heimreise,* the shopgirl Mali in *Eduard und die Mädchen* and Moll Flanders in the film sketch *Defoe* are among the women who keep caged birds and who depend on men for their support. In *Die ägyptische Helene* Altair, the impetuous prince, likens Helena to a splendid

---

65 Miles' interpretation of the bird as representative of the "realm of the spirit" misleads him to conclude that this image suggests "that Andreas' deeper spiritual self still awaits liberation" (*Hofmannsthal's Novel Andreas,* p. 106).
66 "Themes and Symbols in Hofmannsthal's Novel Andreas," p. 16.

bird trapped in his net (D, 4:281). Hofmannsthal varies the image in the following lines, comparing the heart of his beloved to a captive bird:

> Wär nicht die Blume ganz zerfallen
> hätt irgendwie ein Ding Bestand
> müßt immer wie ein kleiner Vogel
> dein Herz mir klopfen in der Hand.[67]

It is interesting to note that this comparison of the lover to a caged bird is anything but original. It forms, to name one example, the basis of the Middle High German poem "Ich zoch mir einen valken" by Der von Kürenberg, where the analogy is implied but never directly stated. There is, however, one major difference between the medieval lyric and Hofmannsthal's use of the image: the former is a *Frauenstrophe,* the lament of a girl whose lover has left her: "er huop sich uf vil hohe und fluog in anderie lant." Hofmannsthal, on the other hand, uses the caged bird exclusively to symbolize the captivity of women.

Although Romana, consistent with her freedom from bondage, does not keep a caged bird herself, she does show Andreas the eagle captured by her grandfather, who was adept at robbing eagles' nests and wooing beautiful women. Wolfram Mauser attempts to define the significance of the eagle in the novel as encompassing

> ... den Bereich männlich-aktiven, lustbetonten Schaffens, geistigen Wirkens, vitalen Bezwingens und gebieterischen Beherrschens.[68]

Though it is tempting to view the grandfather's deed as evidence of his courage and vitality and to regard Romana's forebearer as a contrasting figure to Andreas' uncle Leopold, from whom the youth inherited tendencies toward violence and improvidence, the interpretation is more facile than valid. Hofmannsthal does not draw the contrast so sharply. Romana herself tells Andreas that her grandfather did little else beside prey on eagles and court women. Nor can the eagle in his present state be regarded as an embodiment of life-

---

67 "Gedichtfragmente, Skizzen zu Gedichten in Prosa, Aufzeichnungen," *Die neue Rundschau* 70 (1959), 372.
68 *Bild und Gebärde in der Sprache Hofmannsthals,* p. 41.

giving energy and strength; he has lived entirely in captivity, his face is "versteint," the eyes "wie erstorben" and he is capable of envincing only "matte Freude" to welcome Romana (SW, 30:57; E, p. 136).

It is, of course, possible to regard other eagles in Hofmannsthal's work as regal sacred birds. When one of Sacramozo's crises coincides with a crisis in which Maria speaks to him mockingly as Mariquita, he experiences a period of self-hatred and degradation, but rises above his condition to the highest spiritual purity. He asks himself how "aus der unwerten Substanz die würdige Substanz werden [kann], aus dem Chamäleon der Adler, aus dem Unflat der Edelstein" (SW, 30: 147; E, p. 237). The chameleon represents changeability or even fickleness, in this context the sexual promiscuity of Mariquita and of Nina, who also humiliates Sacramozo during this crisis. In contrast the eagle stands for constancy, fidelity to ideal love, personified in Maria, but at the same time a faithfulness to one's self, to higher spiritual truths.

Elsewhere in Hofmannsthal's work the eagle fulfills more standard symbolic functions. Because of its unusually high flight, the bird was thought to accompany the human soul into the afterlife[69] and plays exactly this role in *Alkestis*. Admet looks at his veiled wife, brought back from the underworld by Heracles, and senses that he too has left earthly life behind:

> Als trüge mich der Adler in die Luft
> und unter meinem Fuß versänken die
> verlassnen Lebensfluten dieser Welt! (D, 1:45)

Paul Gerhard Klussman finds that the eagle may signify for Hofmannsthal fantasy and poetic truth, associated, as we have just seen, with other birds as well:

> Die Nähe zum Licht macht den Adler zum Wissenden, von dem der Dichter wesentliche Weisung erhält über das Verhältnis von Wort und Schöpfung, von dem göttlichen und irdischen Begriff, von Name und Ding.[70]

---

69 *Handwörterbuch des deutschen Aberglaubens*, vol. 1, cols. 175-76. Further explanations of the eagle symbol are given by Richard Exner, *Hugo von Hofmannsthals "Lebenslied,"* pp. 86-87.

70 "Hugo von Hofmannsthals 'Lebenslied,' " *Hugo von Hofmannsthal*, ed. Sibylle Bauer, p. 236.

The "Dichter und Sehervogel"[71] in the essay "Über Charaktere im Roman und im Drama" serves in this manner as an embodiment of the spirit of poetic creativity. The poet, aware of the limits of his imagination, becomes

> ein verzweifelnder Dämon in einem engen gläsernen Gefängnis, durch dessen unüberwindliche Wände er mit grinsender Qual die Welt draußen liegen sieht, über der er vor einer Stunde brütend schwebte, eine Wolke, ein ungeheurer Adler, ein Gott. (P, 2:40)

This comparison of the poet, confined by the strictures of reality, echoes Baudelaire's poem "L'Albatross," in which the poet's fantasy is likened to the grace and controlled strength of the majestic sea bird in flight, while the genius' unsuitability for daily terrestial existence is demonstrated by the bird's awkward gait on the deck of a ship where it is mocked and tortured by the seamen.

Extracting the essence of the above passages, we conclude that the eagle represents spiritual forces transcending this earthly life. It stands for ideals such as constancy, ascendance to the after-life, and the artist's creative power. But how do these attributes relate to the eagle imprisoned in one of the towers of the Finazzer estate? That captive eagle suggests not, as Mauser would have it, that Romana's family possesses such qualities as creativity, vitality and dominance, but rather that the potential for these traits once existed among the Finazzers. The difference between that weary bird and the eagle in "Über Charaktere im Roman und im Drama" makes the contrast even clearer: in the essay, the poet whose fantasy can not surmount the obstacles presented by his actual situation views himself as a desperate prisoner of his circumstances and envies the free bird soaring overhead. In the novel, on the other hand, it is the once majestic bird who has been confined, and whose years of imprisonment have inured him to all sensation. His presence foreshadows the appearance of the eagle at Andreas' departure from the valley, a vision whose implications may be examined only after a discussion of the youth's relationship to Romana.

Vital clues about their love are hidden in the hunt imagery interspersed with the bird imagery surrounding Romana. Gotthelf brings

---

71 Ibid.

the hunt motif into the novel; his view of women as base, purely physical creatures is aptly expressed through his use of animal similes to describe various erotic adventures. He relates how a Pormberg countess enamored of his former master crept to their stand at a hunt and how his master ordered Gotthelf to shoot in his place, so that his absence from the hunt while entertaining the countess might not be noticed. Gotthelf, shooting in his master's stead and aiming for a stag, accidentally shot his own mistress, a Carinthian innkeeper's wife whom he describes as "verliebt ... wie eine Füchsin" (SW, 30:50; E, p. 127). Jealousy over his suspected alliance with the countess' maid has made her "abgemagert und hohläugig ... wie eine kranke Hündin" (SW, 30:50; E, p. 127), and has driven her to seek out Gotthelf. Both similes stress the unbridled passion which Gotthelf perceives to be the woman's dominant feature.

His conception of women soon extends itself to Andreas, who, like Euseb, derives the strongest erotic impulse not from his own experience, but from vicarious participation in the exploits of others. He imagines himself entertaining the countess during the hunt: "wie er schießt, spielt ihr Blick so mit ihm wie er mit dem Leben der Waldtiere" (E, p. 129). But under the spell of his servant's lewd stories, this tryst loses its charm and frightens him:

> Ihm graust, daß es ein Weib ist und nicht mehr eine Gräfin, auch nicht der junge Cavalier, nichts Galantes, Ehrbares mehr, und nichts Schönes sondern ein wildes Tun, ein Morden im Dunkeln. (SW, 30:51; E, p. 129)

It would be a mistake to concur with Chapple's summary dismissal of these past or imagined hunting scenes as "a trite motif,"[72] for they reveal a great deal about Andreas' conception of physical love and about his feeling for Romana. It is while imagining himself alone in the dark with this woman who is no longer a countess but simply female that Andreas sharply reins in his horse in a futile attempt to halt his passionate and increasingly violent fantasies. Nonetheless the conception of the erotic encounter as a kind of murder returns to trouble his dream during the first night at the Finazzer estate.

During Andreas' acquaintance with her, Romana assumes some aspects of the hunted animal suggested by Gotthelf's lewd stories.

---

72 "Themes and Symbols in Hofmannsthal's *Andreas*," p. 14.

Her gaze is a steady as that of an animal, Andreas observes (E, p. 134). In his second dream and again as he watches the eagle soaring over the valley she appears to him as a deer. A closer examination of both incidents will further our understanding of Andreas' future.

During his last night at the Finazzer estate, Andreas dreams of finding Romana on an island meadow encircled with luminous water. She has been haymaking and has fallen asleep near her sickle and rake. David Miles argues quite convincingly that "the landscape of the dream suggests very clearly that of an earthly paradise" which "had been portrayed from the time of antiquity through the Renaissance, as a 'safe place across the water.' "[73] In Hauptmann's *Ketzer von Soana,* an example not given by Miles, the island in the middle of a river where Francesco and Agatha consummate their love is explicitly likened to an earthly paradise.[74]

Although Hofmannsthal was doubtless familiar with the traditional description of the earthly paradise, the landscape of Andreas' dream may also be interpreted as expressing something quite different. While Andreas overhears the conversation of Finazzer and his wife in bed, they describe a scene resembling in some respects that of the dream:

> So seien doch die zwei alten Leut glücklich zu preisen, die der angeschwollene Schwarzbach im April mitgenommen habe [;] zusammen seien sie auf einer Bettstatt dahin geschwommen, hätten einander bei den Händen, und mitsammen hätt sie's in den Tobel hinuntergerissen und ihr weißes Haar hätt geleuchtet wie Silber unter den Weiden. (SW, 30:61; E, p. 152)

This *Liebestod* is reminiscent of that of Sali and Vrenchen in Gottfried Keller's "Romeo und Julia auf dem Dorfe." Like the old couple, the young lovers die floating together without struggling to save their lives. The hay wagon on which Sali and Vrenchen drift to their watery death becomes in the case of the old couple a bed, but in Andreas' dream is reflected as the hayfield where he finds Romana.[75]

---

73 *Hofmannsthal's Novel Andreas,* p. 139.
74 Hauptmann, *Erzählungen; Theoretische Prosa,* p. 160.
75 The reflection of Keller's story in Andreas' dream is confirmed by Michael Hamburger's statement that Hofmannsthal read the second volume of *Die Leute von Seldwyla* and made notes for Andreas' dream in the back of the book. Although "Romeo und Julia auf dem Dorfe" appears in the first

The dream weaves together various threads within the novel itsself, not only the Finazzer's bedtime conversation, but Gotthelf's adventures as well. As Andreas approaches Romana, she backs away from him, trips in a pile of hay, and sinks half to the ground "like a wounded deer" (SW, 30:73; E, p. 157). Bearing in mind the sickle and rake near where Romana had fallen asleep, the reader recalls Gotthelf's story of the Carinthian innkeeper's wife whom he accidentally shot wile aiming at a deer. Afraid to admit that she was wounded while pursuing an illicit love affair, the woman claims to have fallen on a sickle and cut herself above the knee. Andreas' dream reworks the details of Gotthelf's narration; Romana sinks to the ground like the deer for whom Gotthelf mistook his spurned mistress. Instead of merely pretending to have been cut by a sickle, Romana is actually wounded, in all likelihood by the sickle near which she had fallen asleept. The implication of the dream is clear: Andreas, made aware of his kinship with Gotthelf when his servant poisons the dog, desperately fears that the animal violence of passion will cause him to inadvertently harm Romana as Gotthelf wounded his mistress. The terror of sex as "murder in the dark" which tormented Andreas in his first dream haunts him still.

Andreas projects his dread of these characteristics he shares with Gotthelf onto Romana, who mistakes him for Gotthelf and begs him not to tie her to her bed as his servant did the stable girl and ride away on a stolen horse. Romana's telling Andreas that she does not know where the dog lies buried implies that he must know, or perhaps even that he had some part in the dog's death. Although she can know nothing of his childhood misdeeds, Andreas' conviction of his own evil nature is so all pervasive that he dreams she senses all his past guilt.

Yet the impression left by the dream is a happy one, for Andreas dreams that, although Romana knows the very worst about him, she declares herself ready to follow him, even to the gallows (SW, 30:73; E, p. 157). Her willingness to accompany him, in the dream, indicates that Andreas believes Romana ready to accept even those sins

volume of Keller's collection. Hofmannsthal certainly knew the story. (See Hamburger, "Hofmannsthals Bibliothek, ein Bericht," p. 59.)

which, like the crippling of his little dog, he can scarcely bear to acknowledge, to say nothing of communicating them. It is this certainty of her complete acceptance of him provided by the dream which leaves him, upon awakening, with the joyous conviction: "In ihm oder außer ihm, er konnte sie nicht verlieren. Er hatte das Wissen noch mehr er hatte den Glauben, daß sie für ihn lebte" (SW, 30: 83; E, p. 158).

The dreamer is awakened by a sharp blow on the windowpane which he takes for a messenger from Romana. Instead he finds a small bird killed by its impact on the glass, and he lays it on his pillow:

> Der kleine Leichnam durchströmte seinen Puls mit Wonne, ihm war, er hätte leicht dem Tier das Leben zurückgeben können, wenn er es nur an sein Herz genommen hätte. (SW, 30:73-74; E, p. 158)

Andreas understands the bird as a token of Romana, who has been associated with the farmyard poultry and with the family's eagle. His confidence that he could restore the bird to life reveals his new sense of creative power. The youth who maimed and killed animals has become capable of restoring animal life. The power of his body as the source of life-generating warmth has been touched upon earlier in the novel: while contemplating how he will satisfy his parents through a happy marriage, Andreas regrets that they have never taken much pleasure in him: "er dachte dies so lebhaft, als wären sie todt er müßte sich auf sie legen, sie mit seinem Leib erwärmen" (SW, 30:63; E, p. 144). The wish to restore his parents to life through bodily warmth motivates the gesture with which he flings himself down on the grave of the Finazzer dog he has identified with his father.

In connection with the passage just quoted above, Miles cites parallels to Dante's *Vita Nuova* where the birds fall dead to earth at the death of Beatrice.[76] He develops his thesis that birds function as a cipher of spiritual love and that Romana, like Beatrice (both are linked to bird imagery) is destined to serve as a spiritual leader of her lover. He deals at length with the appearance of the swallow in the stable where Andreas takes leave of Romana and compares that incident to the following passage from "Die Wege und die Begegnun-

---

76 *Hofmannsthal's Novel Andreas,* pp. 142-43.

gen" in which Hofmannsthal writes that the return of the mysterious figure, Agur, will be remarkable

> ...aber nicht seltsamer eigentlich als vorgestern nachmittags das Hereinstürzen der zurückgekehrten jungen Schwalbe, durch die Luft, durch die halboffne Haustür, ins alte Nest, einschlagend wie ein dunkler Blitz. Und eine Minute darauf, wie ein zweiter dunkler Blitz, aus dem Scheitelpunkt des Äthers, nachschlagend dem ersten, kam das Weibchen, die junge Schwester, und jetzt die Frau. Denn es sind Geschwister, ausgebrütet im vorigen Sommer in diesem Nest hinter unsrer Haustür. Wie wußten sie den Weg, herabfahrend aus der Unendlichkeit der Himmel? (P, 2–264-65).

The chiaroscuro whose symbolic function as the embodiment of the conjunction of extremes Miles has traced throughout the novel and which we have observed in the vision of the sea bird whose appearance heralds the dawn of thought occurs again here. In contrast to the stable scene in *Andreas,* however, these swallows do not accompany the only source of light in a darkened space, rather they are at once part of light and darkness, "ein dunkler Blitz." The oxymoron further allies them with Agur's young wife, who is repeatedly characterized as "von dunkler Blässe" (P, 2:268). The swallows signify not spiritual love, as Miles would have it, but through their link with Agur's young wife "die Geheimnisse des Eros" binding man and woman together (P, 2:265). The infallibility with which they mate and return to their nest symbolizes the inevitability of the binding sexual union.[77]

If the swallow darting into the stable where Andreas awaits Romana is juxtaposed with the swallow image from "Die Wege und die Begegnungen," it becomes apparent that Hofmannsthal intends to suggest a strong romantic tie, physical as well as spiritual, between

---

[77] Dieter-Olaf Schmalsteig deals with "Die Wege und die Begegnungen" in his essay "Eros und Vogelflug. Hugo von Hofmannsthal als Hermeneut alttestamentarischer Weisheit," *Deutsche Vierteljahresschrift* 53 (1969), 274-88. He compares the impressionistic essay to "Ad me ipsum," defining "Begegnung als der Schnittpunkt von Präexistenz und Existenz" (p. 285), and continues to interpret "Begegnung" not in the sense of spiritual love, as does Miles, but as the erotic encounter which leads, through love, to "Verknüpfung mit der Welt," citing "Ad me ipsum" in this connection: "Präexistenz: Bedrohung durch den Eros."

the two lovers. The question whether or not Andreas' love will liberate him from his dread of violent sexual passion remains an open one at the conclusion of the Carinthian episode. Again the bird symbol, this time the eagle soaring above the valley, offers the only clue.

Hofmannsthal's critics concur in regarding the circling eagle as an image of the mystical unity with Romana and with the world granted Andreas in one fleeting moment of heightened perception. Miles writes that the eagle "becomes the focus of Andreas' realization that all things, when viewed from high enough, are united."[78] Gautschi emphasizes the mystical quality of the experience:

> Andreas erkennt in diesem Augenblick die Landschaft als Ausdruck seiner Seele. Innen und Außen verschmelzen auf wunderbare Weise. So wird die Landschaft für Andreas zum Wesen seiner selbst. In mystischer Versenkung spürt er, daß er und die Welt eigentlich eins sind, daß er in allen Dingen enthalten ist.[79]

Chapple particularly stresses the implication of the vision for Andreas' future:

> Since the eagle sees both him and Romana simultaneously, the mountain does not separate the two lovers; ... and if the eagle can see backwards and forwards geographically, then it can, by extension, do so temporally; thus the present, the past and the future may be seen on the same plane at the same time. Andreas' despair at his separation from Romana is overcome by the realization that a higher vision can envisage their reunion at the same time as their separation, and the future is now almost tangibly present in his hopes.[80]

In contrast to the optimistic impression of mystical union with Romana and the landscape of which she is a part transmitted by Hofmannsthal's critics, an examination of the animal imagery associated with the soaring eagle reveals that the shadow of cruelty and animal passion still hovers over Andreas' love for Romana. Bearing in mind the significance of the goat and deer symbols connected with Romana earlier, we observe their recurrence here.

---

78 *Hofmannsthal's Novel Andreas,* p. 166.
79 "Hugo von Hofmannsthal's Romanfragement 'Andreas,' " p. 45.
80 "Themes and Symbols in Hofmannsthal's *Andreas,*" pp. 56-57.

> Der herrliche Vogel schwebte oben allein noch im Licht, ... und der Hof, das Dorf, die Gräber von Romanas Geschwistern waren seinen durchdringenden Blicken nahe wie diese Bergschluchten, in deren bläuliche Schatten er hinabäugte, nach einem jungen Reh oder einer verlaufenen Ziege. Andreas umfing den Vogel, ja er schwang sich auf zu ihm mit einem beseligten Gefühl. Nicht in das Tier hinein zwang es ihn diesmal, nur des Tieres höchste Gewalt und Gabe fühlte er auch in seine Seele fließen. (SW, 30:76; E, pp. 161-62)

Andreas no longer loses his self awareness in complete identification with the bird, as he lost himself in contemplation of the death agonies of the Finazzer dog. Nonetheless he feels the power of the eagle, the predator scanning the earth for a deer or stray goat, for the very animals that have been linked to Romana. The mention of the goat recalls both the scene in which Romana lay down beneath the goat and its reflection in the bedroom scene where she lay guilelessly under Andreas. Her unquestioning trust in him and in the whole natural world crystallizes in the goat image, yet this very trust seems betrayed or at least threatened by Andreas' feeling of kinship with the eagle. In an early note for the novel, his fantasies about Romana did in fact approach rape:

> Leopold [Andreas'] Gedanken spazierengehend: ob das Faunische Überwältigen Romanas nicht auch straflos und herrlich sein könnte. (SW, 30:12)

The mention of a young deer as possible prey for the eagle evokes the connection of Romana with a wounded deer in Andreas' second dream with the Carinthian innkeeper's wife wounded by Gotthelf. Andreas, feeling the eagle's power in himself, becomes the hunter after his victim, the deer Romana. This recapitulation of the lover and his beloved as hunter and prey seems to have some basis in folklore, for in West Prussia bride and bridegroom have been known to play the roles of hunter and deer.[81] The entire scene, the eagle soaring above the young girl as deer, calls to mind events preceding the opening of "Die Frau ohne Schatten." The empress tells her nurse how she, having taken the form of a gazelle, was seized by the emperor's red falcon which beat its wings against her eyes.[82] When

---

80 *Handwörterbuch des deutschen Aberglaubens*, vol. 8, col. 618.
82 Wolfgang Köhler identifies the source of this hunting scene as the "Geschichte von König Sinibad" in the *Arabian Nights*. In the source, however

she changed herself into human form, the emperor, moments before her hunter, was overcome with love for her. The same tension between love and violence, the opposite poles of sexual passion, recurs here in the novel.

But coupled with this urge to overpower Romana, Andreas feels a simultaneous desire to protect her. It is this longing to shield and care for her, reminiscent of his conviction that he could restore life to the little bird found at his window, that indicates new hope for his future:

> Wie jener [Berg] in gewaltigen Räumen das zarte Reh hegte, mit Schattenkühle es deckte, mit bläulichem Dunkel es vor dem Verfolger barg, so lebte in ihm Romana. (SW, 30:76; E, p. 162)

Andreas has become, instead of the eagle waiting to seize Romana, the mountain protecting and concealing her from her pursuer. Indeed, Romana has become part of himself:

> Er sah in sich hinein und sah Romana niederknien und beten: sie bog ihre Knie wie das Reh, wenn es sich zur Ruh bettet, die zarten Ständer kreuzt, und die Geberde war ihm unsagbar. (SW, 30:76; E, p. 162)

Not only is the deer's attitude consonant with the Finazzers' religiosity, it compounds the piety ascribed to Romana and her family. The deer's religiosity and helpfulness to mankind is attested to by the legend of Saint Genevieve, in which a doe suckles the outcast mother's son, a tale undoubtedly familiar to Hofmannsthal through its treatment in Tieck's *Leben und Tod der Heiligen Genovefa* and Hebbel's *Golo und Genoveva.*

The image of the eagle circling overhead as Andreas leaves the valley encompasses the rival tendencies toward love and toward violence revealed in the imagery of horseback riding and in Andreas' involvement with the death of the Finazzer dog. More than the language of the novel, these symbols embody, though they do not al-

---

the incident revolves around the king's unjust punishment of his faithful falcon, and no mention is made of the gazelle's transformation into human form. (See *Hugo von Hofmannsthal und "Tausendundeine Nacht,"* pp. 132-33). It is characteristic of Hofmannsthal's fascination with the hunting motif that he altered the scene to depict a first erotic encounter.

ways reveal, the fundamental tension at the root of Hofmannsthal's conception of love. If, as David Miles maintains, the dead bird at the window is intended to suggest spiritual love, then the evocation of animal passion and cruelty in the hunt motif introduced by Gotthelf and coloring Andreas' later fantasies of Romana must be given equal weight.

Miles contends that the novel was meant to contain that promise of rebirth through ideal love which is a central theme of such Bildungsromane as *Wilhelm Meister, Hyperion,* and *Heinrich von Ofterdingen.* In the light shed upon Hofmannsthal's view of love and women through our examination of dog imagery and the hunt motif, we must question the applicability of the very concept of spiritual love to Hofmannsthal's work. Even leaving aside those women such as Vuic, the Semele figure and Mariquita, who are directly compared to animals, or those women such as Dianora and the pregnant servant girl of "Knabengeschichte" who are the helpless victims of some hunter, can Hofmannsthal's woman figures be interpreted as exercising an ennobling influence on the men who love them? Miles finds expression of Hofmannsthal's "complex ideas of an immanent-transcendant ideal love and an allomatic constancy within change" in the opera libretti *Ariadne auf Naxos, Die Frau ohne Schatten,* and *Die ägyptische Helena.*[83] In the case of Ariadne and Bacchus, mutual transformation, although not equivalent to spiritual love, does indeed occur. Yet in *Die Frau ohne Schatten,* the empress's love for her husband appears distorted by her memory of that first encounter between the eager hunter and the terrified gazelle. Furthermore, the empress must sacrifice her supernatural powers, in modern terms her very selfhood, in order to remain with her husband. She must succumb to the earthly bondage of motherhood, which can hardly be equated with the transcendence implied, for example, in Wilhelm's "Entsagung" of Nathalie, home and family. And finally, does *Die ägyptische Helena,* whose sexual imagery is laden with Freudian overtones, present any evidence of spiritual love? Does it not deal, instead, precisely with the resolution of such sexual conflicts as physical infidelity?

[83] *Hofmannsthal's Novel Andreas,* p. 203.

Miles points in a fruitful direction when he suggests that Hofmannsthal left the novel unfinished because of the "innate difficulty of portraying Andreas' ideal love for Romana in such a realistic form as that of the novel."[84] The multiplicity and complexity of the animal images pertaining to the relationship between the sexes does indeed confirm that the portrayal of love created a significant obstacle to the novel's completion.

It seems probable however that the difficulty lay not in the tension between ideal love and realistic prose, but rather in the portrayal of ideal love itself. If, as Miles assumes, Hofmannsthal recognized elevating spiritual love as an essential component of the *Bildungsroman,* his inability to reconcile literary tradition with his own troubled concept of a love threatened by violence and animal passion may have forced him to give up work on the novel. The dichotomy between the two aspects of love is reflected in the split personality of Maria-Mariquita and the little dog they share, as well as in the eagle image concluding the Carinthian episode.

As Hofmannsthal continued to work on the draft of the novel, he created a more extensive genealogy for Andreas and for his and Romana's children. The novel's editor in the new critical edition, Manfred Pape, suggests that this "genealogische Zersplitterung" led to the ultimate collapse of the projected novel.[85] A clue to the real nature of Hofmannsthal's difficulties does indeed lie in his preoccupation with genealogy: biographical details took the place of the portrayal of Andreas' and Romana's emotions, character development, and intimacy, which would have been necessary to continue the novel through the resolution of Andreas' identity crises by means of union with Romana.[86] Such a portrayal of a mature, emotionally complete,

---

84 Ibid., p. 202.
85 "Die Vita des Herrn von Ferschengelder; zur Vorgeschichte und genealogischen Konzeption von Hofmannsthals Andreas," *Etudes Germaniques* (Jan.-Mar. 1982), pp. 25-33.
86 Juliette Sperling, who views romantic love as the key to solving Andreas' identity crisis, points out that Romana, like several of Hofmannsthal's figures who form the healing or transforming half of an "allomatische Beziehung," is without duality, possessed of a total, harmonious self concept. For Andreas, such a partner "kann der Gefahr der Selbstauflösung entgegentreten. Das Ich kann letztlich Geborgenheit im Gegenüber des/der Geliebten fin-

lasting "marriage of true minds" is as completely absent from Hofmannsthal's work as is the portrayal of a secure, mutually satisfying father-son relationship. The last few years of Hofmannsthal's life were occupied with work on the novel and on *Der Turm,* where the absence of any success in these two relationships darkens into tragedy.

---

den." See "das Ich und das Gegenüber: Hofmannsthal und Proust," *Arcadia,* 18 (1983), 146-54.

CHAPTER X

DER TURM

Hofmannsthal's last great tragedy shares several important characteristics with some of his earlier works in which animal symbolism predominates. Like the novel, "Knabengeschichte," and *Jupiter und Semele, Der Turm* failed to achieve a definite version and retained some of the tentative nature of the fragments. As in the earlier works, animal imagery serves to shroud critical issues in a protective veil of discretion. The conflict between father and son, a central concern of the narratives cited above, once again becomes the focal point of a major work. The dehumanization of man in times of war forms a common theme and a major source of animal symbolism in *Der Turm* and "Reitergeschichte." The poet's fascination with the magical power of language and the function of animals as the antithesis of that power link *Der Turm* to "Ein Traum von großer Magie." The same reluctance to reveal too much of his own character which led Hofmannsthal to mask themes about which he felt so deeply in the ciphers of animal imagery prompted him, during the lengthy composition of the drama, to reduce substantially the variety and frequency of those images which were his chief means of dealing with those irresolvable questions. Therefore the earlier stages of his adaptation of Calderon are far richer in animal imagery than the play prepared as a theater production in collaboration with Max Reinhardt.[1] Because the version of *Der Turm* composed between 1923

---

[1] Georgina A. Clark describes Reinhardt's role in the development of the play's stage version in "Max Reinhardt and the Genesis of Hugo von Hofmannsthals *Der Turm*," *Modern Austrian Literature*, 17 (1984), 1-32. See also Brian Coghlan, *Hofmannsthal's Festival Dramas* (Cambridge: Cambridge University Press, 1964), pp. 298-302; and Jakob Laubach, "Hugo von Hofmannsthals Turm-Dichtungen," Diss. Freiburg, Switzerland, 1954, pp. 38-42 and 76-78.

and 1925 (in the Steiner edition, D, 4:8-208) offers the widest range of animal symbols, it will form the basis of our discussion here.

The extraordinarily frequent occurrence of metaphoric language and pejoratives linked to animals begins with the opening expository scene of the first act.[2] Several deformed or unusual animals serve as omens of the approaching catastrophe: a three-legged rabbit, a gaunt pig and a calf with glowing eyes have been sighted (D, 4:13). A similar discussion of such unnatural phenomena presages the fateful events in Shakespeare's *Julius Caesar.* In both cases the disturbances in nature mirror the anarchy of political upheaval in human society. Hofmannsthal's adoption of such imagery enhances the Baroque flavor of his work, for the assumption that natural phenomena reflect or correspond to human events rests upon the Baroque concept of a hierarchical world order. In this "great chain of being" man occupies a position between the heavenly ranks and the animal kingdom. Disruption on one level of the cosmos is inevitably reflected in disturbances in the other levels as well.[3] As in Shakespeare's plays (*Macbeth* is another example) a criminal perversion of the natural or divine — the two being synonymous during the Baroque — order of monarchy lies at the root of the cosmic upheaval.

Sigismund demonstrates his grasp of the cosmic order now threatened by events in the kingdom when he comments: "Ist alles durcheinander, blast ein Engel, bringt alles in Reih und Glied" (D, 4: 26). Basilius, likewise cognizant of the disruption of hierarchical order in his realm, expresses through his juxtaposition of social and

---

[2] Heinz Politzer comments: "Nach Kleists Penthisilea kenne ich kein Stück, dessen Bildersprache mit ähnlicher Vehemenz die Zoologie geplündert hätte." See "Der Turm und das Tier aus dem Abgrund," *Grillparzer Forum* (Heidelberg: Lothar Stiehm Verlag, 1969), p. 34.

[3] Most of Hofmannsthal's critics overlook the reflection of political chaos in nature, regarding the anarchy in the play merely as a reflex of the contemporary European condition. See, for example, Laubach, "Hofmannsthals Turm-Dichtungen," p. 96; and Gerhard Meyer-Sichting, "Hofmannsthals Turm," *Merkur* 8 (1954): 210. Lothar Wittmann, however, does mention the Baroque concept of a hierarchical world order and its relation to the animal motifs. See *Sprachthematik und dramatische Form im Werk Hofmannsthals,* Studien zur Poetik und Geschichte der Literatur, vol. 2 (Stuttgart: W. Kohlhammer Verlag, 1966), p. 95.

natural phenomena his conviction that the animal world mirrors disorder on the human plane:

> ... der Soldat, der die Fahn abreißt und seinem Oberen die Pferdehalfter ums Maul schlägt, der Bauer, der vom Pflug läuft und seine Sense umnagelt zur blutigen Pike, die Kometen, die Erde, die sich spaltet, die Haufen herrenloser Hunde, die Raben, kreisend Tag und Nacht überm blachen Feld — es ist alles in der Prophezeiung. (D, 4:63)

The packs of stray dogs function, as in "Reitergeschichte," as a symbol of the chaos brought on by war and its attendant evils, pestilence and starvation. Like the dogs, the ravens multiply in times of death because they feed on carrion. In folklore, the appearance of flocks of ravens forbodes sickness, fire, and inflation, all of which figure in the prophecy to Basilius.[4] Because of their dependence on carrion, ravens may even appear eager for death, as in the old English ballad, "Three Ravens." Their senselessly repeated circling above the field left barren by war creates an image of futility and sterility.

In the fourth act similar birds of prey rare again associated with destruction. Olivier, ordering the complete destruction of the upper and middle classes, proclaims:

> Die Zucht soll verschwinden! Es sollen hinter uns die Geier und Wölfe kommen und sie sollen nicht sagen, daß wir halbe Arbeit getan haben. (D, 4: 163)[5]

The bird motif related to Sigismund has, however, an altogether different significance. Because he is the oppressed victim of Basilius' injustice, of the anarchy in the kingdom, and of Olivier and his rebels as well, he does not identify with those agents of destruction in the animal world, the ravens and the vultures, but rather with those creatures whose lives have been thrown into disarray by sudden violence. He tells the rebels:

> Horch, Jetzt flattern die Dohlen um den Turm und schreien über ihre Nester, in denen die Brut verbrennt — aber der Wanderer, der zehn Stunden weit

---

4 *Handwörterbuch des deutschen Aberglaubens*, vol. 7, col. 444.
5 The vulture personifies death in the slaves' song mourning the dead Alkestis: "Nicht des Geiers Schwingen schlage/ ihr ums Haupt, die wilden, Tod,/ flieg ihr auf den Mund, ein Falter,/ schwarz und still im Abendrot!" (D, 1:26).

> übern Hochpaß geht, sieht nur ein kleines, glimmendes Fünkchen. So bescheiden ist alles! (D, 4:151)

He pities the creatures suffering the effects of human upheaval, yet at the same time his belief in the invalidity of human institutions and machinations causes him to share the wanderer's perspective and deny that either the rebellion or the havoc it wreaks is of any lasting importance. The only permanent fixture in Sigismund's world is the steadfast tower of his own soul.

The unnatural phenomena brought on by the injustice of Sigismund's captivity and by the general distress of the nation culminate in the appearance of the serpent's egg. The recruit warns Olivier not to approach Sigismund and claims that he will be blinded if he disobeys. He explains:

> Wenn eine menschliche Kreatur ins Blutschwitzen kommt, so erbarmen sich die Schlangen, sie werfen sich in die Luft in einem Knäuel und gebären alle zusammen ein Ei, – das macht die Blinden sehend und die Sehenden blind! (D, 4:14)

Hofmannsthal may have been familiar with the following description of the magical serpent's egg in Pliny's *Natural History*:

> Snakes intertwined in great numbers in a studied embrace make these round objects with the saliva from their jaws and the foam from their bodies. It is called a "wind egg." The Druids say that it is tossed aloft by the snakes' hisses, and that it ought to be caught in a military cloak before it can touch the earth.[6]

Pliny records nothing of the healing quality of this egg, ascribing to it only the power to win lawsuits and gain access to potentates. In Bohemia, however, the stone or egg is believed an effective antidote to poison, and prophetic powers, the prevention of epidemics and enchantment are attributed to it as well.[7] Hofmannsthal may have derived the idea that the snakes' egg restored sight from the tale of the blind emperor Theodosius in the *Gesta Romanorum*. He provided a

---

[6] Pliny, *Natural History*, trans. W. H. S. Jones, Loeb Classical Library, 10 vols. (Cambridge, Mass.: Harvard University Press, 1963), vol. 8 p. 217. Book XXIX, xii.

[7] *Handwörterbuch des deutschen Aberglaubens*, vol. 7, col. 1199.

bell of justice to be rung by any having a complaint. A snake which had made her nest under the bell rope rang it to protest that a toad had usurped her nest. The emperor heard the case, and judged that the toad should be driven out and killed and the snake restored to her nest. Later as the emperor lay in bed, the snake glided in, bearing a precious stone in her mouth; when she let the stone fall on his eyes, his sight was restored.[8] Antiquity seems also to have esteemed the snake for its healing powers, a belief attested to by the caduceus of Aesculapius. The recruit implies that the snakes conjoin to aid Sigismund in his acute distress. Olivier's submission to the recruit's desire to protect the prisoner through his threat of blindness proves him to be of a superstitious peasant nature like his troops in spite of his defiant boldness. At the same time, however, the allusion to classical belief in the healing powers of the snake introduces an alien and not readily comprehensible element into the Baroque-Catholic atmosphere of the play.

The animal imagery of the first scene exposes, as we have just observed, the chaotic situation of the nation. Olivier, leader of the rebels, is a major force behind this dehumanization and is therefore described in animal terms by Sigismund:

> Die Geräte des Ackers sind entfremdet ihrem Dienst und müssen jetzt die Welt reinigen. Das erkenne ich. Und ich erkenne auch, daß du der Rechte bist für ein blutiges Werk, genau so wie du bist. Denn du hast einen Stiernacken und die Zähne eines Hundes. (D, 4:151)

Sigismund reverses the Biblical prophecy that peace shall come and swords shall be beaten into plowshares. Instead he foresees a time of war. Olivier's "Stiernacken" signifies the brute strength of a draft animal drawing a plow, but now his power will serve a bloody work. That he has dog's teeth suggests destruction and a tearing apart of carrion; he belongs among the packs of stray dogs appearing in the prophecy to Basilius and in the war-wasted village of "Reitergeschichte."

In the second act, Basilius consults his former spiritual advisor, the Grand Almoner, about the state of the kingdom. Since the Grand

---

[8] *Gesta Romanorum*, pp. 182-83.

Almoner represents the highest spiritual power, he stands at the opposite pole from Olivier, yet not beyond the pale of animal imagery. He has completely withdrawn from worldly existence, and is therefore not compared to animals of this earth, but to imaginary creatures, the griffin and basilisk.

Basilius, who stands in awe of the Grand Almoner, remarks: "Seine Augen gehen wie die Augen des Greifen durch und durch und das Eingeweide hält ihnen nicht stand" (D, 4:64). The griffin, formed with the body of a loin and head and wings of an eagle, appeared in Assyrian and Egyptian art.[9] Hofmannsthal mentions the griffin as a sculptural ornament in *Der Tor und der Tod* (GLD, p. 203; SW, 3:66) and in the story of Amgiad and Assad (A, p. 111). In the legend of Alexander the Great, griffins drew Alexander's chariot toward heaven, and it is in this connection that the merchant's son thinks longingly of Alexander's bed, "getragen von Greifen und geflügelten Stieren" (E, p. 24; SW, 28:27). The griffin appears in religious imagery as a symbol of Christ, possibly because it combines two of the most powerful animals, the eagle, and lion.[10] It was also supposed to guard gold and treasure, and to chastise human greed by devouring strangers who tried to gather such precious stones.[11] Its function as chastizer of human greed particularly applies to the Grand Almoner, who accuses Basilius of these very failings. The "Wahnsinniger" of *Das kleine Welttheater* is also compared to a griffin:

> In der kahlen Kammer, kaum der Nahrung,
> Die ein zahmer Vogel nimmt, bedürftig,
> Wirft sich seine Seele mit den Flügeln,
> Mit den Krallen kühner als eine Greife,
> Wilder als ein Greife, auf die neue
> Schattengleiche, körperlose Beute.
> (GLD, p. 313; SW, 3:145-46)

Here the griffin appears as a fierce predator, but the prey which he seizes is the knowledge contained in the writings of Paracelsus. The

---

9 White, *The Beastiary, A Book of Beasts*, pp. 22-24.
10 George Ferguson, *Signs and Symbols in Christian Art* (New York: Oxford University Press, 1966), p. 20.
11 *Encyclopedia Britannica*, 11th ed., s.v. "griffin."

youth's passion for such knowledge causes him to spurn attachment to this world, as does the Grand Almoner. The youth lives remote from ordinary life isolated in his tower, just as the Grand Almoner has withdrawn to the monastery. The griffin, an imaginary creature, is more appropriate as a symbol of these figures than real animals, for both have purposefully abandoned real life for the imagination or for pursuits of the mind.

Basilius also addresses the Grand Almoner as "Du Basilisk" (D, 4:71). The basilisk became confused with the cockatrice so that the two were virtually synonymous. It was believed to hatch from an egg laid by an old cock from corrupted seed within him.[12] Its glance was deadly, and it could supposedly be killed by regarding its own reflection in a mirror, a belief to which Hofmannsthal alludes in *Dame Kobold:*

> ... O Basilisk,
> ist die Fabel wahr, daß du
> nicht ertragen kannst den Spiegel,
> der dein eigen Bild zurückgibt?
> (L, 4:194)

The basilisk's reputation for its powerful gaze applies to the Grand Almoner, whose regard Basilius dreads.

Basilius himself is directly connected to the imaginary creature, for the word "basilius," from the Greek meaning "king," has given its name to both.[13] The basilisk's corrupt origin and its reputation for destruction ally it with Basilius. The connection also implies that Basilius may be identified with the Antichrist:

> In early symbolism the basilisk was commonly accepted as the symbol of the Devil or the Antichrist, an interpretation based upon a passage from Psalm 91:31, which reads in the Douay version:

---

12 *Gesta Romanorum*, p. 399, note 18, and p. 400.
13 White, *The Bestiary*, p. 169, note. See also Hartmut Zelinsky's study, *Brahman und Basilisk; Hugo von Hofmannsthals poetisches System und sein lyrisches Drama "Der Kaiser und die Hexe,"* (Munich: Wilhelm Fink, 1974), pp. 128-34. Zelinsky examines the basilisk imagery in *Der Kaiser und die Hexe, Der Turm* and *Der Schwierige* and concludes that it represents the Antichrist, deceit or dishonesty, melancholy and "Erstarrung," all attributes which characterize Basilius (p. 129).

"... thou shalt tread upon the adder and the basilisk and trample under foot the lion and the dragon." These four animals were interpreted by St. Augustine as four aspects of the Devil, who was trodden down by the triumphing Christ.[14]

According to a superstition of which Hofmannsthal may have been aware, the basilisk could be killed by the sound of a cock's crowing.[15] Therefore it may be significant that Sigismund, who is instrumental in Basilius' downfall, compares himself to a cock: "Wie der Hahn auf dem Hofe rieche ich den grauenden Morgen und die Stunde wo die Sterne von ihrem Wachposten abtreten" (D, 4:169). Of course the cock is also connected with Christ's passion because of St. Peter's denying him three times before the cock crowed. The association of Basilius with the basilisk and Sigismund with the cock forms part of the imagery linking Sigismund to Christ, a topic which will be discussed later.

The basilisk image is further complicated by the comparison of Sigismund to a basilisk. Olivier commands: "Achtet mir auf den [B]asilisken da und hängt ihm einen Maulkorb um, wofern er seine Zunge nicht im Zaum hält (D, 4:163). Olivier is concerned, of course, that Sigismund might speak and turn his followers against him. The basilisk was by all accounts so poisonous that it could kill merely through its breath; Olivier fears that Sigismund might poison his success through speech. The common denominator which makes the basilisk image applicable to the Grand Almoner, Basilius and Sigismund seems to be its deadly gaze; because it paralyzes or kills whatever it looks upon, the creature stands for isolation and petrifaction. Thus the Grand Almoner has not only retreated to a monastery to divorce himself from life, but also sleeps in a coffin as a sign that he is dead to all human contact. Sigismund, isolated in his tower prison, has never known a friend, as Julian reminds Basilius. And thereupon Basilius compares his own barren existence to that of his son (D, 4:107). Furthermore these three figures are doomed to isolation because of their potential for exercising extraordinary power; they have sacrificed, willingly or unwillingly, the human closeness of

14 Ferguson, *Signs and Symbols in Christian Art*, pp. 11-12.
15 *Encyclopedia Britannica*, 11th ed., s. v. "cockatrice."

love and family to their offices as spiritual or political rulers. Thus the basilisk, symbolizing both kinship and sterility, is a fitting emblem of all three.

In both the first and second acts, animal symbols disclose that the country's inhabitants have sunk to the level of brutes; it is significant that not only the peasants, but the king and Grand Almoner as well are described in animal or non-human terms. Olivier, at once a representative of man's bestial nature and chief exponent of a brutally contemptuous attitude toward his fellow creatures, addresses his men with animal pejoratives ranging from the general "maledetta bestia" to the specific, "Eselskopf." He directs his insults not only to his peers, but refers to the prisoner as "das Vieh" and to Julian as "ein gesalbter Lauskerl." The preponderance of animal epithets in his speech springs of course in part, as was the case with Gotthelf, from a tendency to regard all humans as purely physical, and therefore bestial creatures. Yet Basilius' speech in the second act makes it clear that internal warfare, inflation and pestilence have reduced his subjects to the animal level. Man as brute is not an attitude unique to Olivier, but characteristic of the actual state of the realm. Social order has collapsed, and the peasants have reverted to the unstructured primitive state of forest creatures. Basilius laments:

> Die Wälder, in denen ich jage, sind voller Bettler: sie fressen die Rinde von den Bäumen und stopfen sich die Bäuche mit Klumpen Erde. (D, 4:62)

This degradation of humanity in times of war is reminiscent of the conditions of the desolate village of "Reitergeschichte," where fighting rats, the repulsive dogs and the unsuspecting cow being led to her death mirrored the situation of Anton Lerch, or perhaps even of mankind. It is important to note, however, that the short story preserved the distinction between the animal and human spheres: if the abandoned village encompassed the animal sphere, then Milan depicted the human plane. Just as Lerch's ride through the village presents a mirror image of his ride through Milan, the animal condition reflects that of humanity, yet may not be fittingly equated with it. Lerch's unawareness of his inevitably approaching death resembles the unsuspecting greed of the cow, but the two are not equal, for one is human and the other animal. In *Der Turm,* by contrast, the distinction between human and animal modes of existence is threatened with obliteration; the beggars' struggle for survival hardly differs from that of the forest animals.

The dehumanization of man, though characteristic of the entire kingdom, centers about Sigismund. To his guards, he is only a captive beast, the human body grown together with the pelt which clothes it. Any evidence of human physical characteristics or attitudes, such as piety, is greeted with astonishment:

> Aus dem Wolfsleib ist ein Menschenkopf gewachsen! Er reckt fünffingerige Hand und faltets wie ein Mensch! (D, 4:14)

In the doctor's conversation with Anton, Sigismund's existence is repeatedly compared to that of a dog. The doctor finds the cell "zu schlecht für einen Hundezwinger" (D, 4:19), and Anton tells him that the prince's rations are "für einen räudigen Hund zu gering" (D, 4:27). In spite of his sympathy for the prisoner, Anton too tends to regard him as an animal. He refers to Sigismund as "die Kreatur" and when the doctor asks how the captive passes his time, Anton replies, "Wie ein Herr oder wie ein Hund" (D, 4:20). When he fears that Julian intends to kill Sigismund, he pleads for his life arguing that a muzzle will prevent him from doing any harm (D, 4:96). Later one of the rebels asks Sigismund to identify Julian as "der dich, unsern König, an der Kette gehalten hat, ärger wie einen Hund" (D, 4:152). The dog imagery here does not, as is usually the case in Hofmannsthal's works, connect with the theme of sexuality. Rather it expresses the degradation of man's physical existence to an animal level and simultaneously underscores the helpless state of the prince as a prisoner.

If the first act has been primarily descriptive of man's reversion to the animal state, the second explores the causes of his plight. The Grand Almoner expounds on the irreconcilable disharmony of body and soul, insisting that all bodily urges must be curbed in order to prevent man from sinking into the bestial condition:

> Denn ein Mensch fängt dort an, wo ein viehisch gelüstender Leib überwältigt ist und unter die Füße gebracht von Wesenheit. (D, 4:70)

Within the play these opposing categories, body and soul, seem personified in Basilius, to whom the Grand Almoner addresses his tirade, and Julian, respectively.

The Grand Almoner accuses Basilius of gross sexual appetites, of entertaining himself with adulteresses and hunting dogs (D, 4:72). Here the dog image carries the usual connotation of female sexuality, and may further suggest that the chaos symbolized by the packs of stray dogs roaming in the kingdom results in part from the king's promiscuity, indicative of the same fateful lack of self control which led him, in the Grand Almoner's opinion, into the war which has devastated his land. The link between promiscuity and chaos allies Basilius with Mariquita, whose carefree amorality was represented by the little spaniel she shared with Maria, as both shared the chaotic elements in their personalities.

The dog motif recurs when the Grand Almoner foretells Basilius' subservience to his son: "Aber du wirst wackeln mit dem Steiß vor ihm, wie ein Hund vor seinem Herren [sic] (D, 4:72). He expresses himself through the same image, a dog fawning on its master, which Hofmannsthal used to describe the behavior of the repudiated young Greek before his wealthy uncle in *Andreas.* Basilius is already conscious of his dog-like obsequiousness: "Ich trete hin und her wie ein gefangenes Tier! Ich winde mich!" (D, 4:74). The dog-metaphor communicates the King's base nature, his readiness to submit to any stronger will — such as that of his mentor, before whom he writhes ingratiatingly. His characterization of himself as a trapped animal reveals that he, like his son, is a captive, and, like his subjects, reduced to the animal plane.

Basilius' unnatural lasciviousness lies at the root of his association with the fox. Here, as in connection with Gotthelf, the fox signifies lewdness, treachery and greed. It is Sigismund who first likens Basilius to a fox in the court scene: "Ich habe schon einmal einen alten Fuchs mit Händen erwürgen müssen! Er hat gerochen wie du! (D, 4:123). Sigismund is referring to an incident which Anton has related earlier in the play:

> Er leidet nicht, daß man ihn angeht. Er hat sich einmal mit einem Fuchs verbissen, den die Wächter ihm zur Kurzweil übers Gitter werfen taten. (D, 4:21)

The incident demonstrates not only the cruelty of Sigismund's guards, but also the savagery latent within him and thus serves to prepare the audience for his increasing violence later on in the play. Sigismund alludes to the strangling of the fox to warn his father of his potentially destructive nature. In keeping with his licentious habits Basilius appears as a fox in the conjuring scene of the fifth act. His protruding tongue suggests desire and greed, reminiscent of Gotthelf licking his thick moist lips like a cat. Basilius' adultery had condemned him to a life in the underworld, as is seen from the fact that the fox which the gypsy holds in her arms is suddenly transformed into the king, who rises from the earth.

The fox image is secondarily associated with Basilius' subjects. A courtier, blaming the Jews for the nation's monetary woes, declares:

> Sie liegen auf königlichen Schuldverschreibungen, wie auf Gansdaunen, ihr stinkender Fuchsbau ist tapeziert mit Pfandscheinen von Grafen und Bannerherren... (D, 4:62)

In this instance the fox is associated with avarice, and we recall that the fox-like Gotthelf possessed a similar affinity for money. In the phrase "stinkender Fuchsbau" the courtier alludes to the popular belief that the fox is accompanied by an unpleasant odor. Julian, boasting of his activity in arousing the rebels, again connects the fox with greed:

> ... das Tier mit Zähnen und Klauen habe ich aufgestört, aus Schweinsschnauze und Fuchsrachen stößt es deinen Namen hervor... (D, 4:137)

The pig-fox combination — the two animals are linked by their common reputation for greed — repeats Hofmannsthal's characterization of Baron Ochs in the *Rosenkavalier* as "halb Fuchs, halb Schwein."[16] It implies not only avarice, but a hunger for the gratification of all physical appetites. Julian views the rebels only as a collective mass united by a single purpose; he has no awareness of his inferiors as individuals, only a respect for their unbounded destructiveness suggested by the synecdoche of teeth and claws. The fact that Basilius shares the attributes of greed and lust with the peasant rebels indicates that the dichotomy between body and soul pervades his nation, that a mass of ravaging bodies alone dominates the course of events.

---

16 Hofmannsthal and Kessler, *Briefwechsel*, p. 226.

Basilius, defamed by the comparison with dog and fox, attempts to give himself a more impressive countenance by associating himself with the stag in a lengthy passage of self-glorification:

> Heut ist St. Aegydi Tag: da geht der Hirsch in die Brunft ... groß und fürstlich tritt der Hirsch aus dem Holz, und löst die Lippen, daß es scheint, als ob er lache, und schreit machtvoll, daß die Tiere im Jungholz ihre zitternden Flanken aneinanderdrücken vor Schreck und Verlangen. — Wir waren wie er und haben majestätische Tage genossen, ehe das Wetter umschlug, und den schönen Weibern lösten sich die Knie beim Laut Unseres Kommens, ... (D, 4:60)

Basilius evokes in the stag image precisely those qualities he lacks: regality, unquestioned command over others, and virility. The stag's self-contained and dignified bearing justify its association with nobility. Its sexual prowess is attested to by superstitious belief in the power of medicaments concocted from its organs to produce sexual arousal or alleviate impotence.[17] Once these associations are recognized, the king's invocation of the stag only draws attention to his own infertility.

Like the fox and dog images, the stag symbol is not unique to Basilius. Sigismund calls forth Olivier's spirit and remarks, "Er stinkt nach Brand und Blut wie der Brunfthirsch!" (D, 4:183). He ignores the stag's nobler connotations and sees in him only repulsively excessive sexual desire, a trait common to both Olivier and Basilius. Sigismund himself is associated with the stag earlier in the play. Count Adam announces: "Ich habe ihm von hinten die Sehne durchschnitten wie einem Hirsch. Er liegt" (D, 4:127). Although the text does not elaborate on this particular use of the metaphor, it seems consistent with the depiction of Sigismund as a passive Christ figure which will be examined below. The stag is linked in the writings of the church fathers with Christ himself. According to religious legend, a stag with a glowing cross between his antlers appeared to St. Hubertus during a hunt and caused him to give up worldly pleasures for a religious life.[18] In Flaubert's *Légende de Saint Julien l'Hospitalier* a

---

17 *Handwörterbuch des deutschen Aberglaubens*, vol. 4, col. 104.
18 Ibid., col. 97. The stag bearing a cross between its antlers appears in the bas-relief depicting the conversion of St. Hubertus above the chapel door at the chateau of Amboise.

white stag appears to warn the hunter Julien that he will kill his father. As applied to Sigismund, the stag image endows him with the god-like nobility Basilius seeks through his application of the stag metaphor to himself.

Finally, Basilius is briefly compared to a he-goat. After the disastrous court scene, Julian repulses the attentions of the doctor, saying, "nicht mich laßt zum Ader — aber das Tier mit Hörnern, bis es weiß wird und umfällt: den alten Bock mit einer Krone auf!" (D, 4:129). Here, as in the comparison of Gotthelf to a goat, the animal symbolizes excessive lewdness. It is interesting to note that both Basilius and Gotthelf are compared to both fox and goat; the animal imagery reveals a similarity of character — lasciviousness and duplicity — not immediately discernible.[19]

The fire and light imagery surrounding Julian has given rise to the assumption that he, as the incorporation of asceticism and piety, is intended as the antithesis of Basilius.[20] Unlike the king, who has gratified every physical desire, Julian has renounced the pleasures of love and family in the service of his ambition. Further examination shows, however, that his goal is not altruistic service to his country, but merely self-aggrandizement. Because of the internal struggle between ambition and conscience, he is repeatedly associated with the snake. The doctor recognizes the inner conflict in Julian:

> In furchtbarem Schlangenkampf ringen Gut und Bös in diesen gebieterischen Mienen. (D, 4:43)

The snake image immediately draws attention to Julian's unsatisfied sexuality and negates the aura of complete self-control surrounding him. The Grand Almoner compares man's awareness of his own body

---

19 The comparison of Sigismund to a goat (D, 4:89) refers to the goat as a creature of the devil. His pious foster mother points to the crucifix commanding, "Schau hin, Bock du, widerspenstiger!"

20 Lothar Wittmann contrasts Basilius, representative of Sigismund's "animal nature," with Julian, his spiritual father, and interprets the fire and light imagery as "Symbole des Engelhaften" and of the miracle of language. Although his interpretation of *Der Turm* is generally sound, he places too little emphasis on Julian's sinister and self-serving ambition (*Sprachthematik und dramatische Form im Werk Hofmannsthals*, pp. 96-97).

to "Wälzen von Schlangen mit schlagendem End ..." (D, 4:75), and although he addresses himself to Basilius, Julian is bound to his physical being in the same manner. The snake metaphor also suggests Julian's treachery; Basilius tells Sigismund:

> Eines ist Königen not: daß sie sich ihrer bösen Ratgeber zu erwehren lernen. Sie sind die Schlangen an unserem Busen.

And then he requests, "Mache uns frei von der Schlange Julian, der uns beide umstrickt hat" (D, 4:121). The same connotations of evil and falseness surround Klytemnästra:

> Eine gelbe Gestalt, ... einer Ägypterin ähnlich, mit glattem Gesicht einer aufgerichteten Schlange gleichend, trägt ihr die Schleppe. (D, 2:24)

Like Basilius and Julian, Sigismund ist characterized through the use of animal imagery. The choice of symbols links him to the earthly corporeal sphere of Basilius and simultaneously to the ideal or divine sphere imperfectly represented by Julian. He presents, then, one example of the Baroque dichotomy of body and spirit, failing to achieve a complete synthesis of the two poles. His holy soul suffers terribly from the association with the lowest forms of animal life and seeks to affirm its god-like nature through a search for the boundary separating man and beast.

Examining first the animal imagery linking Sigismund to the spiritual world, we find that it belongs to the larger complex of allusions to the passion of Christ, a complex greatly expanded in the 1927 version of the play. The comparison of the prince to a calf with bound feet points to his role as a sacrifice, not, as in the Bible, to God, but to political reality (D, 4:140). He likens himself to a lamb when pleading with Julian for knowledge of his true identity: "Sag mir zuvor, wer ich bin, und ich folge dir wie ein Lamm" (D, 4:95). Although Sigismund intends docility as the basis of his simile, he again implies that he is a passive sacrifice to Julian's political machinations. At the same time, the image connects him with Christ, a theme repeated when the doctor begs Julian not to betray his charge before the cock crows thrice, and when Sigismund imitates Christ's position on the cross.[21] Both the calf and lamb symbols depend for

---

21 For a study of the Biblical allusions in the play see Erwin Kobel, *Hugo von Hofmannsthal*, p. 234.

their effect not on the image of the animals themselves, but merely on their traditional Christian connotations.

The comparison of Sigismund to an eagle revolves around the majestic bird's association with divinity and royalty. Exner points out that royal persons are supposedly born under the constellation of Aquila, and reminds us that Zeus transformed himself into an eagle to capture Ganymede.[22] Hofmannsthal attributes eagle-like qualities to other royal characters in his work, notably to Oedipus, to whom Kreon exclaims:

> Du bist ein Gott! es schwebte der ungeheure Blitz aus blauer Nacht hernieder wie ein goldner Adler hinter dir! (D, 2:406)

The hero of Hofmannsthal's biographical essay "Prinz Eugen der edle Ritter" is frequently associated with the eagle and becomes identified with the two-headed eagle, the emblem of Austria (P, 3:293, 297, 299). The silver eagle appears on the Polish flag and on the medallion Basilius awards to Julian and later reclaims. Basilius, who considers his royal person synonymous with the monarchy, attempts to reassert his majesty when intimidated by the memory of the Grand Almoner's piercing gaze:

> Wir sind noch König in Polen! Wir wollen jetzt, wo nicht sogleich Unserem Wunsch willfahrt wird — so werden Wir diesem Mönchsloch den Rücken kehren und reiten, wohin Unserem Adlerblick zu reiten gelüstet! (D, 4:64)

But like the stag image, the eagle metaphor is appropriate not to Basilius, but to Sigismund, a born ruler, Julian informs him that he will be brought "So nah ans Licht, daß nur ein junger Adler nicht blind wird" (D, 4:94). He describes the sleeping potion he wishes to administer to the prince as that "wonach Hirsch und Adler und Schlange lechzen" (D, 4:94), implying that the three rivals in a position to impose their rule on the kingdom, namely, Basilius, Sigismund, and Julian himself, thirst for rebirth as the chosen king.

The symbols connecting Sigismund with Christ and with the Polish throne indicate his potential, while his real existence, a debasing captivity, relegates him to the plane of the lowliest creatures.

---

22 Exner, *Hugo von Hofmannsthal's "Lebenslied,"* pp. 86-87.

We have already discussed the dog imagery applied to the captive Sigismund. He is so imbued with his identity as animal that even when freed from his prison, Sigismund speaks of himself in animal terms. While threatening the courtiers, he declares: "An mir ist nichts vom Weib! Mein Haar ist kurz und sträubt sich. Ich zeige meine Tatzen" (D, 4:124). This image recalls the picture of Sigismund dressed in a wolf's pelt, for now he seems a predatory animal. Next he warns them: "Ich will mit euch hausen wie der Sperber im Hühnerhof" (D, 4:125-26). He calls forth not only the vision of a bird of prey, but suggests to the courtiers an insulting parallel between the royal "Hof" and a "Hühnerhof."

Sigismund's desire for escape from reality is likewise expressed in animal terms. Resisting Julian's demands that he re-enter the world outside his tower as figurehead of the rebel forces, he says:

> Ich liege hier und dennoch zugleich fliege ich dahin, ... und im Fluß, unter dem silbernen Schimmer stehen die Fische und freuen sich an der lauen fließenden Tiefe und ich spiele in ihrer Mitte, ... (D, 4:136)

It is significant that Sigismund has no real association with fish; vermim have plagued him, he has strangled a fox, he wears a wolf's pelt, but his fish exist totally apart from his present state. Therefore he imagines their world as one of pure fantasy, and as so different from his own that they inhabit a realm, "in dem alles von Schmach befreit ist" (D, 4:136). His longing for refuge in their non-human sphere recalls Dianora's similar desire for the underwater world.

Later the fish image reappears; Sigismund tells the rebels:

> Ich sage dir: es ist kein Ding anderer Natur als unsere Träume, — das Wasser, das aus diesem irdenen Quellbrunnen rinnt, — Er zeigt auf seinen Krug — was ist wirklicher? Aber auch diesem ist das beigemischt — und die Sterne schwimmen wie Fische im gleichen. (D, 4:155)

The water in his pitcher represents reality, as he points out, and the water in which fish swim his dreams or fantasies. It remains questionable whether Sigismund is, at this point, capable of distinguishing fantasy from reality. When he speaks of stars as well as fish swimming in water, he is thinking, of course, of stars reflected and therefore "swimming" in water occupied by fish. But is he able to differentiate clearly the stars in the sky from their reflection, or to perceive that the swimming of fish in water differs from the appearance of stars mirrored on its surface? Peter A. Stenberg, dealing primarily with the earliest (1901-04) stages of *Der Turm*, compares the prince's mystical visions to those of the "poet-aesthetes" of Hofmannsthal's early work. Both are isolated from the real world, he finds, but the "poet-aesthetes" express dream truths arising from inspiration, while Sigismund reacts to the external pressure, the captivity imposed by his father. Stenberg concludes that Sigismund's mystical visions are clearly described as symptoms of insanity.[23]

The whole problem of distinguishing reality from fantasy becomes particularly acute in the passages dealing with animal torture. Several of these passages make it clear that Sigismund willingly obliterates the distinction between his self and other creatures, identifying with their suffering, which is only a smaller reflection of his own. On the other hand, his psychological survival necessitates some awareness that he is separate from them, for he derives his only gratification from assuming his father's role and torturing the vermin who share his miserable existence. We have repeatedly emphasized the fragmentary character of those works in which animal torture plays a major part; it is therefore interesting to note that its role was far greater in the earlier stages of *Der Turm*. One of Sigismund's most explicit monologues is cited below:

>Stöhnen lernt ich da und Schäumen
>und die langen, leeren Tage
>in der Kammer hinzuträumen,
>erst am Abend auszugehen
>mit den Käuzchen, mit den Kröten.
>Grauts mich, ihnen zuzusehen,
>freuts mich doppelt, sie zu töten.
>Und wie die da drin mit mir,
>also spiel ich mit den Tieren.
>Seh ich zwei voll Saft und Leben
>zärtlich aneinanderkleben,
>seh ich eines flink sich regen,
>töt ich sie mit kurzen, schrägen
>Würfen oder jähen Schlägen.

---

23 Peter A. Stenberg, "Hofmannsthal und Sigismund: The Move from the Tower," *Monatshefte* 67 (1975), 22.

> Wären sie nicht blöd und stumm,
> fragten etwa sie, warum?
> Ihr seid lauter Sigismunde,
> ihr elenden, blinden Kröten,
> ich bin Sigismunds Geschick,
> mich gelüstets, euch zu töten. (D, 3:351-52)

Here Sigismund clearly detaches himself from his own position as tortured creature and assumes the superior role. He does not speak directly of his father, but identifies himself only as "Sigismunds Geschick." He feels a particular hostility toward sexual relationships ("Seh ich zwei voll Saft und Leben/ zärtlich aneinanderkleben"), a trait marked in later versions of the play only by his declaration "An mir ist nichts vom Weib!" (D, 4:124). His father's cruelty has destroyed not only his sense of family origin, of being born from a woman, but has somehow made sexual relationships so abhorrent to him that he struggles against their existence, even among animals.

In later versions of the play Sigismund's discourses on his own aberrations are significantly diminished. The causal relationship between the prince's mistreatment by Basilius and his tendency to mistreat in turn creatures weaker than he is expressed first not by Sigismund himself, but by one of his guards:

> Sie kujonieren ihn seit er am Leben ist, so kujoniert er was ihm unter die Hände kommt. (D, 4:12)

Julian, preparing Sigismund to confront his father, calls attention to the parallel once again:

> Du begreifst, daß deines Vaters Wege unerforschlich sein mußten, wie dem Getier deine Wege übers Getier. (D, 4:115)

Finally Sigismund reveals his own recognition of the correspondence between his father's cruel authority over him and his brutal domination of the animals; he exclaims:

> Daß ist eines Königs Großheit! die ich mir zu ahnen vermeinte, wenn ich einen Roßknochen schwang überm Getier! (D, 4:122)

Hofmannsthal's explicitness in explaining Sigismund's reason for persecuting weaker creatures confirms the thesis presented in the discussion of the hunting scene of *Das kleine Welttheater,* with the crucifixion of the sparrow-hawk in "Knabengeschichte" and with "Andreas' mistreatment of his little puppy; cruelty toward or sacrifice of animals is frequently exercised by one who feels himself the helpless victim of a greater, more forceful cruelty, be it that of the gods, as in the "Gespräch über Gedichte," or of the father, as in the other works cited. Jakob Laubach concurs with this interpretation of the motivation for mistreatment of animals, he writes:

> Spuren für diesen Zug. Schmerzen zuzufügen, weil man Schmerzen zu leiden hat, lassen sich besonders in dem frühen Schaffensabschnitt des Dichters nachweisen – In den *Stadien,* vermutlich von 1893, werden Erlebniss eines Knaben beschrieben, die einen merkwürdigen Hang zur Selbstquälerei verraten ... Nach einer Briefstelle von 1906 darf man vermuten, daß diese dichterischen Aussagen (Euseb's crucifixion of the sparrow-hawk, Andreas' cruelty toward his puppy) auch biographische Elemente enthalten. Hofmannsthal schreibt damals an seinen Vater: "Je älter ich werde, desto mehr fühle ich, wie seltsam ähnlich ich mit der guten Mama bin; dazu gehört auch diese unnatürlich gesteigerte Fähigkeit, in anderen zu leben (die freilich gerade den Dichter ausmacht), verbunden mit einer dämonischen Gabe, die liebsten und nächsten Menschen auf vielerlei Art (und zwar in einer Art Selbstquälerei) zu quälen, was sie ja auch so sehr gehabt hat" (B, 2:233).[24]

Although Sigismund's struggle to eradicate the vermin infesting his cell predominates in the 1925 version of the play, earlier stages are concerned primarily with the prisoner's sympathy and identification with these creatures. The notes relate that Sigismund, grieved by the murder of his favorite animal, a spider or a worm, refuses food until his governor Clotald (later renamed Julian) leads him out into the starry night:

> Da verspricht er, überwältigt, zu leben, um das Königreich zu erwerben, das über diesen Sternen ist (– sein Sprechen über die armseligen Tiere großartig, königlich: sich ein mystisches Königreich in der Einöde schaffend ...) (D, 3:428)

Sigismund's desire to attain the kingdom under the stars indicates his realization of the heavenly or divine kingdom as the antithesis of the animal world. He feels that his own person encompasses animal life, a belief symbolically represented through the function of the tower as

---

24 "Hugo von Hofmannsthals Turm-Dichtungen," p. 29.

an image of the self;[25] because it imprisons him in the company of vermin, they become part of his very being:

> Das Stadium der Megalomanie: der Wind ist ein Stück von ihm, und die Vögel sind er, auch die Mäuse: alles was er früher als Objekt der Qual in sich hineingeschluckt hat, assimiliert er sich jetzt. Die Kröten, die diesen Garten beleben, der nur eine Art Anhäufung seiner Absonderungen ist, erscheinen ihm wie Ungeziefer seines eigenen Leibes. In gehobenen Stunden hat er den Größenwahn, zu glauben, daß alles nur aus ihm herausgewachsen ist. (D, 3:429)

In the 1925 version of the play, Sigismund has lost the glorious aspects of his identification with toads and insects: he no longer feels that they have gone forth out of him, but rather that they are forcing their way into him:

> Vieher sind vielerlei, wollen alle los auf mich. Ich schrei: Nicht zu nah! Asseln, Würmer, Kröten, Feldteufeln, Vipern! Sie wollen alle auf mich. Ich schlag sie tot, sinds erlöst, kommen harte schwarze Käfer, vergrabens. (D, 4:25)

Because the tower representing Sigismund's selfhood also encompasses these creatures, they become an inseparable part of him: "Es wächst mit mir zusammen. Unken und Asseln, Mauern und Turm" (D, 4:86). His attempt to defend himself against their intrusion is an attempt to defend his very humanity from the process of reversion to the animal state now menacing the entire kingdom, from Basilius, who falls prey to his animal appetites, to the beggars in the forest who battle animals for their food.

The various creatures named as co-inhabitants of the tower may call forth certain associations. The wood lice evoke the realistically shabby atmosphere of "Reitergeschichte" and of "Knabengeschichte" where they also appear. In each case the protagonist has been condemned by external circumstances to a grim animal-like existence and his observation of the wood lice indicates preoccupation with his physical condition, a state of mind devoid of any transcendence of reality. The worms suggest, in the Baroque Catholic atmosphere of

---

25 See J. H. Reid's interpretation of the tower as symbol, " 'Draußen sind wir zu finden...' the Development of a Hofmannsthal Symbol," *German Life and Letters*, n. s., 27 (1973): 47.

the play, the decay of the body frequently invoked to urge man to greater piety. The aggregation of various insects and reptiles seems intended as a corporate mass revealing that even Sigismund's pure Christ-like soul is imprisoned in a material body.[26] This awareness of his corporeal existence is strengthened by his foster mother's definition of body and soul. She tells Sigismund:

> Deine Seele ist ein Web aus reinem unverlöschlichem Licht, so wie das Linnen, das gebunden war an seinen vier Zipfeln, darin das Gewürm war und die Tiere der Erde. Bind es auf, fällt das Getier heraus, das weiße Tuch aber bleibt rein und fährt leuchtend wieder hinauf zum Himmel, ... (D, 4:86)

Sigismund remains unable to separate body and soul and consequently fails to grasp exactly how he, possessed of an immortal soul, differs from those creatures sharing his cell and whom the peasant woman equates with his body. His failure to resolve the conflict inherent in his intermediary position between the divine beings and the animal world places him at the center of the irresolvable human dilemma and elevates him to a representative of occidental man, seeking an equilibrium between the hungers of the body and the longing for immortality.

Hofmannsthal's emphasis on the corporeal rather than the divine components in Sigismund appears to have shifted during the composition of the play. The earlier stages stress the threat of reversion to the animal state posed by Sigismund's captivity among worms, toads and insects. He was originally even connected with Hofmannsthal's chosen symbol of the earthly and sexual forces, the dog. Frightened by the prophecy that his son would overthrow him, Basilius according to notes for the first version of the play, proclaimed that the child had been stillborn: "Das Kind wurde weggeschafft und statt seiner das tote Kind einer Hundwärtersfrau beerdigt" (D, 3:430). The link, however indirect between the royal child and the dog, is remi-

---

[26] It would be fallacious to characterize Sigismund, as does Karl. J. Naef, as "die immaterielle Lichtseele" revealing in his struggle against the vermin his "Abscheu gegen eine Verbindung mit dem Materiellen und Endlichem" *(Hugo von Hofmannsthals Wesen und Werk,* p. 255). By the very fact of his physical existence, Sigismund is irrevocably bound to the corporeal and material.

niscent of Hofmannsthal's frequent juxtaposition of dogs and children in his letters, a juxtaposition which suggests that the very young child, lacking complete command of language and without spiritual enlightment, particulary resembles the mute dog.

In the final stage version of the play, the vermin signify only the degradation of Sigismund's captivity; he is no longer grown part of them and triumphs as a hero over all desires of the flesh. In the version with which we are concerned, however, Sigismund is obsessed with his search for the criteria distinguishing man from beast.

In contrast to Sigismund's foster mother who equates his body with "Gewürm" infesting his tower prison, Julian insists on a fundamental essential difference between man and beast as physical entities. He states:

> Kriechende und reissende Getiere, an denen dein kindlicher Sinn hängt, sind aus der Erde gewirkt, Bäume und Fische aus Wasser, Vögel aus Luft, Sterne aus Feuer, du aus noch reinerem Feuer. (D, 4:94)

Julian affirms the Baroque concept of world order, viewing each stage of animal life as corresponding to one of the four medieval elements. He does not concern himself with the soul of man as a distinguishing criterion, but rather declares man and beast different by nature of the material from which they are created. Sigismund's familiarity with the physical nature of the baser creatures prevents him from accepting such a distinction.

In the conversation with his foster mother, Sigismund attempts to comprehend the intangible soul, which her Christian teaching has presented as the critical difference:

> Weißt du noch das Schwein, das der Vater geschlachtet hat, und es schrie so stark und ich schrie mit — und wie ich dann kein Fleisch hab anrühren können, und hättet ihr mir mit Gewalt die Zähn aufgebrochen, auch nicht. Dann ist es an einem Kreuzholz gehangen, im Flur an meiner Kammertür; das Innere so finster, ich verlor mich darin. — War das die Seele, die aus ihm geflohen war in dem Letzten schrecklichen Schrei? Und ist meine Seele dafür hinein in das tote Tier? (D, 4:87) [27]

---

[27] The aversion to eating meat produced by Sigismund's intense identification with the animal continues long after he has left the tower and restricts him to vegetable food:

While the youths of Hofmannsthal's earlier works, Lucidor and Andreas, took pleasure in losing self-awareness through identification with an animal, the same process has become a source of acute suffering for Sigismund. Whereas the euphoric unio mystica enjoyed by the aesthetes of the early work ended abruptly when confronted with death or animal suffering, as in "Der Jüngling und die Spinne," Sigismund's tormenting identification with the animal continues through that experience. He too has become a suffering creature, like Euseb; as his anguish is indistinguishable from that of the animal, so his existence converges with that of the tortured animal.

Furthermore, suffering brings about the identification with Christ as well as with the animal. Recalling the pig hung on a "Kreuzholz," Sigismund imitates the position of Christ on the cross, then referring to both crucifixions, he tells his foster mother:

> Ich brings nicht auseinander, mich mit dem und aber mich mit dem Tier, das aufgehangen war an einem queren Holz und ausgenommen und innen voller blutiger Finsternis. Mutter, wo ist mein End und wo ist dem Tier sein End. (D, 4:88)

Through the experience of suffering, animal, human, and divine existence converge.[28] The possession or lack of an immortal soul is immaterial to the question of physical suffering, thus Sigismund rejects it as the essential criterion.

Sigismund next ponders moral conscience as a possible distinction. Because he can relate it directly to his own rejection and im-

> "Nicht was die Vogelschlinge noch was der Angelhaken geschafft hat, noch das Messer an der Kehle des Schweines, — aber dies da aus weißem Mehl ist eine schöne Speise." (D, 4:168)
>
> His reverence for his fellow creatures contrasts sharply with the omnivorous greed of Olivier, who commands for his troops "die Kälber und Schwein, die Lämmer, die Ziegen, Hühner und Gäns, Salz und Schmalz, Störe und Hecht..." (D, 4:154).

28 Grete Schaeder comments on Sigismund's identification with the slaughtered pig:
Die Atmosphäre des Spiels wird von diesem Wort bestimmt: der Mensch als leidende Kreatur in einer von Christus nicht erlösten Welt...
("Hugo von Hofmannsthals Weg zur Tragödie. Die drei Stufen der 'Turm' Dichtung," *Deutsche Vierteljahresschrift* 23, no. 3 (1949): 347.)

prisonment by his father, the consciousness of right and wrong is more germane to his situation:

> Grausig ist das Tier. Es frißt die eigenen Jungen, noch feucht aus dem Mutterleib. Meine Augen habens gesehen. Und doch ist es unschuldig. (D, 4:93)

Sigismund appears to excuse the animal's cannibalism because it lacks such abstract concepts as parent and offspring, right and wrong. By contrast his father, possessed of a full knowledge of their relationship and its attendant moral obligations, is guilty of a crime too heinous to be reconciled with his humanity.

Elektra, who like Sigismund has been reduced through imprisonment to an animal-like state and is also repeatedly compared to a dog, raises the same question as to the distinction separating man from beast and expresses herself through the same image of the animal devouring its own young. She addresses Chrysothemis:

> Vergessen? Was? Bin ich ein Tier? Vergessen? Das Vieh schläft ein, von halbgefressner Beute die Lefze noch behängt, das Vieh vergißt sich und fängt zu kauen an, indes der Tod schon würgend auf ihn sitzt, das Vieh vergißt, was aus dem Leib ihm kroch, und stillt den Hunger am eignen Kind — ich bin kein Vieh, ich kann nicht vergessen! (D, 2:20-21)

Unlike Sigismund, Elektra makes no asumption of the animal's guilt or innocence; she stresses only its lack of memory as the criterion distinguishing animal from man.

In his cogent analysis of *Elektra,* Lothar Wittmann maintains that language is the indispensable tool of memory which prevents Elektra from reverting to the dumb animal state and forgetting the murder of her father:

> Dieses Halten, Bewahren, Nichtvergessen aber — und damit das Menschbleiben — ist Elektra nur möglich durch die unwiderstehliche Gewalt ihres Wortes, mit dem sie "von alten Dingen" redet, "wie wenn sie gestern geschehen wären"...[29]

He quotes "Wert und Ehre deutscher Sprache" where Hofmannsthal writes: "indem er spricht, bekennt der Mensch sich als das Wesen, das nicht zu vergessen vermag" (P, 4:439). In *Der Turm* as well, it is

---

[29] *Sprachthematik und dramatische Form im Werk Hofmannsthals,* p. 75.

finally language which enables man to formulate such abstract concepts as paternity and which makes possible social organization.

Oddly enough, it is Anton who first expresses the social function of language:

> Jetzt wird der Sigismund auch sprechen. Alle werden wir miteinander diskutieren. Mit reden kommen die Leut zusammen. (D, 4:24)

True to his maxim, "An der Red erkennt man den Mann" Anton adapts his speech to the listeners at hand. While Sigismund's imprisonment has caused him to lose almost all speech, Anton speaks to him as if to a child who can understand only the simplest utterances. Yet his conversation with Julian after they have been notified of the Woiwode's visit is full of puns; he warns Julian:

> Das bedeutet doch nicht mehr und nicht weniger, als daß man Sie zurückholt an den Hof, daß man Ihnen aufdrängt die Ehren, soll heißen die Beschweren, die Würden, soll heißen die Bürden, die Vertrauensstellen, die Sinekuren und Sekkaturen... (D, 4:39).

Here Anton's language presages the way that language is used at the court to which his master has been summoned. One phrase leads glibly to the next, words become playthings, and the listener must decode the implicit message behind what is actually said.

In his statement, "Mit Reden kommen die Leut zusammen," Anton makes no distinction between language as the definitive characteristic of man and language as an instrument of social organization. These two functions also coincide in Aristotle's *Politics:*

> For nature, as we declare, does nothing without purpose; and man alone of the animals possesses speech. The mere voice, it is true, can indicate pain and pleasure, and is possessed by the other animals as well... but speech is designed to indicate the advantageous and the harmful, and therefore also the right and the wrong; for it is the special property of man in distinction from the other animals that he alone has perception of good and bad and right and wrong and the other moral qualities, and it is partnership in these things that makes a household and a city-state.[30]

---

30 Aristotle, *Politics,* trans. H. Rackham, Loeb Classical Library (Cambridge, Mass.: Harvard University Press, 1959), p. 11.

Hofmannsthal was surely familiar with this concept of language; in his essay "Französische Redensarten" he writes:

> Die Sprachen gehören zu den schönsten Dingen, die es auf der Welt gibt. Man sagt, sie sind es, die unser Dasein vom Dasein der Tiere unterscheiden. (P, 1:300)

Aristotle appears to have influenced Elektra's and Sigismund's remarks about the animal's lack of conscience: without the linguistic facility for formulating and remembering such abstractions as parent, child, right, wrong, the animal cannot be judged guilty of transgression against these principles. As Aristotle points out, expression and communication of such concepts as just, unjust forms the basis of common moral principles and of communal justice. Elsewhere Hofmannsthal affirms that language is the keystone of social organization because it transcends the isolation of the individual:

> Das Individuum ist unaussprechlich. Was sich ausspricht, geht schon ins Allgemeine über, ist nicht mehr im strengen Sinne individuell. Sprache und Individuum heben sich gegenseitig auf. (A, p. 194)

Returning for a moment to our depiction of man suspended between the bestial and the divine, we observe that language is allied throughout the play with the divine aspect of man. Thus Julian boasts to Sigismund:

> Zum Betrachter der Gestirne hab ich dich gemacht, zum Genossen der Engel! Einen gewaltigen Magier habe ich aus dir gemacht, gleich Adam und Moses! denn ich habe das Wunder der Sprache in deinen Mund gelegt. (D, 4:92-93)

Adam, who first named the newly created animals, and Moses, who communicated divine law to mankind, were among the first contributors to social organization. Elsewhere Hofmannsthal confirms that language elevates man toward heaven:

> Die romantischen Dichter nannten die Natur den chaoswärts gesehenen Menschen — ist nicht die Sprache der Mensch, gottwärts gesehen? (A, p. 292)

Within the drama itself, the fabric of social organization woven by language is constantly threatened with destruction. Man is in danger of being cast down into the chaotic state represented consistently throughout Hofmannsthal's works by means of animal imagery. The courtier warning Julian that he has been confined to the environs of the tower declares that anyone sighting him outside its pale shall throw his tongue to the dogs (D, 4:131), symbols of the preconscious, non-speaking state. One of the rebels threatens to punish Julian and Anton for the imprisonment of Sigismund by hanging them where ravens can hack out their tongues (D, 4:155). Bearing in mind the roaming dogs and the circling ravens as images of chaos in the prophecy to Basilius, it becomes obvious that both sentences express the danger that internal warfare will break all social bonds. Olivier, the personification of the anarchy threatening the kingdom, speaks in disjointed phrases, mixes several languages in his epithets, barks sharp commands, but never engages in a communicative conversation.[31] It is significant that he ignores the distinction between the human mouth, an organ capable of speech, and that of the animal, referring to both as "Maul." He commands his followers to watch Sigismund and muzzle him if he fails to control his speech (D, 4:163). Like Anton, who begged Julian to muzzle Sigismund rather than kill him, Olivier confuses the threat posed by an animal capable of biting with that posed by an unfavorable utterance.

Sigismund's own command of language is significant, though not a consistently developed theme in the play. He lacks the superficial facile speech necessary for frictionless social contact, yet his nobility elevates him above the wordless animal plane. The groom describing his horsemanship announces to Basilius:

> Dieser fremde Prinz ist ein schlechter Redner, denn er tut beinahe den Mund nicht auf, aber das kann ich beschwören, ein geborener Reiter. (D, 4:104)

Regardless of critics who detect in the passage the influence of Egmont[32] or of Kaspar Hauser,[33] the opposition of horsemanship and

31 See Lothar Wittmann's analysis of Olivier's character and speech, *Sprachthematik und dramatische Form im Werk Hofmannsthals* pp. 98-99.
32 Bruce Coghlan suggests the influence of *Egmont* IV, ii, where Egmont's horsemanship is discussed as he arrives at the summons of the Duke of Alba *(Hofmannsthal's Festival Dramas,* pp. 234-35).
33 Jakob Laubach notes the similarity between Sigismund's unschooled talent as rider and that of Kaspar Hauser as described by Jakob Wassermann in 1908 ("Hofmannsthals Turm-Dichtungen," pp. 51-52).

linguistic facility signifies that Sigismund shares with the great *Magier* and with the youth of "Die Beiden" absolute mastery over himself and his surroundings, a control more readily apparent in gesture than in the spoken word. Unlike the merchant's son and Andreas, who are not truly noble by ancestry and who lack the firmness of will and self-assurance indispensable to a successful rider, Sigismund demonstrates through his mastery of the horse that he is a born king. His horsemanship serves Hofmannsthal as an effective substitute for the characterization of his nobility and power of command through language.[34]

The importance of the dichotomy between horsemanship and the exercise of power through language is significant enough throughout Hofmannsthal's oeuvre to warrant examining more closely the importance of horseback riding in his last great tragedy.

In the beginning of the play, riding can expose the rider to danger; thus Basilius' nephew and heir to the throne has been killed

---

34 My interpretation differs significantly from that offered by Mary E. Gilbert, who writes that the portrayal of Sigismund as a rider suggests that he "has control over his horse because he is in 'in Eintracht mit sich selbst;' his conscious and unconscious drives pull the same way" ("The Image of the Horse in Hofmannsthal's Poetic Works," p. 63). As I have already stated, the animal imagery surrounding Sigismund points up the tension between body and spirit and shows little evidence of an inner harmony. Rather his success as a rider is founded upon the brutal domination of any physical desire by a supreme effort of the will. Later Mary E. Gilbert quotes the words of the Grand Almoner, "ein Mensch fängt dort an, wo ein viehisch gelüstender Leib unter die Füsse gebracht wird von Wesenheit" and continues, "The King himself is forced to subjugate his animal drives for fear of being overrun by their violence. The contrast brought into focus by the horse-rider incident anticipates and epitomizes the clash between father and son" (Ibid.). The contrast of which she speaks here is that between Sigismund's "Eintracht mit sich selbst" and his father's struggle for mastery over his physical desires. I submit, on the other hand, that the contrast implied is between Basilius' failure to control his "viehisch gelüstender Leib" and Sigismund's success in doing so. Sigismund's suffering through the identification with animals, his desire to escape to the innocent world of fish, and the harshness of such statements as "An mir nichts vom Weib" demonstrate, however, that his control over his bodily desires — symbolized by the mastery of his horse — has been brought about forcibly and at tremendous cost to himself.

while hunting when his horse stumbles into a wolf's burrow. After the Woiwode's arrival has been announced, Anton suggests that Julian might still escape: "Wenn Euer Gnaden im Wald verreiten täten?" (D, 4:40). But Julian's escape will be impossible, for the messengers have brought a saddle horse for him to ride to court, exposing him to danger of another sort.

The destruction of all order within the kingdom is depicted through horse imagery as well. Among the perversions of social order which Basilius recites from the prophecy he mentions the soldier, "der die Fahn abreißt und seinem Oberen die Pferdehalfter ums Maul schlägt" (D, 4:63). One of his courtiers suggests that the old order could be reestablished by effective riding: "Lasse die königliche Majestät uns reiten mit unseren getreuen adligen Vasallen gegen die Juden und Judenknecht" (D, 4:62). The courtier speaking here targets the Jewish usurers as source of the kingdom's economic misfortunes; the opposition of the commercial class to the nobles who ride parallels the merchant's son's confession that as son of a merchant he knows nothing of saddles or horses.

Basilius rides as a hunter, but his riding exposes him to direct awareness of the plight of his subjects: "Ich reite an: sie sind Bettler" (D, 4:62) he complains. The Grand Almoner condemns his hunting as trivial entertainment which Basilius has pursued instead of governing as he should have: "Aber leicht war es, das Eitle zu tun, und zu reiten, anstatt zu raten!" (D, 4:70).

Sigismund's riding relates to all of these themes. First, he is exposed to danger as a rider, for he has been sent out riding with Graf Adam as a test of his behavior before the court. The horse he has been given is a "Fuchs," like Hofmannsthal's mare in Göding, and is restless and difficult to control. His instinctive mastery over the animal shows that Sigismund has conquered his torment over the distinction between himself and animals; he handles the horse forcefully even though he has never ridden before. Basilius tells us how to interpret his symbolic success as a rider: "Eine Herrschaft über sich selber ohnegleichen" (D, 4:105); he possesses precisely the self mastery that Andreas, Anton Lerch, and the young lord in *Das kleine Welttheater* lack. The connection between successful riding and the rider's nobility is affirmed by the groom, who relates that Sigismund rides "wie der fürstlichste Kavalier" (D, 4:105) and by Basilius, who speaks later of his son as "ein Prinz, der zu Pferde sitzt wie ein geborener König" (D, 4:111).

Finally, horseback riding is opposed to the power of language. Immediately after the comments on Sigismund's horsemanship, Basilius asks, "Welche Sprache ist von ihm zu erwarten?" (D, 4:105).

Paul Requadt has examined the difficulty of endowing Sigismund with a language at once appropriate to his heritage and to his demeaned condition. He observes that the dramatist intended that the gulf separating the prince's child-like nonviolent "Engelssprache" from Basilius' harsh "Befehlssprache" should disappear under Sigismund's reign. Requadt finds his entanglement in the language of the world inevitable, as is the guilt incurred through the responsibilities of war and kingship.[35]

The animal imagery surrounding Sigismund's entry into political reality reveals his ensnarement in violence and destruction. The role of language, that divine element in man, diminishes before the need for raw power to control the nation. Anton's statement that if wolves and bears were capable of speech they would rule the world implies that, were it not for the social order constructed through the abstractions formulated in language, brute force would hold sway. The wolf has been associated with Sigismund in the early stages of the play, where he wears an old wolf's pelt (D, 4:11), and seems so grown together with it that his guard is surprised to see a human head on a wolf's body (D, 4:14). It seems predestined that the heir to Basilius' throne should be injured when his horse stumbles into a wolf's burrow, for his death opens the way for the wolf-prince. Olivier proclaims that wolves and ravens will follow the rebels to ravage the earth (D, 4:163). Thus the wolf image links Sigismund to the rebels' violence and Anton's statement serves as a reminder that Sigismund owes his ascent not to the superior powers of language or intellect, but to the force of rebellion sweeping him along.

The bear, in physical strength the equal of the wolf, is another link between Sigismund and the rebels. Julian compares the rebellion

---

35 "Sprachverleugnung und Mantelsymbolik" in *Hugo von Hofmannsthal*, ed. Sibylle Bauer, pp. 72-73.

spreading through the unsuspecting kingdom to a bear climbing onto the roof of a sheep pen (D, 4:137). In the fifth act, Sigismund demonstrates his dependence on brute force by dancing like a chained bear while conjuring Olivier to appear from the underworld (D, 4: 184). The wolf and bear images, when connected with Anton's statement of the function of language, contradict his assertion that language and the social structure it formulates are the means of dominance in the world.

The rats, mice and vermin appearing in the conjuring scene furnish additional proof that Sigismund, in spite of exchanging his wolf's pelt for royal raiment, has not transcended the animal plane of his imprisonment. Finally, it must be noted that the viper occurred among the reptiles and insects infesting his cell, and it is by the viper's poison that he dies. The tragic guilt inextricably interwoven with his ascent to the throne is demonstrated, on the one hand, by the violence of his followers, who burn monasteries and villages. On a higher level, however, Sigismund fails to achieve a harmonious equilibrium between the opposing poles, body and soul. His lack of an effective speech idiom corresponding to the absolute mastery demonstrated in his horsemanship is evidence of his failure to ascend toward the divine. And his increasingly frequent connection with carnivorous and destructive animals proves that the creature imprisoned in the tower has become a more powerful animal, but ultimately failed to transcend his own nature.

CONCLUSION

Looking back over the material presented in the foregoing chapters, we are now in a position to draw several conclusions about animal symbolism in Hofmannsthal's work. Hofmannsthal asserted that animal images constitute ciphers which can not be adequately re-expressed through language. Nonetheless, we have established that certain animals evoke certain concepts, although these relationships can not be formulated simply as equations of things with ideas. Rather the animal symbol calls forth in the mind of the reader whole complexes of sensations and experiences.

When discussing the "Märchen der 672. Nacht," we put forth the hypothesis that Hofmannsthal relied on literary or artistic tradition for the symbolic connotations of animals with which he has not directly acquainted. It was suggested that his symbolic use of horse, dog, and other familiar animals might be more original and spring from personal experience. The validity of this hypothesis may now be judged on the basis of information about the possible sources of animal images supplied in the preceding chapters.

One of the major images in Hofmannsthal's work was found to be that of horseback riding. Command of the horse may represent an instinctive intuitive force within the individual, which is somehow an antithesis of the rational power of the word; thus Sigismund is judged a poor speaker, but an excellent horseman. We found a comparable opposition expressed in *Wilhelm Meisters Wanderjahre,* where instruction in language counterbalances Felix's occupation tending horses. Another facet of the image, horseback riding as a metaphor for the rational mind's dominance over physical appetites, was traced through Freud back to medieval theologians.

We observed that the horse, as bearer of the lover to his mistress, is frequently linked with sexual encounters; such is the case in "Die Beiden," "Reitergeschichte" and *Andreas.* The horse's realm, the stable, became the scene of such encounters in *Andreas* and was associated with them in "Der goldene Apfel" and "Vor Tag" as well as in Goethe's *Wanderjahre* and Kafka's "Ein Landarzt." Hofmannsthal uses the horse as an image of adultery in *Die Frau im Fenster,* where the bite Braccio has received from his roan horse symbolizes his wife's unfaithfulness. And in "Idylle" the centaur, half man, half horse, carries the blacksmith's wife toward an adulterous affair. Although our study of the horse imagery in *Der Turm* focused on riding as a symbol of nobility and a counterweight to speech, the sexual aspect of horse imagery is by no means lacking in the drama. Sigismund combats the vermin in the tower, which represent the physical side of his own nature, with a "Roßknochen," showing that he has overcome the sexual desires symbolized by the horse. In discussing Andreas' failings as a rider we established a clear link between the rider reining in his horse and the ego restricting the id's sexuality. In the same way, Sigismund's perfect horsemanship demonstrates complete mastery of his libido. He proclaims his total repression of all things feminine: "An mir ist nichts vom Weib!" (D, 4:124). His revulsion against the carnal sexuality of Basilius and Olivier culminates in an unnatural rejection of even the sexual activity necessary for procreation.[1] Preparing to confront Olivier's gypsy mistress he regrets, "Wir haben nichts anderes, das uns Mutter werden konnte, als dieses Geschlecht, und dies ist der Stoff, aus dem die Welt gemacht ist" (D, 4:180). The gypsy, who is pregnant, has been forced to run barefoot behind her captor's horse, three further details

---

1   Sigismund's misogyny was even more pronounced in earlier drafts of the play. Werner Bellmann tells us that by early 1922 Hofmannsthal had created a scene in the fifth act in which Sigismund confronts Olivier and his women, declaring:
>Ich bin gekommen, die Werke des Weiblichen aufzulösen – ... Ich habe euch nicht erkannt und ihr habet mich nicht erkannt.

Bellmann states that his enmity toward the feminine principle was intended to portray Sigismund as an androgynous, Christ-like figure incorporating characteristics of both sexes. The doctor, in this draft of the play, describes Sigismund as "weder Mann noch Weib, sondern über beiden." (Bellmann, "Eine Quelle zu Hofmannsthal's 'Großem Welttheater' und zum 'Turm'," *Jahrbuch des Freien deutschen Hochstiftes* [1984], p. 292).

calling attention to her sexuality. When Sigismund scorns her conjuring up mice and rats, he challenges her: "Du kannst nichts aus deinem Schoß schütteln, schwarzer Engel, womit ich nicht auf du und du wäre!" (D, 4:182). In response she brings forth "etwas wie ein Weib, mit einem entfleischten Pferdekopf an Stelle des Kopfes," a creature Sigismund recognizes and addresses as "Bettschatz." The gypsy and Olivier are repeatedly associated with the swamp, whose rank vegetation and chaotic state make it an appropriate symbol of their asocial promiscuity.

The swamp image also occurs in *Der Schwierige* as Hans-Karl discusses love and marriage with Antoinette Hechingen. He abhors random sexual encounters, as does Sigismund:

> Es ist nicht zum Ausdenken, wie zufällig wir alle sind, und wie uns der Zufall zueinander jagt und auseinanderjagt, und wie jeder mit jedem hausen konnte, wenn der Zufall es wollte... Darin ist so ein Grausen, das der Mensch etwas hat finden müssen, um sich aus diesem Sumpf herauszuziehen ... (L, 2:243).

The solution, he continues, is marriage. In *Der Turm* the swamp image, linked to the gypsy and the horse, can be traced to Bachofen, who documents the horse's connection with the procreative power:

> Das Pferd ist das Bild der im Sumpf waltenden, die Erde wild befruchtenden Wasserkraft, ... mithin auch das Bild des ehebrecherischen Lebens.[2]

These aspects of the horse image in Hofmannsthal's work, representing the antithesis of language, man's struggle for dominance of his sexuality, or the procreative power itself, then, are not wholly original or unique, for their significance coincides with their significance in literary and cultural tradition.

A second major set of images described man's relationship to women as that of hunter and prey. This analogy proved significant in interpreting the relationships at the center of *Die Frau im Fenster,* "Knabengeschichte," "Die Frau ohne Schatten," and *Andreas.* Its origin was traced back as far as Ovid's *Art of Love.*

A third complex of animal symbolism in which a youth tortures an animal as surrogate for his father frequently occurs in combina-

---

2 *Das Mutterrecht,* vol. 1, p. 125.

tion with the imagery of the hunt. In these instances the love or sexual relationship depicted through hunt imagery is likely to fail because the youth confronts sexual maturity without a suitable parental model, without a vision of his own parents as man and wife. Euseb, who fantasizes about father-torture and hunts the pregnant servant girl never knew his father, and Sigismund never knew his mother, who died at his birth. Andreas, who struggles to overcome his own brutality as embodied in his alter-ego, Gotthelf, has no vision of his parents together as lovers, as he perceives the Finazzers.

In mature love, the male partner must be able to envisage himself as both lover and father, and his beloved as both lover and mother. Hofmannsthal never portrayed complete fulfillment in this most fundamental of human relationships; (at best it is intimated at the close of his dramas): aberrations abound. The merchant's son, able to imagine a woman only as mother, has memories of both his parents, but not in union, and he retreats into Oedipal fantasies. Elektra's family tragedy has left her with a horror of woman's sexuality as embodied in her mother. Madonna Dianora, who enjoys her role as Messer Palla's prey, saw her mother only on her deathbed and knew almost nothing about her father. The young lord in *Das kleine Welttheater* envisages his father (source of his social responsibilities) as target of his hunt, but tells us nothing about his mother, and shuns the "Netze und Fußangeln" of romantic involvement which leads to integration into society.

If the woman appears too fully as mother, obscuring her role as lover, her partner pursues other women; the emperor of *Der Kaiser und die Hexe* hunts and hunts the witch because his wife appears to him only as mother. The same is true of Jaromir's wife in *Der Unbestechliche*. On the other hand, women who are desired uniquely as lovers become trapped in this role and fail to make the transition to motherhood. Vittoria in *Der Abenteurer und die Sängerin* plays the role of Cesarino's sister; while Lorenzo and Weidenstamm adore her as a lover, neither is prepared to accept the knowledge of her motherhood. Weidenstamm (who wore a hunter's green clothing when he was with Vittoria) never knew his father and thus remains incapable of the transition from Vittoria's lover to father of her child. The Marschallin in *Der Rosenkavalier,* although childless, is transformed during the opera from Oktavian's lover (and the prey of his hunt while her husband is hunting elsewhere) through the recognition that she is old enough to be his mother, and relinquishes him to a younger woman.

These troubling implications for the man-woman relationship constitute perhaps the most significant revelation achieved through our analysis of animal imagery. The problem continues from the earliest through the latest of Hofmannsthal's works. Development of the theme may be discerned; in the earliest works ("Das Märchen der 672. Nacht," *Das kleine Welttheater*) the youth shuns involvement with women. In the later works, biological fatherhood is partially transcended by spiritual paternity. While Sigismund's lack of a suitable parental model dooms him to sterility and hatred of women, the appearance of the Kinderkönig (likewise without parents) was perhaps intended, like Sacramozo's mentoring of Andreas, to suggest a transcendant spiritual fatherhood in which women play no part.

Our original question whether the sources of Hofmannsthal's animal images are unique and biographical or coincide with literary and cultural tradition must be posed again here. While the deeper roots of hunting imagery and father-torture by the son may lie in portions of the author's biography which remain sealed in his unpublished correspondence, we have found antecedents for both. Freud maintained in *Totem und Tabu* that patricide (and the conquest of women) lay at the root of animal sacrifice. The son's sacrifice by his father is familiar from the Biblical story of Abraham and Isaac. In an earlier note for *Das Leben ein Traum* Basilius alludes to them as he describes a nightmare:

> ... dort lag ich vor meinem Sohn: alle standen um mich, und niemand half mir ... keine Hand von Engeln tauchte nieder, mich verkehrten Abraham zu retten. (D, 3:432)

The image of animal sacrifice and torture, then, also has its roots deep in cultural tradition.

The awareness that Hofmannsthal's symbols are neither unique nor original raises another question: Did Hofmannsthal consciously and deliberately make use of animal symbols for his artistic purpose? The emphasis placed in the opening chapters on Hofmannsthal's contact with animals during military service would suggest that some of his animal imagery grew out of his own experience. On the other hand, he was undoubtedly aware of some literary or cultural precedents, of the parallel between Euseb's crucifixion of the sparrowhawk and Christ's death on the cross, for example. The answer to this question, then, must be both yes and no. Hofmannsthal's use of animals such as lion, dolphin, snake, spider and eagle depends to a large extent on the traditional function of these animals in art and literature. Certain aspects of his horse and dog symbols, on the other hand, regardless of their consonance with tradition, derive directly from his own experience.

Hofmannsthal's difficulties with his mare in Göding became a source for his horse imagery, some of it certainly unconscious. The horse as a factor in financial gain or loss has already been treated in connection with *Andreas* and "Reitergeschichte." The horse serves similarly in *Das Bergwerk zu Falun* as an indicator of financial standing. Elis arrives at Dahlsjö's house when the family's fortune is at its nadir; as the son, Christian, prepares to leave, a groom announces that his mare has gone lame. After Elis has lived with the family for some time, Dahlsjö has prospered so that he is able to buy a handsome stallion.

It has already been suggested, when analyzing "Ein Traum von großer Magie," that Hofmannsthal, because of his mare's defiance of his control, considers the riderless horse a symbol of chaos. Even years after his defeat as a rider, Hofmannsthal, perhaps involuntarily, chooses the riderless horse to symbolize anarchy. Oedipus addresses the populace of Thebes using this very image:

> ... Du Volk aus dieser Stadt, was schnaubst du hier vor dem verschlossenen Tor und bäumst dich wie ein reiterloses Roß? Wo ist dein König, daß er dir den Zaum nicht auflegt? (D, 2:382)

It may be argued that the horse as a measure of financial security, or as a symbol of uncontrolled forces, is a logical choice for communicating the things it represents to the reader and, regardless of the closeness of such images to Hofmannsthal's experience, does not necessarily constitute an unconscious symbol. Yet there is no explanation, other than the psychic wound inflicted by Hofmannsthal's loss of control over his roan mare and the subconscious need to confess his own helplessness, for the intrusion of the incident into *Der Bürger als Edelmann*. In the second act a nobleman recounts for Jourdain his conversation with Dorante about Jourdain himself:

> Der reiche Kerl frißt, aber er weiß nicht zu schmecken! Er sauft – aber – da haben Sie den Soldaten, Herr Jourdain, dem eher das Maul durchgeht als eine feurige Fuchsstute. (L, 3:325)

Molière's *Le bourgeois gentilhomme* offers no source for the "feurige Fuchsstute."

Other mentions of a horse of this color occur in works from every period of Hofmannsthal's career. In an unfinished "Soldatengeschichte" probably begun between 1895 and 1896, the soldier Schwendar is chased toward a forest by a young officer riding a "großen heftig athmenden Fuchsen" (SW, 29:57). Andreas' own horse which he thoughtlessly reins in, setting off the chain of events which leads to Romana and the disaster at the Finazzer estate is also a "Fuchs." And finally when Anton in *Der Turm* announces the arrival of the Woiwode of Lublin, he tells Julian that the emissary has brought a saddle horse for him, "ein russischer Goldfuchs." Although the reader or viewer may ignore this detail, the horse's color forbodes risk and treachery once he is reminded of Hofmannsthal's mare in Göding.

The psychological defeat brought on by his rebellious mare never left Hofmannsthal's subconscious; the runaway horse as an image of danger may thus be identified as having a biographical source. A second image which apparently springs from an incident in Hofmannsthal's life is the dying dog.

During the summer of 1896 he worked at a short story, "Geschichte der beiden Leibespaare," in which the narrator and his friend observe the latter's fatally ill wife as she sleeps:

> Wie im Schmerz zog sich Oberlippe hinauf und entblößte die ganze milchweiße Reihe der oberen Zähne. Zugleich erschien ein böser und leidender Zug zwischen den Augenbrauen. Allmählich wurde der Ausdruck des Gesichts entsetzlich. (SW, 39:71-72)

The woman's facial expression is much like that of the merchant's son, whose teeth are exposed at the moment of his death, causing him to resemble the ugly cavalry horses. The dying woman's face assumes an evil rapacious expression which, through her recounting of the following dream, is revealed to be that of a dog:

> Ich hab geträumt, ich bin dann geworden wie der Hund von dem ihr erzählt habt. Der Hund, von dem da eine Photographie ist, ... der ertrunken ist. Zuerst bin ich gestorben. Ich hab gespürt, wie ich geworden bin, ganz, und nur die Zähne sind weiß und schön geblieben. (SW, 29:72)

The editor of the critical edition identifies this passage as "eine Reminiszenz an den Tod des Hundes von Richard Beer-Hofmann im Comer See, ein Erlebnis, das Hofmannsthal in September 1894 in einem Gedicht festhielt" (SW, 29:313). The poem is a juvenile attempt at justifying the suitability of the animal's death by asserting that the dog's advancing age would have constantly reminded his owner of the inevitable presence of death and physical decay everywhere in life.[3] The details of the dog's drowning — unspecified in either the story or the poem — might explain the subsequent association of a dying dog with a woman. Possibly Hofmannsthal found female sexuality repugnant in the same way that the dog repelled him by reminding him too insistently of the frailty of flesh, whether human or animal. In any case, the poet's mistress in *Jupiter und Semele,* implicitly compares herself, as "stumme Kreatur," to the poisoned dog which has appeared at the lovers' bedside. Andreas observes the poisoned watchdog while listening to Frau Finazzer's conversation with her husband, and envisaging his own future relationship with Romana; at the same time Gotthelf is presumably occupied with the stable girl.

Both the runaway horse which represents uncontrollable forces and the suffering dog which is connected with a sexually active woman reappear in essentially the same form at various periods throughout Hofmannsthal's career. In general, the significance of Hofmannsthal's individual animal images undergoes little real development.[4] Rather, the major symbols acquire a cumulative power pre-

---

3 The poem appears among Hofmannsthal's letters (B, 1:115, see also Hofmannsthal and Beer-Hofmann, *Briefwechsel,* p. 38).

4 Mary E. Gilbert attempts to define the development of the horse image, stating that its negative variant is restricted to the years 1895-1912, that is,

cisely because their meaning remains constant. It may be difficult to grasp the significance of the dogs intruding in "Ein Traum von großer Magie," but their meaning becomes apparent through the more obvious significance of the dogs in "Reitergeschichte," and these in turn illuminate the presence of the packs of stray dogs in the prophecy to Basilius.

Although the significance of Hofmannsthal's animal images remains more or less fixed, the way in which they are used does show certain changes. In the early work, that is, until about 1901, animals represent the antithesis of artistic or rational power. The great *Magier* emerges triumphant from his confrontation with the dogs and horses representing the powers of chaos. *Das Bergwerk zu Falun* shows a sharply drawn contrast between the Dahlsjö household (to which dog, cat, birds and horses belong) and the underground world of the *Bergkönigin*. This fundamental opposition between reality — the animal world — and the inner world — the creative imagination or the fantasy world of art — leads to a violent clash in the "Märchen." There the cavalry horses not only present the antithesis of the harmonious flux of nature depicted in the merchant's son's art treasures, but ultimately negate that vision through killing the youth who was deluded by it. The animals in the village of "Reitergeschichte" counterbalance the rationally ordered discipline of the Austrian squadron.

After about 1901, the identification with the tortured suffering animals begins its ascendancy. The main characters of the early work relinquished their self-awareness in a fantasy experience of oneness with all creation, including animals. The youths of the later work, in contrast, appear to lose awareness of self only through identification with some animal. Grete Schaeder writes of this period: "Es gibt in

from the "Märchen" through *Andreas*. (The Image of the Horse in Hofmannsthal's Poetic Works," p. 70). Actually, however, the horse as an image of disruption and disorder appears as early as 1893 with the centaur in "Idylle" and continues through *Der Turm;* an orderly succession to the throne is jeopardized when Basilius' nephew dies as a result of a hunting accident in which his horse stumbled into a wolf's den.

jenen Jahren kein Allheitserlebnis für Hofmannsthal, das nicht durch den Tierleib der Schöpfung gewonnen wird..."[5]

The watershed in this development appears to be the Chandos letter written in 1901. Chandos describes experiencing total loss of self through mystical union with the cosmos, but the major example he cites is that of identification with poisoned and dying rats:

> Es war viel mehr und viel weniger als Mitleid: ein ungeheures Anteilnehmen, ein Hinüberfließen in jene Geschöpfe oder ein Fühlen, daß ein Fluidum des Lebens und Todes, des Traumes und Todes, des Traumes und Wachens für einen Augenblick in sie hinübergeflossen ist... (P, 2:15).

His mystical experiences are not yet the occasion for suffering, as they will be later for Sigismund, but fill him with wonder and joy:

> In diesen Augenblicken wird eine nichtige Kreatur, ein Hund, eine Ratte, ein Käfer, ein verkümmerter Apfelbaum ... mir mehr, als die schönste, hingebendste Geliebte der glücklichsten Nacht mir je gewesen ist. (P, 2:16)

In the Chandos letter the mystical experience is for the first time attached to suffering animals, yet joy in the experience still outweighs the consciousness of their shared torment.

The "Gespräch über Gedichte" draws an analogy between animal sacrifice and poetic symbolism. Here again the sensation of the human identifying with the sacrificial animal is ultimately one of pleasure, or at least relief. In the fragments of the following years, however, the presence of a dying animal brings a darker note into the work, as in *Jupiter und Semele*. Euseb's crucifixion of the sparrowhawk hardly rewards him with any pleasurable sensations, rather he loses his grasp of his father's role and tortures himself with the tormented bird. Andreas' youthful experiments with animal torture have left him a burden of guilt still unresolved in the completed portion of the novel and in the notes for its continuation.

Can any explanation be found for the predominance of identification with a suffering animal in Hofmannsthal's later work? A biographical basis for the phenomenon may at least be suggested. His earlier poems and lyrical dramas attest to Hofmannsthal's confidence

---

5 Grete Schaeder, "Hugo von Hofmannsthals Weg zur Tragödie. Die drei Stufen der Turm-Dichtung," *Deutsche Vierteljahresschrift* 23 (1949), 324.

in that power he called *Magie,* the power to call characters and situations into being, to create atmosphere, to substitute for reality a richer inner life of the mind. In May of 1895 he believes he possesses this power: "Ich glaub' immer noch, daß ich imstand sein werde, mir eine Welt in die Welt hineinzubauen" (B, 1:130).[6] His year of military service, the sharper acquaintance with reality, and the difficulties with his horse begin to undermine this confidence. In May of 1896 he describes the ugliness and discomfort of his surroundings and continues: "Ich begreife nicht, wie all diese Dinge eine solche Gewalt über mich haben können."[7] As external circumstances gain increasing power over him, financial and professional worries no longer yield to the command of *Magie.* Nor can the experience of unity with the cosmos, once a source of such pleasure, be called forth at will; Chandos explains that the ability to induce such moments stands in no way within his power (P, 2:14). Particularly in the later work such mystical experiences, now bound up with animal suffering, overcome the individual against his will. Thus the loss of self-awareness, an eagerly sought pleasure in the early years, becomes an agony which leaves Sigismund groping for the boundaries which separate man from beast.

It is ironic, yet inevitable, that the triumphant *Magie* of Hofmannsthal's youth, the power of the word, has been reduced in *Der Turm* to the final criterion distinguishing man from beast. The aesthetes of the early work used *Magie* to induce the vision of a harmonious union of all living creatures, human, animal and even vegetable. The purely imaginary existence of this mystical union might be suddenly negated by the forces of reality, which present animals rebelling against or totally separate from human domination. Sigismund, on the other hand, is tormented immeasurably by this very vision of his oneness with all creatures, including vermin and slaughtered animals. Yet in Hofmannsthal's final drama, the reality outside Sigismund's tower no longer negates, but rather confirms this oneness of man and beast: Basilius' subjects and Olivier's troops are repeatedly compared to wild animals. Now the function of language

---

6   Hofmannsthal and Beer-Hofmann, *Briefwechsel,* p. 47.
7   Hofmannsthal and von Andrian, *Briefwechsel,* pp. 63-64.

is to set man, who rules through the word, through its power to express social concepts, apart from the animals, which hold sway by brute force alone. *Magie* no longer serves to conjure into being the never-never land of artistic fantasy, but to evoke reality, the political reality of social organization, for language creates as it formulates such abstractions as self, society and nation. The changing use to which the conjuring power of language is put constitutes only one aspect of Hofmannsthal's total development; it is complemented by the cessation of his purely lyrical productivity and his increased political or nationalistic activity during World War I.

SELECTED BIBLIOGRAPHY

Hofmannsthal's Works

"Gedichtfragmente, Skizzen zu Gedichten in Prosa, Aufzeichnungen." *Die neue Rundschau* 70 (1959) : 367–74.

Gesammelte Werke in Einzelausgaben. Edited by Herbert Steiner. 15 vols. Frankfurt: S. Fischer, 1946–73.

Sämtliche Werke, kritische Ausgabe. Edited by Heinz Burger et al. 38 vols. Frankfurt: S. Fischer, 1975ff.

Hofmannsthal's Correspondence

Briefe, 1890–1901. Berlin: S. Fischer, 1935.

Briefe, 1900–1909. Vienna: Bermann–Fischer, 1937.

Briefe an Marie Herzfeld. Edited by Horst Weber, Poesie und Wissenschaft, vol. 1. Heidelberg: Lothar Stiehm, 1967.

With Leopold von Andrian. *Briefwechsel.* Frankfurt: S. Fischer, 1968.

With Richard Beer–Hofmann. *Briefwechsel.* Edited by Eugene Weber. Frankfurt: S. Fischer, 1972.

With Eberhard von Bodenhausen. *Briefe der Freundschaft.* Edited by Dora von Bodenhausen. Düsseldorf: Eugen Diederichs, 1953.

With Rudolf Borchhardt. *Briefwechsel.* Frankfurt: S. Fischer, 1954.

With Carl J. Burckhardt. *Briefwechsel.* Frankfurt: S. Fischer, 1956.

With Hans Carossa. "Briefwechsel, 1907–1929." *Die neue Rundschau* 71 (1960): 357–409 and 573–84.

With Stefan George. *Briefwechsel zwischen George und Hofmannsthal.* 2d ed. Edited by Robert Boehringer. Munich: Helmut Kupper, 1953.

With Willy Haas. *Ein Briefwechsel.* Berlin: Propyläen Verlag. 1968.

With Edgar Karg von Bebenburg. *Briefwechsel.* Edited by Mary E. Gilbert. Frankfurt: S. Fischer, 1966.

With Harry Graf Kessler. *Briefwechsel, 1898–1929.* Edited by Hilde Burger. Frankfurt: Insel Verlag, 1968.

With Helene von Nostitz. *Briefwechsel.* Edited by Oswalt von Nostitz. Frankfurt: S. Fischer, 1965.

With Florens Christian Rang. "Briefwechsel, 1905–1924." *Die Neue Rundschau* 70 (1959): 402–48.

With Josef Redlich. *Briefwechsel.* Frankfurt: S. Fischer, 1971.

With Arthur Schnitzler. *Briefwechsel.* Frankfurt: S. Fischer, 1964.

With Richard Strauss. *Briefwechsel.* Edited by Willi Schuh. Zurich: Atlantis, 1964.

With Anton Wildgans. *Briefwechsel.* Edited by Norbert Altenhofer. Heidelberg: Lothar Stiehm, 1971.

Secondary Literature about Hofmannsthal

Alewyn, Richard. *Über Hugo von Hofmannsthal* 4th ed. Kleine Vandenhoeck Reihe, nos. 57, 57a, 57b. Göttingen: Vandenhoeck & Ruprecht, 1967.

Altenhofer, Norbert. " 'Wenn die Zeit uns wird erwecken...' Hofmannsthals *Turm* als politisches Trauerspiel." *Hofmannsthal Forschungen* 7 (1983): 1–17.

Austin, Gerhard. Phänomenologie der Gebärde bei Hugo von Hofmannsthal. Heidelberg: Winter, 1981.

Bahr, Hermann. *Studien zur Kritik der Moderne.* Frankfurt: Ruiten & Loening, 1894.

Barker, Andrew. "The Triumph of Life in Hofmannsthal's 'Das Märchen der 672. Nacht'." *MLR* 74 (1979): 341–48.

Bauer, Sibylle, ed. *Hugo von Hofmannsthal*. Wege der Forschung, vol. 183. Darmstadt: Wissenschaftliche Buchgesellschaft, 1968.

Baumann, Gerhart. "Hugo von Hofmannsthal: *Das kleine Welttheater*," *Germanische–Romanische Monatsschrift*, n.s. 7 (1957): 106-30.

Bellmann, Werner. Eine Quelle zu Hofmannsthal's 'Großem Welttheater' und zum 'Turm' " *Jahrbuch des Freien deutschen Hochstifts* (1984): 289–94.

Böker, Uwe. "Hugo von Hofmannsthals 'Märchen der 672. Nacht' " *Archiv für das Studium der neueren Sprachen und Literaturen* 206, no. 1 (1969–70): 16–38.

Böschenstein, Bernhard. "Der junge Hofmannsthal heute." *Etudes Germaniques* 29 (1974): 149–69.

Brion, Marcel. "Hugo von Hofmannsthal: elucidation d'un conte." *Nouvelle Revue des Deux Mondes* (Mars 1975): 526–40.

Broch, Hermann. *Hofmannsthal und seine Zeit; eine Studie*. Munich: R. Piper, 1964.

Burkhard, Marianne. "Hofmannsthals *Reitergeschichte* – ein Gegenstück zum Chandosbrief." *Amsterdamer Beiträge zur neueren Germanistik* 4:27–53.

Chapple, Clement Gerald. "Themes and Symbols in Hofmannsthal's *Andreas*." Ph.D. dissertation, Harvard University, 1967.

Chelius-Göbbels, Annemarie. *Formen mittelbarer Darstellung im dramatischen Werk Hugo von Hofmannsthals*. Deutsche Studien, vol. 6. Meisenheim am Glan: Anton Hain, 1968.

Clark, Georgina A. "Max Reinhardt and the Genesis of Hugo von Hofmannsthal's *Der Turm*." *Modern Austrian Literature* 17 (1984): 1–32.

Coghlan, Brian. *Hofmannsthal's Festival Dramas*. Cambridge, Eng.: Cambridge University Press, 1964.

Cohn, Dorrit. " 'Als Traum erzählt': The Case for a Freudian Reading of Hofmannsthal's 'Märchen der 672. Nacht'." *Deutsche Vierteljahresschrift* 54 (1980): 284–305.

David, Claude. "Hofmannsthals letztes Drama." *Wirkendes Wort* 9 (1959): 206–16.

Derungs, Werner. "Form und Weltbild der Gedichte Hugo von Hofmannsthals in ihrer Entwicklung." Ph.D. Dissertation, Freiburg, Switzerland, 1960.

Dotzler, Bernhard F. "Beschreibung eines Briefes; zum handlungsauslösenden Moment in Hugo von Hofmannsthal's *Märchen der 672. Nacht.*" Hofmannsthal Forschungen 8 (1985): 49–54.

Donop, William R. "Archetypal Vision in Hofmannsthal's 'Reitergeschichte.' " *German Life and Letters,* n.s. 22 (1969): 126–34.

Durr, Volker O. "Der Tod des Wachtmeisters Anton Lerch und die Revolution von 1849: zu Hofmannsthals 'Reitergeschichte.' " *German Quarterly* 45 (1972): 33–46.

Erken, Gunther. "Hofmannsthal-Chronik; Beitrag zu einer Bibliographie." *Literaturwissenschaftliches Jahrbuch.* n.s. 3 (1962): 239–313.

—.— *Hofmannsthals dramatischer Stil*; Untersuchungen zur Symbolik und Dramaturgie. Hermaea; germanistische Forschungen, n.s., vol. 20. Tübingen: Max Niemeyer, 1967.

Erken, Gunther. "Hugo von Hofmannsthal." In *Dichter der Moderne,* Edited by Benno von Wiese. Berlin: Erich Schmidt, 1965, pp. 213–36.

Ernst, Erhard. "Das Karma-Thema und der *Turm* Stoff bei Hugo von Hofmannsthal." *Wirkendes Wort* 21 (1971): 14–24.

Exner, Richard. *Hugo von Hofmannsthals "Lebenslied;" eine Studie.* Heidelberg: Carl Winter, 1964.

—.— "Arabella: Verkauft, verlobt, verwandelt?" Hofmannsthal Forschungen 8 (1985): 55–80.

Fetzer, Günther. *Das Briefwerk Hugo von Hofmannsthals.* Deutsches Literaturarchiv: Verzeichnisse, Berichte, Informationen, 6. Marbach: Deutsche Schillergesellschaft, 1980.

Fiechtner, Helmut A., ed. *Hugo von Hofmannsthal*; der Dichter im Spiegel der Freunde. 2d ed. Bern: Francke, 1963.

Fiedler, Theodore. "Hofmannsthals 'Reitergeschichte' und ihre Leser: zur Politik der Ironie." *Germanische-romanische Monatsschrift* n.s. 26 (1976): 140–63.

Gautschi, Karl. "Hugo von Hofmannsthals Romanfragment *Andreas.*" Ph.D. dissertation, Zurich, 1965.

Gilbert, Mary E. "The Image of the Horse in Hofmannsthal's Poetic Works." *Modern Austrian Literature* 7 (1974): 58–76.

—.– "Recent Trends in the Criticism of Hofmannsthal." *German Life and Letters,* n.s. 5 (1952): 255–68.

—.– "Some Observations on Hofmannsthal's Two 'Novellen:' 'Reitergeschichte' and 'Das Erlebnis des Marschalls von Bassompierre.' " *German Life and Letters,* n.s. 11 (1958): 102–11.

Goff, Penrith. "Hugo von Hofmannsthal: the Symbol as Experience." *Kentucky Foreign Language Quarterly* 7 (1960): 196–200.

Hagedorn, Gunther. "Die Märchendichtung Hugo von Hofmannsthals." Ph.D. dissertation, Cologne, 1967.

Hamburger, Michael. "Hofmannsthals Bibliothek: ein Bericht." *Euphorion* 55 (1961): 15–76.

—.– *Hugo von Hofmannsthal: zwei Studien.* Schriften zur Literatur, vol. 6. Göttingen: Sachse & Pohl, 1964.

Hansen, Carl V. "The Death of First Sergeant Anton Lerch in Hofmannsthals *Reitergeschichte*: A Military Analysis." *Modern Austrian Literature* 13 (1980): 17–26.

Heimrath, Ulrich. Hugo von Hofmannsthals 'Reitergeschichte,' eine Interpretation." *Wirkendes Wort* 21 (1971): 318–18.

Hirsch, Rudolf. "Hofmannsthal und Frankreich; zwei Beiträge." *Etudes Germaniques* 29 (1974): 145–53.

Hoppe, Manfred. *Literatentum, Magie und Mystik im Frühwerk Hugo von Hofmannsthals.* Quellen und Forschungen zur Sprache und Literaturgeschichte der germanischen Völker, n.s. 28 (152). Berlin: de Gruyter, 1968.

Hudson, Frank L. " 'Böser Dinge hübsche Formel.'; Some Thoughts on Hofmannsthal's Judgment of Aestheticism." *German Studies Review* 6 (1983): 59–74.

Ittenbach, Max. "Hugo von Hofmannsthals *Kleines Welttheater.*" *Germanische–Romanische Monatsschrift* 20 (1932): 192–99.

Jenkinson, D.E. "The Poetry of Transition; Some Aspects of the Interpretation of Hofmannsthal's Lyrics." *German Life and Letters,* n.s. 27 (1974): 294–302.

Kern, Peter C. *Zur Gedankenwelt des späten Hofmannsthals;* die Idee einer schöpferischen Restauration. Beiträge zur neueren Literaturgeschichte, 3d series, vol. 6. Heidelberg: Carl Winter, 1969.

Klieneberger, H.R. "Hofmannsthal and Leopold Andrian." *MLR* 80 (1985): 619–36.

Kobel, Erwin. *Hugo von Hofmannsthal.* Berlin: de Gruyter, 1970.

—.– "Arbeitskreis: Philosophische Grundfragen: 'Magie und Ewigkeit' " In *Hofmannsthal-Forschungen* 5 (1977): 111-118.

Köhler, Wolfgang. *Hugo von Hofmannsthal und "Tausendundeine Nacht."* Europäische Hochschulschriften, series 1, Deutsche Literatur und Germanistik, vol. 77. Bern: Herbert Lang, 1972.

Kohler, Stephen. " 'Ein Traum von großer Magie.' Anmerkungen zu Hugo von Hofmannsthal." In *Literarische Profile:* Deutsche Dichter von Grimmelshausen bis Brecht. Edited by Walter Hinderer. Königstein: Athenäum, 1982, pp. 238-253.

Kovach, Thomas A. *Die Frau ohne Schatten:* Hofmannsthal's Response to the Symbolist Dilemma." *German Quarterly* 57 (1984): 377–391.

—.— *Hofmannsthal and Symbolism; Art and Life in the Work of a Modern Poet.* American University Studies, Series III, Comparative Literature, 18. New York: Peter Lang, 1985.

Krämer, Eckhart. "Die Metaphorik in Hugo von Hofmannsthals Lyrik und ihr Verhältnis zum modernen Gedicht." Ph.D. dissertation. Marburg/Lahn, 1963.

Lakin, Michael. "Hofmannsthal's 'Reitergeschichte' and Kafka's 'Ein Landarzt.' " *Modern Austrian Literature* 3 (1970): 39–50.

Laubach, Jakob. "Hugo von Hofmannsthals *Turm*-Dichtungen." Ph. D. Dissertation. Freiburg, Switzerland 1954.

Lewis, Hanna B. "Hofmannsthal, Shelley and Keats." *German Life and Letters,* n.s. 27 (1974): 220–33.

—.— "The *Arabian Nights* and the Young Hofmannsthal." *German Life and Letters* (1984): 186–196.

Martini, Fritz. *Das Wagnis der Sprache.* Stuttgart: Ernst Klett, 1954.

Mathes, Jürg. Überlegungen zur Verwendung der Zahlen in Hofmannsthal's Erzählungen – 'Die 672. Nacht.' *Germanisch-Romanische Monatsschrift* 32 (1982): 202–204.

Mauser, Wolfgang. *Bild und Gebärde in der Sprache Hofmannsthals.* Österreichische Akademie der Wissenschaften, philosophisch-historische Klasse, Sitzungsberichte, vol. 238, no. 1 Vienna: Hermann Böhlau, 1961.

—.— *Hugo von Hofmannsthal; Konfliktbewältigung und Werkstruktur, eine psychologische Interpretation.* Munich: Wilhelm Fink, 1977.

Mennemeir, Fritz Norbert. "Hugo von Hofmannsthal, 'Vor Tag.' " In *Die deutsche Lyrik, Form und Geschichte. Interpretation,* 2 vols., 2: 292–302. Edited by Benno von Wiese. Düsseldorf, August Bagel, 1957.

Metzeler, Werner. *Ursprung und Krise von Hofmannsthals Mystik.* Munich: Wilh. Gottl. Korn, 1956.

Meyer-Sichting, Gerhard. "Hofmannsthals *Turm*; eine Einführung und Deutung." *Merkur* 8 (1953): 209–26.

Miles, David H. "Hofmannsthals 'dänischer Schriftsteller' und das Bild des sterbenden Tieres." *Hofmannsthal Blätter,* 12 (1974): 462–63.

—.— *Hofmannsthal's Novel Andreas: Memory and Self.* Princeton, N.J.: Princeton University Press, 1972.

Mollenhauer, Peter. "Wahrnehmung und Wirklichkeitsbewußtsein in Hofmannsthals Reitergeschichte." *German Quarterly* 50 (1977): 283–97.

Muerdel-Dormer, Lore. *Hugo von Hofmannsthal; das Problem der Ehe und seine Bedeutung in den frühen Dramen.* Abhandlungen zur Kunst-, Musik-, und Literaturwissenschaft, vol. 164. Bonn: H. Bouvier, 1975.

—.— "Die Truggestalt der Kaiserin und Oscar Wilde. Zur Metaphorik in Hofmannsthals Drama *Der Kaiser und die Hexe.*" *Deutsche Philologie* 96 (1977): 579–86.

Naef, Karl J. *Hugo von Hofmannsthals Wesen und Werk.* Zurich: Max Niehans, 1938.

Naumann, Walter. Hofmannsthals Lyrik und das moderne Gedicht." *Wirkendes Wort 9* (1959): 155-60.

Norton, Roger C. "Hofmannsthal's 'Magische Werkstätte:' Unpublished Notebooks from the Harvard Collection." *German Review* 36 (1961): 50–64.

Pape, Manfred. "Die Vita des Herrn von Ferschengelder. Zur Vorgeschichte und genealogischen Konzeption von Hofmannsthal's *Andreas." Etudes Germaniques* (1982): 25–33.

Pestalozzi, Karl. *Sprachskepsis und Sprachmagie im Werk des jungen Hofmannsthal.* Zürcher Beiträge zur deutschen Sprach- und Stilgeschichte, no. 6. Zurich: Atlantis, 1958.

Politzer, Heinz. "Der Turm und das Tier aus dem Abgrund; zur Bildsprache der österreichischen Dichtung bei Grillparzer, Hofmannsthal und Kafka." In *Grillparzer Forum* Forchtenstein: Vorträge, Forschungen, Berichte, 1968. Heidelberg: Lothar Stiehm, 1969, pp. 24–42.

Porter, Michael. "Elements of Hofmannsthal's Lyric Style: 'Erlebnis' and 'Vor Tag.' " *Modern Austrian Literature* 7 (1974): 87–108.

—.— " 'Leicht' und 'Schwer' in the Poetry of Hugo von Hofmannsthal." *Monatshefte* 65 (1973): 241–48.

Reid, J.H. " 'Draußen sind wir zu finden...' – the Development of a Hofmannsthal Symbol." *German Life and Letters*, n.s. 27 (1973): 35–51.

Renner-Henke, Ursula. "...das auf einem gesunden Selbstgefühl das ganze Dasein ruht' ... Opposition gegen die Vaterwelt und Suche nach dem wahren Selbst in Hofmannsthal's *Andreas* – Fragment." *Hofmannsthal Forschungen* 8 (1985): 233–262.

Resch, Margit. *Das Symbol als Prozeß bei Hugo von Hofmannsthal*. Hochschulschriften Literaturwissenschaft, 48. Königstein/Ts.: Forum Academicum, 1980.

Rieckmann, Jens. "Von der menschlichen Unzulänglichkeit: zu Hofmannsthal's 'Das Märchen der 672. Nacht." *German Quarterly* 54 (1981): 298–310.

Rieder, Heinz. "Hugo von Hofmannsthals 'Reitergeschichte.' " In: *Marginalien zur poetischen Welt. Festschrift für Robert Mülherr zum 60. Geburtstag*. Edited by Alois Eder et al. Berlin: Dunker & Humbolt, 1971. pp. 311–23.

Rölleke, Heinz. "Ein Grimm 'Zitat' in Hofmannsthal's 'Märchen der 672. Nacht' ". *Wirkendes Wort* 34 (1984): 65–66.

—.— "Nochmals zum Rätsel der 672. Nacht bei Hofmannsthal." *Germanisch-Romanische Monatsschrift* N.F. 33 (1983): 344–45.

Schaeder, Grete. "Hugo von Hofmannsthals Weg zur Tragödie; die drei Stufen der Turm Dichtung." *Deutsche Vierteljahresschrift* 23 (1949): 306–50.

Schaefer, Rudolf H. *Hofmannsthals Arabella: Wege zum Verständnis des Werkes.* Bern: Lang, 1967.

Schings, Hans-Jürgen. "Allegorie des Lebens, zum Formproblem von Hofmannsthals 'Märchen der 672. Nacht.' " *Zeitschrift für deutsche Philologie* 86 (1967): 533-61.

Schmalstieg, Dieter-Olaf. "Eros und Vogelflug. Hugo von Hofmannsthal als Hermeneut alttestamentlicher Weisheit." *Deutsche Vierteljahresschrift* 43 (1969): 274-88.

Schoolfield, George C. "The Pool, the Bath, the Dive: the Water Image in Hofmannsthal." *Monatshefte* 45 (1953): 379–88.

Schultz, H. Stefan. "Some Notes on Hofmannsthal's *Die Frau im Fenster.*" *Modern Austrian Literature* 7 (1974): 29–57.

Schunicht, Manfred. "Die frühen Erzählungen Hugo von Hofmannsthals." *Germanisch-Romanische Monatsschrift*, n.s., 15 (1965): 275–92.

Schurig, Arthur. "Hugo von Hofmannsthal." In *Hugo von Hofmannsthal; die Gestalt des Dichters im Spiegel der Freunde.* Edited by Helmut A. Fiechtner. Vienna: Humboldt, 1949, pp. 299–304.

Schwalbe, Jürgen. *Sprache und Gebärde im Werk Hugo von Hofmannsthals.* Studien zur deutschen Sprache und Literatur, vol. 2. Freiburg, Germany: Klaus Schwarz, 1971.

Schwarz, Egon. "The Nobility and the Cult of the Nobility in the German Novel around 1900." *German Quarterly* 52 (1979): 171–217.

Sondrup, Steven P. "Three Notes on Symbolism by Hugo von Hofmannsthal." *Modern Austrian Literature* 9 (1976): 1–9.

Sperling, Juliette. "Das Ich und das Gegenüber: Hofmannsthal und Proust." *Arcadia,* 18 (1983): 139–57.

Steffen, Hans. "Wahre Sprachliebe ist nicht möglich ohne Sprachverleugnung." *Germanisch-Romanische Monatsschrift* 24 (1974): 430–45.

Steffen, Hans. "Das sich selbst erlebende Ich. Hugo von Hofmannsthal's "Ein Traum von großer Magie." *Jahrbuch der deutschen Schillergesellschaft* 18 (1974): 506–20.

Stenberg, Peter A. "Hofmannsthal and Sigismund: the Move from the Tower," *Monatshefte* 67 (1975): 21–36.

Stern, Martin. "Zu einem Gedicht Hugo von Hofmannsthals: 'Ein Traum von großer Magie.' " In *Festschrift Gottfried Weber*. Edited by Heinz Otto Burger and Klaus von See. Frankfurter Beiträge zur Germanistik, vol. 6. Bad Homburg: Fehlen, 1967, pp. 265–98.

Tarot, Rolf. *Hugo von Hofmannsthal; Daseinsformen und dichterische Struktur*. Tübingen: Max Niemeyer, 1970.

Trabing, Gerhard. "Hugo von Hofmannsthals 'Reitergeschichte;' Beitrag zu einer Phänomenologie der deutschen Augenblicksgeschichte." *Deutsche Vierteljahresschrift* 43 (1969): 707–25.

Vanhelleputte, Michel. "Hofmannsthaliana (1968–1970)." *Etudes Germaniques* 27 (1972): 251–62.

Verhofstadt, Edward. "Hugo von Hofmannsthals Märchen der 672. Nacht. Eine soziopsychologische Interpretation." In *Theatrum Europaeum. Festschrift für Elida Maria Szarota*. Edited by Richard Brinkmann et al. Munich: Wilhelm Fink, 1982, pp. 559-576.

Volke, Werner. *Hugo von Hofmannsthal in Selbstzeugnissen und Bilddokumenten*. Reinek bei Hamburg: Rowohlt, 1967.

Vortriede, Werner. "Hofmannsthal, Gottfried Keller und die Weisheit der Spinne." In *Texte und Kontexte; Studien zur deutschen und vergleichenden Literaturwissenschaft. Festschrift für Norbert Fuerst zum 65. Geburtstag*. Edited by Manfred Durzak, Eberhard Reichmann and Ulrich Weisstein. Bern: Francke, 1973, pp. 295–308.

—.— "Das schöpferische Auge: zu Hofmannsthals Beschreibung eines Bildes von Giorgione." *Monatshefte* 48 (1956): 161–68.

Wampach, Erny. "*Ein Traum von großer Magie* von Hugo von Hofmannsthal; Versuch einer Interpretation." *Mélanges de Lin-*

guistique et de Littérature offerts au Professeur Henri Drave à l'Occasion de son Emeritat. Edited by Jacques Lerot and Rudolf Kern. Lourain: Bibliothèque de l'Université, 1978, pp. 241–57.

Weber, Eugene M. "A Chronology of Hofmannsthal's Poems." *Euphorion* 63 (1969): 284–328.

—.— "Hofmannsthal und Oscar Wilde," *Hofmannsthal Forschungen* 1 (1971): 99–106.

Weinhold, Ulrike. "Die Renaissancefrau des fin de siècle; Untersuchungen zum Frauenbild der Jahrhundertwende am Beispiel von R.M. Rilkes *Die Weiße Fürstin* und Hugo von Hofmannsthal's *Die Frau im Fenster.*" In *Aufsätze zur Literatur und Kunst der Jahrhundertwende.* Edited by Gerhard Klunge. Amsterdam: Rodopi, 1984, pp. 235–71.

Wiese, Benno von. *Das deutsche Drama vom Barock bis zur Gegenwart:* Interpretationen, vol. 2. Düsseldorf: August Bagel, 1962.

—.— *Die deutsche Novelle von Goethe bis Kafka,* part 1. Düsseldorf: August Bagel, 1956.

Wieser, Theodor. "Der Malteser in Hofmannsthals *Andreas.*" *Euphorion* 51 (1957): 397–421.

Wittmann, Lothar. *Sprachthematik und dramatische Form im Werke Hofmannsthals.* Studien zur Poetik und Geschichte der Literatur, 2. Stuttgart: W. Kohlhammer, 1966.

Workman, J.D. "Hofmannsthal's 'Märchen der 672. Nacht.' " *Monatshefte* 53 (1961): 303–14.

Wunberg, Gotthard. *Der frühe Hofmannsthal;* Schizophrenie als dichterische Struktur. Sprache und Literatur, 25. Stuttgart: W. Kohlhammer, 1965.

Wyss, Hugo. *Die Frau in der Dichtung Hofmannsthals;* eine Studie zum dionysischen Welterlebnis. Zurich: Max Niehans, 1954.

Zelinsky, Hartmut. *Brahman und Basilisk; Hugo von Hofmannsthals poetisches System und sein lyrisches Drama "Der Kaiser und die Hexe."* Münchner germanistische Beiträge, vol. 13. Munich: Wilhelm Fink, 1974.

Zimmerman, Werner. *Deutsche Prosadichtung der Gegenwart,* part 1. Düsseldorf: Schwann, 1956.

General Works

Aristotle. *The Generation of Animals.* Translated by A. L. Peck. Loeb classical library. Cambridge, Mass.: Harvard University Press, 1963.

—.— *Politics.* Translated by H. Rackham. Loeb classical library. Cambridge, Mass.: Harvard University Press, 1959.

Bachofen, Johann Jakob. *Gesammelte Werke.* vols. 2 and 3: *Das Mutterrecht.* Edited by Karl Meuli. Basel: Benno Schwabe, 1948.

Bächthold-Stäubli, Hans, ed. *Handwörterbuch des deutschen Aberglaubens.* 10 vols. Berlin: deGruyter, 1927–42.

Collins, Mabel. *The Idyll of the White Lotus.* 3d ed. London: Theosophical Publishing Society, 1910.

Erk, Ludwig. *Deutscher Liederhort.* Edited by Franz Böhme. 3 vols. Leipzig: Breitkopf & Hartel, 1893–94.

Faulkner, William. *Absalom, Absalom!* The Modern Library. New York: Random House, 1964.

Ferguson, George. *Signs and Symbols in Christian Art.* New York: Oxford University Press, 1966.

Fingerhut, Karl-Heinz. *Die Funktion der Tierfiguren im Werke Franz Kafkas.* Abhandlungen zur Kunst-, Musik- und Literaturwissenschaft, vol. 89. Bonn: H. Bouvier, 1969.

Flaubert, Gustave. *Trois Contes.* Paris: Garnier Frères, 1969.

Freud, Sigismund. *Gesammelte Werke.* 18 vols. London: Imago, 1940–68.

Gesta Romanorum. Translated by Charles Swan. Revised and corrected by Wynnard Hooper. New York: Dover, 1959.

Goethe, Johann Wolfgang von. *Goethes Werke.* Hamburg edition in 14 vols. Edited by Erich Trunz. Hamburg: Christian Wegner; Munich: C.H. Beck, 1966–73.

Grohmann, Josef Virgil. *Sagen aus Böhmen.* Prague: Calvesche Buchhandlung, 1863.

Groos, Karl. *Die Spiele der Thiere.* Jena: Gustav Fischer, 1896.

Hauptmann, Gerhart. *Sämtliche Werke.* Edited by Hans-Egon Hass. Vol. 6: *Erzählungen. Theoretische Prosa.* Berlin: Propyläen Verlag, 1963.

Hebbel, Friedrich. *Werke.* Edited by Gerhard Fricke, Werner Keller and Karl Pörnbacher. 5 vols. Munich: Carl Hanser, 1963–67.

Hoffman, E. T. A. *Poetische Werke.* Vol. 9. *Lebensansichten des Katers Murr.* Berlin: deGruyter, 1960.

Jung, Karl J. *Man and His Symbols.* Garden City N.J.: Doubleday, 1964.

Lawrence, David Herbert. *Women in Love.* New York: Viking Press, 1965.

Mann, Thomas. *Gesammelte Werke.* 2d ed. 13 vols. Vol 3: *Der Zauberberg.* Frankfurt: S. Fischer, 1974.

Molière. *Oeuvres Complètes.* 2 vols. Paris: Librairie Gallimard, 1956.

Monnier, Philippe. *Venise au XVIIIe Siècle.* Paris: Perrin et Cie., 1907.

Ovid. *The Art of Love, and Other Poems.* Translated by J. H. Mozley, Loeb classical library. Cambridge, Mass.: Harvard University Press, 1947.

Pliny. *Natural History.* Translated by W. H. S. Jones. 10 vols. Loeb classical library. Vol. 8. Cambridge, Mass.: Harvard University Press, 1963.

Rehder, Helmut, ed. *Literary Symbolism, a Symposium.* Austin, Texas: University of Texas Press, 1965.

Robertson, D. W. *A Preface to Chaucer*; Studies in Medieval Perspectives. Princeton, N.J.: Princeton University Press, 1963.

Silberer, Herbert. *Probleme der Mystik und ihrer Symbolik*. Vienna: Hugo Heller, 1914.

White, T. H. trans. and ed. *The Bestiary, a Book of Beasts.* New York: G. P. Putnam's Sons, Capricorn Books, 1960.

Whitehead, Alfred North. *Symbolism, its Meaning and Effect.* Barbour-Page Lectures, University of Virginia, 1927. New York: G. P. Putnam's Sons, Capricorn Books, 1959.

INDEX OF ANIMALS AND ANIMAL SYMBOLS

animal as antithesis of language, 23, 245-47
animal sacrifice, 8, 142, 149-51, 199, 257
animal torture, 136, 142, 168, 190-91, 197, 238-40, 257, 261-63
basilisk, 226-29
bat, 142
bear, 251-2
bees, 111-12
bird, 16, 71, 93-94, 102, 112, 125-26, 128-29, 131, 142-43, 145, 183, 201-208, 212, 223
calf, 142-44, 153, 222, 235
cat, 17, 136, 149, 157-61, 168, 193-96, 199, 232
centipede, 82, 157
chameleon, 207
cock, 227-28
cow, 81-81, 93, 143, 169, 172, 229
deer, 128, 210-11, 214-16
dog, 13, 17, 18, 19, 24-28, 29, 35-38, 40, 43, 44, 47, 56, 74-81, 93, 105, 112-14, 118, 133-38, 140, 155, 159, 161, 168, 170, 182-200, 205, 211, 212, 216, 219, 223, 225, 229, 242-43, 245, 248, 253, 259-61
dolphin, 48-50, 96, 258
dove, 145, 173
duck, 204
eagle, 17, 54, 147, 201, 206-208, 210, 214-16, 226, 236, 258
ermine, 105
falcon, 108, 206, 215
fish, 100-104, 112, 237-38
fly, 67, 72, 92

fox, 161-62, 209, 231-33, 237
frog, 164
gazelle, 108, 215
geese, 94
goat, 165-68, 200, 204, 214-16, 234
goat-sucker, 142
griffin, 54, 226-27
hedgehog, 106-107, 108, 112
horse, 12-13, 17-23, 26-38, 40, 43-45, 55-58, 61-63, 67-71, 74, 83-86, 89, 93, 105, 118, 128-29, 143, 154-56, 164, 168, 171-81, 209, 211, 253, 258-60
horse as antithesis of speech, 33-34, 87-88, 221, 248, 251, 255
horse leads to erotic encounter, 67, 72, 115, 168-69, 177
horse's mastery as mastery of id, 121-22, 169-70, 180, 254-55
horse's mastery parallels mastery of woman, 116-17, 119
horsemanship as control of one's fate, 116, 145-46, 173-74, 180
horsemanship as sign of nobility, 53, 86, 174-77, 180, 248-51
hunt, 107-10, 123-28, 131, 142, 149, 154, 168, 209-17, 256-57
lamb, 13, 235-36
lark, 67, 165
lion, 39, 49-50, 54, 61, 93, 109, 117, 136, 144, 197, 226
pig, 162, 197, 222, 232, 244
quail, 65-66
rabbit, 16, 222
rat, 72-74, 143, 169, 252, 255
raven, 223, 248
rooster, 204

281

sheep, 112, 167, 252
snake, 46, 192-94, 224-25, 234-35, 236, 238
sparrow-hawk, 141-42, 146-49, 154, 198, 237, 258
spider, 94-95, 112, 156-57, 240, 258
squirrel, 165
stag, 128, 209, 233-34, 236
swallow, 201, 213-14

toad, 144-45, 146, 151, 154, 162-64, 165, 225, 241
viper, 252
weasel, 16, 104-105, 112, 144-45, 146, 151, 154
whippet, 108, 113-14
wolf, 237, 248, 251, 252
woodlice, 82-83, 144, 241-42
worm, 83, 240, 241-42

INDEX OF HOFMANNSTHAL'S WORKS CITED

Ad me ipsum, 26, 247
Age of Innocence, 63, 125, 146, 198
Alkestis, 207
Amgiad und Assad, 23-24, 26-27, 35, 47, 51, 66, 75, 226
Andreas, 17, 21, 30, 52, 57, 62, 72, 91, 105, 113, 122, 133, 136, 140-42, 149, 153, 154, 155-219, 231, 239, 248, 250, 253, 255, 256, 258, 260
Arabella, 52, 177
Ariadne auf Naxos, 79, 82-83, 144, 217
Augenblicke in Griechenland, 167
Brief (poem), 76
Briefe des Zurückgekehrten, 153, 203
Buch der Freunde, 153
Christinas Heimreise, 25, 205
Dame Kobold, 227
Dämmerung und nächtliches Gewitter (see Knabengeschichte)
Danae oder die Vernunftheirat, 177
Das Bergwerk zu Falun, 11, 60, 75, 77, 79, 134, 158, 163-64, 258, 261
Das Dorf im Gebirge, 102-103
Das Erlebnis des Marschalls vom Bassompierre, 72, 135
Das Gerettete Venedig, 25, 73, 79, note 19, 193, 194, 204
Das Gespräch über Gedichte, 7, 8, 14, 80, 91, 149, 240, 260, 262
Das kleine Welttheater, 39, 43-44, 72, 91, 94, 101, 104, 111, 113, 119, 121-32, 149, 170, 187, 226, 230, 239, 250, 256, 257

Das Märchen der 672. Nacht, 9, 12-13, 23, 27, 41-64, 65, 67, 83, 89, 96, 105, 106, 118, 124, 127, 142, 155, 174, 179, 226, 248, 250, 253, 257
Das Märchen von der verschleierten Frau, 12, 147-48
Das Salzburger große Welttheater, 73
Das Tagebuch eines Willenskranken, 100
Defoe, 205
Der Abenteurer und die Sängerin, 48-49, 50, 67, 203, 256
Der Brief des letzten Contarin, 87-88, note 29
Der Bürger als Edelmann, 159, 259
Der Dichter und diese Zeit, 39, 77, 136, 197
Der goldene Apfel, 158, 172, 254
Der Jüngling und die Spinne, 94, 156, 244
Der Kaiser und die Hexe, 60, 104, 124, 125, 256
Der Rosenkavalier, 66, 77, 109-110, 116-17, 162, 177, 232, 256-57
Der Schiffskoch, ein Gefangener, singt, 101
Der Schwierige, 101, 102, 255
Der Tod des Tizian, 21, 111, 125
Der Tor und der Tod, 21, 54-55, 60, 66, 226
Der Turm, 11, 18, 20, 30, 32, 36, 49, 62, 66, 94, 103, 113, 133, 134, 140, 142, 144, 147, 149, 197, 219, 221-52, 259, 263
Der Unbestechliche, 160, 256

283

Der weiße Fächer, 16, 50, 93, 159, 201
Die ägyptische Helena, 101, 110, 124, 205-206, 217
Die Beiden, 32-33, 34, 169, 248, 253
Die Frau im Fenster, 72, 82, 91-120, 122, 124, 136, 145, 149, 153, 168, 172, 184, 193, 196, 255-56
Die Frau ohne Schatten, 26, 49, 73, 78, 101, 108, 140, 163, 192, 215, 217, 255
Die Freunde, 202
Die Hochzeit der Sobeide, 79, 92, 136, 159, 177
Die Josephslegende, 114
Die Rede Gabriele d'Annunzios, 91, note 1
Die Wege und die Begegnungen, 148, 212-13
Eduard und die Mädchen, 205
Ein Brief (des Lord Chandos), 10, 12, 73, 103, 262, 263
Ein Traum von großer Magie, 20, 22, 29-40, 43, 47, 49, 59, 75, 87-89, 105, 106, 117-18, 122, 123, 137, 144, 155-56, 181, 221, 258, 260
Elektra, 59 note 27, 76, 81, 85, 92, 158, 235, 245, 256
Erlebnis, 83, 98, 100
Französische Redensarten, 247
Fuchs (Poil de Carotte), 62
Gerechtigkeit, 111, 114
Geschichte der beiden Liebespaare, 97, 259-60
Gestern, 54, 66
Griechenland, 167
Idylle, 60, 140, 254

Jedermann, 192-94
Jupiter und Semele, 113, 133-40, 153, 184, 197, 221, 260-61, 262
Knabengeschichte, 66, 91, 113, 141-54, 196, 209, 221, 239, 241, 255, 256
König Kandaules, 161
Leben, Traum und Tod, 36
Lebenslied, 17
Leda und der Schwan, 111
Lucidor, 146, 244
Madame de la Vallière, 79
Manche freilich, 39, 87
Mein Garten, 50
Oedipus, 62, 76, 163, 236, 258
Prinz Eugen der edle Ritter, 49, 147, 236
Prolog zu dem Buch Anatol, 49, 50
Reitergeschichte, 21, 23, 24, 32, 33, 36, 44, 47, 65-89, 92, 93, 105, 114, 115, 118, 121, 122, 125, 127, 136, 145, 153, 155, 168, 172, 174, 179, 203, 223, 225, 229-31, 241, 253, 256, 258, 260
Silvia im Stern, 78, 159, 177
Soldatengeschichte, 20, 57, 259
Terzinen über Vergänglichkeit, 25, 138
Über Charaktere im Roman und im Drama, 208
Verse auf ein kleines Kind, 49
Verse zum Gedächtnis des Schauspielers Joseph Kainz, 147, 203
Versuch über Victor Hugo, 75
Vor Tag, 82, 83, 105, 129, 145, 172-73, 254
Vorspiel für ein Puppentheater, 202
Wert und Ehre deutscher Sprache, 245